HIDDEN®

Oahu

HIDDEN®

Oahu

Ray Riegert

Ulysses Press®
BERKELEY, CALIFORNIA

Published by:
ULYSSES PRESS
P.O. Box 3440
Berkeley, CA 94703-3440

Library of Congress Catalog Card Number 97-60637

ISBN 1-56975-086-6

Printed in Canada by Best Book Manufacturers

10 9 8 7 6 5 4 3 2 1

EDITORIAL DIRECTOR: Leslie Henriques
MANAGING EDITOR: Claire Chun
COPY EDITOR: Lily Chou
CONTRIBUTING WRITER: Judy Jacobs
EDITORIAL ASSOCIATES: Nicole O'Hay, Natasha Lay
TYPESETTER: David Wells
CARTOGRAPHY: Phil Gardner, Wendy Ann Logsdon
COVER DESIGN: Sara Glaser
INDEXER: Sayre Van Young
COVER PHOTOGRAPHY: Front: Christopher Freas
    Circle and back: Allan Seiden
    Back: Christopher Freas
ILLUSTRATOR: Jen-Ann Kirchmeier

Distributed in the United States by Publishers
Group West, in Canada by Raincoast Books,
and in Great Britain and Europe by World
Leisure Marketing

The author and publisher have made every effort to
ensure the accuracy of information contained in *Hidden
Oahu*, but can accept no liability for any loss, injury
or inconvenience sustained by any traveler as a result of
information or advice contained in this guide.

For Claire,
my favorite kamaaina

What's Hidden?

At different points throughout this book, you'll find special listings marked with a hidden symbol:

◀ HIDDEN

This means that you have come upon a place off the beaten tourist track, a spot that will carry you a step closer to the local people and natural environment of Oahu.

The goal of this guide is to lead you beyond the realm of everyday tourist facilities. While we include traditional sightseeing listings and popular attractions, we also offer alternative sights and adventure activities. Instead of filling this guide with reviews of standard hotels and chain restaurants, we concentrate on one-of-a-kind places and locally owned establishments.

Our authors seek out locales that are popular with residents but usually overlooked by visitors. Some are more hidden than others (and are marked accordingly), but all the listings in this book are intended to help you discover the true nature of Oahu and put you on the path of adventure.

Write to us!

If in your travels you discover a spot that captures the spirit of Oahu, or if you live in the region and have a favorite place to share, or if you just feel like expressing your views, write to us and we'll pass your note along to the author.

We can't guarantee that the author will add your personal find to the next edition, but if the writer does use the suggestion, we'll acknowledge you in the credits and send you a free autographed copy of the new edition.

ULYSSES PRESS
3286 Adeline Street, Suite 1
Berkeley, CA 94703
E-mail: ulypress@aol.com

Contents

1 THE GATHERING PLACE   I
Where to Go   4
When to Go   5
Seasons   5
Calendar of Events   6
Before You Go   9
Visitors Centers   9
Package Tours   9
Packing   10
Lodging   11
Condos   12
Dining   12
Traveling with Children   13
Women Traveling Alone   14
Gay & Lesbian Travelers   14
Senior Travelers   15
Disabled Travelers   15
Foreign Travelers   16
Mail   17
Transportation   17
Addresses & Phone Numbers   23

2 THE LAND AND OUTDOOR ADVENTURES   25
Geography   25
Geology   26
Flora   26
Fauna   29
Outdoor Adventures   32

3 HISTORY AND CULTURE   49
History   49
Culture   63
People   64
Cuisine   65
Language   66
Music   68
Hula   70

4 WAIKIKI   71
Sights   72
Lodging   77

Condos   83
Dining   84
Groceries   87
Shopping   87
Nightlife   90
Beaches & Parks   93

5 DOWNTOWN HONOLULU   94
Sights   95
Lodging   101
Dining   101
Groceries   107
Shopping   107
Nightlife   109
Beaches & Parks   110

6 GREATER HONOLULU   112
Sights   112
Lodging   118
Dining   120
Groceries   122
Shopping   122
Nightlife   122
Beaches & Parks   122

7 SOUTHEAST OAHU   124
Sights   124
Dining   126
Groceries   129
Beaches & Parks   129

8 WINDWARD COAST   133
Sights   133
Lodging   138
Dining   139
Groceries   141
Shopping   141
Nightlife   142
Beaches & Parks   142

9 NORTH SHORE **147**
Sights 147
Lodging 150
Dining 151
Groceries 153
Shopping 153
Nightlife 154
Beaches & Parks 154

10 CENTRAL OAHU & LEEWARD COAST **157**
Sights 158
Lodging 161
Dining 161
Groceries 162
Nightlife 162
Beaches & Parks 162

Index 167
Lodging Index 172
Dining Index 174
About the Author 180

Maps

Oahu   3
Waikiki   73
Downtown Honolulu   97
Honolulu   115
Southeast Oahu   127
Windward Coast   135
North Shore   149
Leeward Coast and Central Oahu   159

OUTDOOR ADVENTURE SYMBOLS

The following symbols accompany national, state and regional park listings, as well as beach descriptions throughout the text.

Symbol	Activity	Symbol	Activity
▲	Camping		Snorkeling or Scuba Diving
	Hiking		Surfing
	Biking		Windsurfing
	Swimming		Fishing

ONE

The Gathering Place

Oahu is the centerpiece of the Hawaiian archipelago that stretches more than 1500 miles across the North Pacific Ocean. In a sense, Oahu is a small continent. Volcanic mountains rise in the interior, while the coastline is fringed with coral reefs and white-sand beaches. In the parlance of the Pacific, it is a "high island," very different from the low-lying atolls that are found elsewhere in Polynesia.

The northeastern face of the island, buffeted by trade winds, is the wet side. The contrast between this side and the island's southwestern sector is sometimes startling. In the northeast, the landscape teems with exotic tropical plants, while across the island you're liable to see cactus growing in a barren landscape!

Dominated by the capital city of Honolulu, Oahu is the meeting place of East and West. Today, with its highrise cityscape and crowded commercial center, Honolulu is more the place where Hong Kong meets Los Angeles. It's the hub of Hawaii—a city that dominates the political, cultural and economic life of the islands.

And it's the focus of Oahu as well. Honolulu has given Oahu more than its nickname, The Capital Island. The city has drawn three-fourths of Hawaii's population to this third-largest island, making Oahu both a military stronghold and a popular tourist spot.

With military installations at Pearl Harbor and outposts seemingly everywhere, the armed forces control about one-quarter of the island. Most bases are off-limits to civilians; and tourists congregate in Honolulu's famed resort area—Waikiki. Both defense and tourism are big business on Oahu, and it's an ironic fact of island life that the staid, uniformly dressed military peacefully coexist here with crowds of sun-loving, scantily clad visitors.

The tourists are attracted by one of the world's most famous beaches, an endless white-sand ribbon that has drawn sun worshipers and water lovers since the days of Hawaiian royalty. In ancient times Waikiki was a swamp; now it's a spectacular region of world-class resorts.

Indeed, Waikiki is at the center of Pacific tourism, just as Honolulu is the capital of the Pacific. Nowhere else in the world will you find a population more varied or an ambience more vital. There are times when Waikiki's Parisian-size boulevards seem ready to explode from the sheer force of the crowds. People in bikinis and wild-colored aloha shirts stroll the streets, while others flash past on mopeds.

Since the 1980s this sun-splashed destination has also become a focal point for millions of wealthy tourists from Japan. As a result, Waikiki now has money-changing shops, restaurants displaying menus in Japanese only, stores where the clerks speak no English and an entire mall filled with duty-free shops.

Today the development craze that created modern-day Waikiki is continuing on to the southwest corner of the island in an area called Koolina. Here a major tourist facility named Ihilani Resort & Spa opened near Ewa Beach and plans are afoot to create Kapolei, a "second city" of as many as 200,000 people.

So hurry. Visitors can still discover that just beyond Honolulu's bustling thoroughfares stretches a beautiful island, featuring countless beaches and two incredible mountain ranges. Since most of the tourists (and a vast majority of the island's 863,000 population) congregate in the southern regions around Honolulu, the north is rural. You can experience the color and velocity of the city, then head for the slow and enchanting country.

As you begin to explore for yourself, you'll find Oahu also has something else to offer: history. *Oahu* means "gathering place" in Hawaiian, and for centuries it has been an important commercial area and cultural center. First populated by Marquesans around 500 A.D., the island was later settled by seafaring immigrants from Tahiti. Waikiki, with its white-sand beaches and luxurious coconut groves, became a favored spot among early monarchs.

Warring chiefs long battled for control of the island. According to legend, Kamehameha I seized power in 1795 by sweeping an opposing army over the cliffs of Nuuanu Pali north of Honolulu. Several years earlier the British had "discovered" Honolulu Harbor, a natural anchorage destined to be one of the Pacific's key seaports. Over the years the harbor proved ideal first for whalers and sandalwood traders and eventually for freighters and ocean liners.

In 1850 the city, which had grown up around the shipping port and become the focus of Hawaii, became the archipelago's capital as well. Here in 1893 a band of white businessmen illegally overthrew the native monarchy. Almost a half-century later, in an ill-advised but brilliantly executed military maneuver, the Japanese drew the United States into World War II with a devastating air strike against the huge naval base at Pearl Harbor.

There are some fascinating historical monuments to tour throughout Honolulu, but I recommend you also venture outside the city to Oahu's less congested regions. Major highways lead from the capital along the east and west coasts of this 608-square-mile island, and several roads bisect the central plateau en route to the North Shore. Except for a five-mile strip in Oahu's northwest corner, you can drive completely around the island.

Closest to Honolulu is the east coast, where a spectacular seascape is paralleled by the Koolaus, a jagged and awesomely steep mountain range. This is Oahu's rain-swept Windward Coast. Here, traveling up the coast past the bedroom communi-

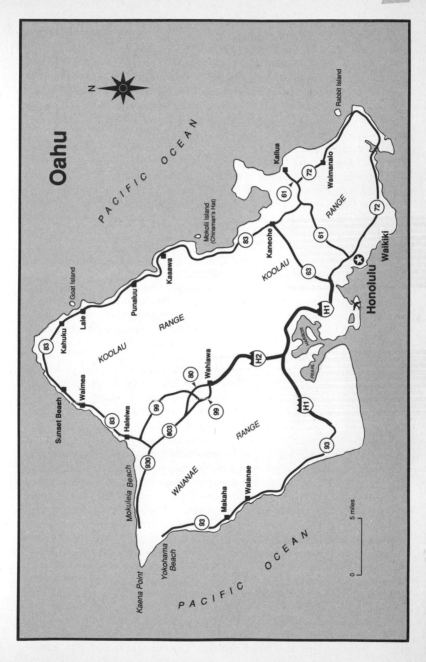

ties of Kailua and Kaneohe, you'll discover beautiful and relatively untouched white-sand beaches. On the North Shore are some of the world's most famous surfing spots—Waimea Bay, Sunset, the Banzai Pipeline—where winter waves 20 and 30 feet high roll in with crushing force.

The Waianae Range, rising to 4040 feet, shadows Oahu's western coast. The sands are as white here, the beaches as uncrowded, but I've always felt slightly uncomfortable on the Leeward Coast. Theft can be a problem here. Wherever you go on Oahu you have to be careful not to leave valuables unattended, but be particularly watchful along this coast.

Between the Koolau and Waianae ranges, remnants of the two volcanoes that created Oahu, spreads the Leilehua Plateau. This fertile region is occupied by sugar and pineapple plantations as well as several large military bases.

Geologically, Oahu is the second-oldest island in the chain; two million years ago it was two individual islands, which eventually were joined by the Leilehua Plateau. Among its geographic features is the *pali*, an awesome wall of sheer cliffs along the windward coastline, and three famous tuff-cone volcanoes—Diamond Head, Punchbowl and Koko Head.

▼▼▼▼▼▼▼▼▼▼
Where to Go

Although many visitors bypass Oahu to vacation on the Neighbor Islands, it has much to offer. From the hustle and bustle of the largest city in the South Pacific to the quiet beaches of the Leeward Coast and the mountains of the interior, the island's diversity allows a variety of experiences unavailable elsewhere in Hawaii.

Waikiki is where the action is. People come from all over the world to stroll along its beaches, shop in its malls and be part of the scene. The competition among the vast number of hotels means there are good bargains in accommodations, which means most people stay here. Restaurants range from inexpensive fast food to elegant five-star hotel dining rooms, and the shopping opportunities are endless.

The buildings of **Downtown Honolulu** trace the city's history from its early days as a mission outpost and royal capital to its current incarnation as a modern port and commercial center. This eclectic collection of architectural treasures includes old homes, commercial buildings, churches, the shops of Chinatown and the only royal palace ever to be built in the United States.

Greater Honolulu is the Honolulu of the locals. It is where they live and play in neighborhoods like Kalihi, a working class enclave to the west of downtown, inhabited by Hawaiians and Samoans, among others. Or in Kahala, the toney coastal district with its beachside homes and perfectly manicured lawns. Or Manoa, a neighborhood that stretches from the University of Hawaii campus to a valley verdant with tropical rainforest.

Beyond the hustle and bustle of Honolulu lies the rural tropical terrain of **Southeast Oahu**. This region of volcanic craters towering overhead, cliffs plunging into the sea and beaches strung out along the shoreline is waiting to be explored. Waimanalo, a rural town of fruit farmers and cowboys, sports another side of Oahu's many faceted personality.

Heading north along the **Windward Coast**, the spectacular scenery continues. The bedroom community of Kailua has become a low-key windsurfing resort with lots of bed-and-breakfasts and restaurants catering to the sailboard crowd. Kamehameha Highway hugs the coast, passing a series of sandy beaches on one side and small farms on the other. The Mormons developed the town of Laie with its branch of Brigham Young University and the Polynesian Cultural Center, which brings to life the traditional customs of the Pacific islanders.

Seeking a cooler climate? Head up to the mountains; for every thousand feet in elevation, the temperature drops about 3°.

Perhaps nowhere is more legendary among surfers than Oahu's **North Shore**. Surfers from around the world come to try their skills at Waimea Bay and Sunset Beach. The area is also noted for its farms and ranches. Haleiwa, a restored plantation town, serves as the commercial center of the North Shore and has scores of shops and restaurants that cater to the surfers, farmers and counterculturalists, all who call this beautiful coastal region home.

Central Oahu and the **Leeward Coast**, which together comprise the western half of Oahu, are the only part of the island that have been relatively untouched by tourism. The last of Oahu's major plantations occupy the high central plateau that is nestled between two mountain ranges. The isolated Leeward Coast, with its rugged landscape, has some of the most beautiful beaches on Oahu. The area also serves as home to rugged, independent people, who are determined to preserve the customs and traditions of the past that have disappeared elsewhere.

There are two types of seasons on Oahu, one keyed to tourists and the other to the climate. The peak tourist seasons run from mid-December until Easter, then again from mid-June through Labor Day. Particularly around the Christmas holidays and in August, the visitors centers are crowded. Prices increase, hotel rooms and rental cars become harder to reserve, and everything moves a bit more rapidly.

When to Go

SEASONS

If you plan to explore Oahu during these seasons, make reservations several months in advance; actually, it's a good idea to make advance reservations whenever you visit. Without doubt, the off-season is the best time to hit the island. Not only are hotels more readily available, but campsites and hiking trails are also less crowded.

Climatologically, the ancient Hawaiians distinguished between two seasons—*kau*, or summer, and *hooilo*, or winter. Summer extends from May to October, when the sun is overhead and the temperatures are slightly higher. Winter brings more variable winds and cooler weather.

The important rule to remember about Oahu's beautiful weather is that it changes very little from season to season but varies dramatically from place to place. The average yearly temperature is about 75°, and during the coldest weather in January and the warmest in August, the thermometer rarely moves more than 5° or 6° in either direction. Similarly, seawater temperatures range comfortably between 74° and 80° year-round.

A key aspect to this luxurious semitropical environment is the trade wind that blows with welcome regularity from the northeast, providing a natural form of air-conditioning. When the trades stop blowing, they are sometimes replaced by *kona* winds carrying rain and humid weather from the southwest. These are most frequent in the winter, when the Hawaiian islands receive their heaviest rainfall.

While summer showers are less frequent and shorter in duration, winter storms are sometimes quite nasty. I've seen it pour for five consecutive days, until hiking trails disappeared and city streets were awash. If you visit in winter, particularly from December to March, you're risking the chance of rain.

A wonderful factor to remember about this wet weather is that if it's raining where you are, you can often simply go someplace else. And I don't mean another part of the world, or even a different island. Since the rains generally batter the northeastern sections of each island, you can usually head over to the south or west coast for warm, sunny weather.

CALENDAR OF EVENTS

Something else to consider in planning a visit to Oahu is the amazing lineup of annual cultural events. For a thumbnail idea of what's happening when, check the calendar below. You might just find that special occasion to climax an already dynamic vacation.

JANUARY

Mid-January   The opening of **Hawaii's legislature** on the third Wednesday in January is marked by traditional pageantry.

Mid-January   The **Hula Bowl** football game, a competition between various college all-stars from around the nation, is preceded by golf tournaments, dinner cruises and a boat parade.

Mid-January or February   The month-long **Narcissus Festival** begins with the Chinese New Year. During the weeks of festivities there are open houses, street parties and parades in Honolulu's Chinatown.

Late January   In Waikiki, people come from throughout the islands to compete in ancient games, a quarter-mile outrigger canoe race and tug-of-war competitions at the **Ala Wai Challenge** at Ala Wai Park.

Late January through March The Japanese community in Honolulu celebrates the **Cherry Blossom Festival** with tea ceremonies, kabuki theater presentations, martial arts demonstrations and crafts exhibits.

During February Architecture students from the University of Hawaii challenge local professionals in the annual **Sandcastle Building Contest** at Kailua Beach Park in Kailua.

Early March The longest running sportkite competition brings together competitors from around the world for the **Hawaiian Challenge International Sportkite Championship** at Kapiolani Park.
Mid-March Japanese street performers, food booths, sumo wrestling and dancing celebrate Japanese culture during the **Honolulu Festival**, which also includes a major parade and an international kite festival.
March 17 The **St. Patrick's Day Parade** makes its way from Ala Moana to Kapiolani Park in honor of the state's large Hawaiian-Irish population.

Early April Buddhist temples on all the islands mark **Buddha Day**, the luminary's birthday, with special services. Included among the events are pageants, dances and a flower festival.
Mid-April Bed teams from Hawaii and as far away as Australia come to Honolulu to compete in the **International Bed Race Festival**. This unique event includes the race, as well as a carnival with food booths, rides, games and live entertainment. In honor of the event, **The Waikiki Electric Light Parade** and fireworks takes place the night before.

May 1 **Lei Day** is celebrated in the islands by people wearing flower leis and colorful Hawaiian garb. The Brothers Cazimero, one of Hawaii's most popular singing groups, gives an annual **Lei Day Concert** at the Waikiki Shell.
Mid-May Top dancers from Hawaii, Samoa and the mainland compete in the **World Fire Knife Dance Competition** at the Polynesian Cultural Center in Laie.

During June Starting on Memorial Day and lasting for four weekends, the **50th State Fair** highlights Hawaii's agriculture, farm animals, flowers and products in Aloha Stadium. There are also rides, games and commercial booths.
During June On the weekend when the best surf is up, the **Hawaiian Bodysurfing Championships** are held at Point Panic.
June 11 A wide range of activities make up the **King Kamehameha Celebration** in honor of Hawaii's first king. A floral parade with floats and marching bands, a ceremony decorating Ka-

mehameha's statue with leis, and an all-day festival of Hawaiian entertainment in Kapiolani Park commemorate the island ruler.

Mid-June Athletes from throughout the state come to compete in 40 various Olympic sports at 50 locations around the island as part of the **Aloha State Games**.

Mid-June More than 20 hula *halau* from around the islands compete in the **King Kamehameha Hula Competition**, an annual event that showcases chanting as well as both traditional and contemporary hula styles.

JULY

Early July Military and high school bands interspersed with floral floats make their way through the streets of Kailua, during the city's **4th of July Weekend Parade**.

Mid-July The contestants in the **Transpacific Yacht Race** start arriving in Honolulu to be greeted by festivities and parties at the city's marinas.

Mid-July Oahu's biggest watersports carnival, **Bayfest**, takes place at Kaneohe Bay. The three-day event includes live entertainment, food booths and a carnival, in addition to, you guessed it, watersports events.

Late July Dancers from all the islands come to participate in the **Prince Lot Hula Festival** in honor of Prince Lot, who revived hula after it was banned by the missionaries.

Late July Hundreds of ukelele players gather to strum their instruments at Kapiolani Park in Waikiki at the **Annual Ukelele Festival**.

AUGUST

During August The dramatic **Hawaii State Surfing Championships** and the **Wahini Bodyboard Championships** take place on designated beaches on the island.

During August In Honolulu, dancers six to twelve years old gather to compete in the **Queen Liliuokalani Keiki Hula Festival**.

August 21 Local residents celebrate **Admission Day**, the date when Hawaii became the 50th state in 1959.

SEPTEMBER

September 6 Iolani Palace celebrates **Queen Liliuokalani's Birthday** with island entertainment.

Mid-September and October The highlight of Hawaii's cultural season is the **Aloha Week** festival, a series of week-long celebrations featuring parades, street parties and pageants.

Late September The Bishop Museum hosts the annual festival of Hawaiian women's music and dance known as **Bankoh na Wahine o Hawaii**.

OCTOBER

During October The **Honolulu Orchid Society Show** presents a display of thousands of orchids and other tropical plants at the Neal S. Blaisdell Center.

Early October   About 100 teams of the top male outrigger canoe paddlers in the world compete in the 40.8-mile Molokai-to-Oahu outrigger canoe race, the **Annual Bankoh Molokai Hoe**, which ends at Fort DeRussy Beach in Waikiki.

Late October   In honor of Halloween, the Mission Houses Museum sponsors the **Spooky Stories Tour** of downtown historic sites, including the capitol, Iolani Palace, the Royal Tomb and Cemetery and the Mission Houses.

NOVEMBER

Early November   The **Hawaii International Film Festival** provides a showcase of 100 foreign, independent, short and premiere films, seminars and workshops.

Early November   The **Kaneohe Bay Fall Craft and Plant Fair** takes place on the Windward Coast.

November through December   The world's greatest surfers compete on Oahu's north shore in a series of contests, including the **Triple Crown of Surfing**.

Late November   Mission House Museums re-creates an 1800's Thanksgiving feast at their **Giving Thanks** celebration, with storytelling, games, hymns and food prepared over an open fire and baked in a beehive oven.

DECEMBER

During December   The **Festival of Trees** at Honolulu's Amfax Plaza marks the start of the Christmas Season. **A Candlelight Christmas** at Mission Houses is an old-fashioned celebration of the season.

Early December   Buddha's enlightenment is commemorated with **Bodhi Day** ceremonies and religious services.

Mid-December   Runners by the thousands turn out for the **Honolulu Marathon**.

▼▼▼▼▼▼▼▼▼▼
Before You Go

The **Hawaii Visitors & Convention Bureau**, a state-run agency, is a valuable resource from which to obtain free information on Oahu. With offices nationwide the Bureau can help plan your trip and then offer advice once you reach the island. ~ 2270 Kalakaua Avenue, Room 801, Honolulu; 923-1811.

VISITORS CENTERS

On the mainland, you can contact the **Hawaii Visitors & Convention Bureau**. ~ 180 Montgomery Street, Suite 2360, San Francisco, CA 94104; 415-248-3800, 800-353-5846.

Another excellent resource is the **Hawaii State Library Service**. With a network of libraries, this government agency provides facilities for residents and non-residents alike. The libraries are good places to find light beach-reading material as well as books on Hawaii. Visitors can check out books by simply applying for a library card with a valid identification card.

PACKAGE TOURS

In planning a Hawaiian sojourn, one potential moneysaver is the package tour, which combines air transportation with a hotel room and other amenities. Generally, it is a style of travel that I avoid. However, if you can find a package that provides air transportation, a hotel or condominium accommodation and a rental car, all at one low price—it might be worth considering. Just try to avoid the packages that preplan your entire visit, dragging you around on air-conditioned tour buses. Look for the package that provides only the bare necessities, namely transportation and lodging, while allowing you the greatest freedom.

However you decide to go, be sure to consult a travel agent. They are professionals in the field, possessing the latest information on rates and facilities, and their service to you is usually free.

PACKING   When I get ready to pack for a trip, I sit down and make a list of everything I'll need. It's a very slow, exact procedure: I look in closets, drawers and shelves, and run through in my mind the activities in which I'll participate, determining which items are required for each. After all the planning is complete and when I have the entire inventory collected in one long list, I sit for a minute or two, basking in my wisdom and forethought.

Then I tear the hell out of the list, cut out the ridiculous items I'll never use, halve the number of spares among the necessary items, and reduce the entire contents of my suitcase to the bare essentials.

Before I developed this packing technique, I once traveled overland from London to New Delhi carrying two suitcases and a knapsack. I lugged those damned bundles onto trains, buses, jitneys, taxis and rickshaws. When I reached Turkey, I started shipping things home, but by then I was buying so many market goods that it was all I could do to keep even.

I ended up carrying so much crap that one day, when I was sardined in a crowd pushing its way onto an Indian train, someone managed to pick my pocket. When I felt the wallet slipping out, not only was I unable to chase the culprit—I was so weighted down with baggage that I couldn't even turn around to see who was robbing me!

I'll never travel that way again, and neither should you. Particularly when visiting Oahu, where the weather is mild, you should pack very light. The airlines permit two suitcases and a carry-on bag; try to take one suitcase and maybe an accessory bag that can double as a beach bag. Dress styles are very informal here, and laundromats are frequent, so you don't need a broad range of clothing items.

Remember, you're packing for a semitropical climate. Take along a sweater or light jacket for the mountains, and a poncho to protect against rain. But otherwise, all that travelers on Oahu require are shorts, bathing suits, lightweight slacks, short-sleeved shirts and blouses, and summer dresses or muumuus. Rarely do visitors require sport jackets or formal dresses. Wash-and-wear fabrics are the most convenient.

For footwear, I suggest soft, comfortable shoes. Low-cut hiking boots or walking shoes are preferable for hiking; for beachgoing, there's nothing as good as sandals.

There are several other items to squeeze in the corners of your suitcase—sunscreen, sun glasses, a towel and, of course, your copy of *Hidden Oahu*. You might also consider packing a mask, fins and snorkel, and possibly a camera.

If you plan on camping, you'll need most of the equipment required for mainland overnighting. On Oahu, you can get along quite comfortably with a lightweight tent and sleeping bag. You'll also need a knapsack, canteen, camp stove and fuel, mess kit, first-aid kit (with insect repellent, water purification tablets and Chapstick), toilet kit, a pocket knife, hat, waterproof matches, flashlight and ground cloth.

LODGING

Accommodations on Oahu range from funky cottages to bed-and-breakfast inns to highrise condos. You'll find inexpensive family-run hotels, middle-class tourist facilities and world-class resorts.

Whichever you choose, there are a few guidelines to help save money. Try to visit during the off-season, avoiding the high-rate periods during the summer and from Christmas to Easter. Rooms with mountain views are less expensive than oceanview accommodations. Another way to economize is by reserving a room with a kitchen. In any case, try to reserve far in advance.

To help you decide on a place to stay, I've described the accommodations not only by area but also according to price (prices listed are for double occupancy during the high season; prices may decrease in low season). *Budget* hotels are generally less than $50 per night for two people; the rooms are clean and comfortable, but lack luxury. The *moderately* priced hotels run $50 to $90, and provide larger rooms, plusher furniture and more attractive surroundings. At *deluxe*-priced accommodations you can expect to spend between $90 and $130 for a homey bed and breakfast or a double in a hotel or resort. You'll check into a spacious, well-appointed room with modern facilities; downstairs the lobby will be a fashionable affair, and you'll usually see a restaurant, lounge and a cluster of shops. If you want to spend your time (and money) in the island's very finest hotels, try an *ultra-deluxe* facility, which will include all the amenities and price well above $130.

Generally, the farther a hotel is from the beach, the less it costs.

BED-AND-BREAKFAST INNS The bed-and-breakfast business on Oahu becomes more diverse and sophisticated every year. Today there are several referral services that can find you lodging. Claiming to be the biggest clearinghouse in the state, **Bed & Breakfast**

Honolulu (Statewide) represents over 100 properties on Oahu. ~ 3242 Kaohinani Drive, Honolulu, HI 96817; 595-7533, 800-288-4666, fax 595-2030.

The original association, **Bed & Breakfast Hawaii**, claims about 20 locations on Oahu. This Kauai-based service was founded in 1976 and is well known throughout Hawaii. ~ P.O. Box 449, Kapaa, HI 96746; 822-7771, 800-733-1632, fax 822-2723.

When traveling around Christmas and during the summer high season, it's wise to book reservations as far in advance as possible.

You can also try **Affordable Accommodations**, which is based on Maui and has 20 listings on Oahu. ~ 2825 Kauhale Street, Kihei, HI 96753; 879-7865, fax 874-0831. Or call **All Islands Bed & Breakfast**, an Oahu-based reservation service that represents more than 150 bed-and-breakfasts on the island. ~ 823 Kainui Drive, Kailua, HI 96734; 263-2342, 800-542-0344, fax 263-0308.

While the properties represented by these agencies range widely in price, **Hawaii's Best Bed & Breakfasts** specializes in small, upscale accommodations. With about six establishments to choose from, it places guests in a variety of privately owned facilities; most are deluxe priced. ~ P.O. Box 563, Kamuela, HI 96743; 885-4550, 800-262-9912, fax 885-0559, e-mail bestbnb@aloha.net.

CONDOS

Many people visiting Hawaii, especially those traveling with families, find that condominiums are often cheaper than hotels. While some hotel rooms come with kitchenettes, few provide all the amenities of condominiums. A condo, in essence, is an apartment away from home. Designed as studio, one-, two- or three-bedroom apartments, they come equipped with full kitchen facilities and complete kitchenware collections. Many also feature washer/dryers, dishwashers, air-conditioning, color televisions, telephones, lanais and community swimming pools.

Utilizing the kitchen will save considerably on your food bill; by sharing the accommodations among several people, you'll also cut your lodging bill. While the best way to see Oahu is obviously by hiking and camping, when you're ready to come in from the wilds, consider reserving a place that provides more than a bed and a night table.

DINING

A few guidelines will help you chart a course through Oahu's countless dining places. Within a particular chapter, the restaurants are categorized geographically, with each restaurant entry describing the establishment as budget, moderate, deluxe or ultra-deluxe in price.

To establish a pattern for Oahu's parade of dining places, I've described not only the cuisine but also the ambience of each establishment. Restaurants listed offer lunch and dinner unless otherwise noted.

Dinner entrées at *budget* restaurants usually cost $8 or less. The ambience is informal café style and the crowd is often a local one. *Moderately* priced restaurants range between $8 and $16 at dinner and offer pleasant surroundings, a more varied menu and a slower pace. *Deluxe* establishments tab their entrées above $16, featuring sophisticated cuisines, plush decor and more personalized service. *Ultra-deluxe* restaurants generally price above $24.

Breakfast and lunch menus vary less in price from restaurant to restaurant. Even deluxe-priced kitchens usually offer light breakfasts and lunch sandwiches, which place them within a few dollars of their budget-minded competitors. These early meals can be a good time to test expensive restaurants.

Oahu is an ideal vacation spot for family holidays. The pace is slow, the atmosphere casual. A few guidelines will help ensure that your trip to the islands brings out the joys rather than the strains of parenting, allowing everyone to get into the *aloha* spirit.

TRAVELING WITH CHILDREN

Use a travel agent to help with arrangements; they can reserve spacious bulkhead seats on airlines and determine which flights are least crowded. They can also seek out the best deals on inexpensive condominiums, saving you money on both room and board.

Planning the trip with your kids stimulates their imagination. Books about travel, airplane rides, beaches, whales, volcanoes and Hawaiiana help prepare even a two-year-old for an adventure. This preparation makes the "getting there" part of the trip more exciting for children of all ages.

And "getting there" means a long-distance flight. Plan to bring everything you need on board the plane—diapers, food, toys, books and extra clothing for kids and parents alike. I found it helpful to carry a few new toys and books as treats to distract my son and daughter when they got bored. I also pack a few snacks.

Allow extra time to get places. Book reservations in advance and make sure that the hotel or condominium has the extra crib, cot or bed you require. It's smart to ask for a room at the end of the hall to cut down on noise. And when reserving a rental car, inquire to see if they provide car seats and if there is an added charge. Hawaii has a strictly enforced car seat law.

Besides the car seat you may have to bring along, also pack shorts and T-shirts, a sweater, sun hat, sundresses and waterproof sandals. A stroller with sunshade for little ones helps on sightseeing sojourns; a shovel and pail are essential for sandcastle building. Most importantly, remember to bring a good sunblock. The quickest way to ruin a family vacation is with a bad sunburn. Also plan to bring indoor activities such as books and games for evenings and rainy days.

Most towns have stores that carry diapers, food and other essentials. However, prices are much higher on Oahu. To economize, some people take along an extra suitcase filled with diapers and wipes, baby food, peanut butter and jelly, etc. If you're staying in Waikiki, ABC **stores** carry a limited selection of disposables and baby food. Shopping outside Waikiki in local supermarkets will save you a considerable sum: **Star Market** is open 24 hours. ~ 2470 South King Street, Honolulu; 973-1666.

A first-aid kit is always a good idea. Also check with your pediatrician for special medicines and dosages for colds and diarrhea. If your child does become sick or injured in the Honolulu area, contact **Kapiolani Medical Center** at 973-8511. On the Windward Coast, call **Castle Medical Center** ~ 263-5500; on the North Shore, **Kahuku Hospital** ~ 293-9221; and on the leeward side, **Wahiawa General Hospital** ~ 621-8411. There's also a **Poison Control Center** in Honolulu, which can be reached at 941-4411.

Hotels often provide access to babysitters. On Oahu, a bonded babysitting agency is available: **Aloha Babysitting Service.** ~ 732-2029.

WOMEN TRAVELING ALONE

It is sad commentary on life in the United States, but women traveling alone must take precautions. It's entirely unwise to hitchhike and probably best to avoid inexpensive accommodations on the outskirts of town; the money saved does not outweigh the risk. Bed and breakfasts, youth hostels and YWCAs are generally your safest bet for lodging.

If you are hassled or threatened in some way, never be afraid to scream for assistance. It's a good idea to carry change for a phone call. In case of emergency, contact the **Sex Abuse Treatment Center.** ~ 524-7273.

GAY & LESBIAN TRAVELERS

The **Gay & Lesbian Community Center**, specializing in support groups and community outreach, supplies Oahu visitors with gay-relevant information. Stop by during office hours to pick up lesbian and gay newspapers and brochures. Located in the YWCA, it's open Monday through Friday from 10 a.m. to 2 p.m. ~ 1566 Wilder Avenue; 951-7000.

KEIKI CAMP

Some resorts and hotels have daily programs for kids during the summer and holiday seasons. Hula lessons, lei making, storytelling, sandcastle building and various sports activities keep *keikis* (kids) over six happy while also giving Mom and Dad a break. As an added bonus, these resorts offer family plans, providing discounts for extra rooms or permitting children to share a room with their parents at no extra charge. Check with your travel agent.

For monthly updates on the gay and lesbian scene on Oahu, pick up a copy of *Island Lifestyle Magazine* at any local newsstand. Along with coverage of news and entertainment, it provides a calendar of events and a listing of services. **Lifestyle Publishing** also puts out *The Pages,* an annual publication that includes everything of interest to the gay community. This handy directory can be purchased through the mail for $4. ~ Lifestyle Publishing, P.O. Box 11840, Honolulu, HI 96828; 737-6400, fax 735-8825.

The *Guide to Hawaii,* published by **Pacific Ocean Holidays,** is also helpful for gay travelers. It comes out three times a year and lists the best and hottest establishments and beaches that Hawaii has to offer. Send $5 per copy (via mail only) if ordering from the mainland. This outfit can also help book reservations. ~ P.O. Box 88245, Honolulu, HI 96830-8245; 923-2400, reservations only 800-735-6600.

Hawaiinet Tour & Travel Services Network, Inc. offers special tour packages to both gays and straights. They can help decide on hotels, condos and restaurants. This gay-owned company also delivers Hawaiian food, music and other goodies to the mainland. ~ P.O. Box 15671, Honolulu, HI 96830-5671; 545-1119, 800-992-5642, fax 524-9572, e-mail hinet@hula.net.

For further information, be sure to look under "gay and lesbian travelers" in the index at the end of the book.

SENIOR TRAVELERS

Oahu is a hospitable place for senior citizens to visit. Countless museums, historic sights and even restaurants and hotels offer senior discounts that can cut a substantial chunk off vacation costs.

The **American Association of Retired Persons (AARP)** offers membership to anyone over 50. AARP's benefits include travel discounts with a number of firms. ~ 3200 East Carson Street, Lakewood, CA 90712; 310-496-2277, 800-424-3410.

Elderhostel offers reasonably priced, all-inclusive educational programs in a variety of locations throughout the year. ~ 75 Federal Street, Boston, MA 02110-1941; 617-426-7788.

Be extra careful about health matters. Consider carrying a medical record with you—including your medical history and current medical status as well as your doctor's name, phone number and address. Make sure your insurance covers you while you are away from home.

DISABLED TRAVELERS

The **Commission on Persons with Disabilities** publishes a survey of the city, county, state and federal parks in Hawaii that are accessible to travelers with disabilities. They also provide "Aloha Guides to Accessibility," which covers Oahu and gives information on various hotels, shopping centers, and restaurants that are accessible. ~ 919 Ala Moana Boulevard, Room 101, Honolulu, HI 96814; 586-8121.

The **Society for the Advancement of Travel for the Handicapped** offers information for travelers with disabilities. ~ 347 5th Avenue, Suite #610, New York, NY 10016; 212-447-7284, fax 725-8253, e-mail sathtravel@aol.com. **Travelin' Talk**, a network of people and organizations, also provides assistance. ~ P.O. Box 3534, Clarksville, TN 37043; 615-552-6670, fax 615-552-1182.

Be sure to check in advance when making room reservations. Some hotels feature facilities for those in wheelchairs.

FOREIGN TRAVELERS

Passports and Visas   Most foreign visitors are required to obtain a passport and tourist visa to enter the United States. Contact your nearest United States Embassy or Consulate well in advance to obtain a visa and to check on any other entry requirements.

Customs Requirements   Foreign travelers are allowed to carry in the following: 200 cigarettes (1 carton), 50 cigars or 2 kilograms (4.4 pounds) of smoking tobacco; one liter of alcohol for personal use only (you must be 21 years of age to bring in alcohol); and US$100 worth of duty-free gifts that include an additional quantity of 100 cigars. You may bring in any amount of currency, but must fill out a form if you bring in over US$10,000. Carry any prescription drugs in clearly marked containers. (You may have to produce a written prescription or doctor's statement for the customs officer.) Meat or meat products, seeds, plants, fruits and narcotics are not allowed to be brought into the United States. Contact the **United States Customs Service** for further information. ~ 1301 Constitution Avenue NW, Washington, DC 20229; 202-927-6724.

Donning aloha attire—aloha shirts and muumuus—on Friday is a custom even the most staid businessperson generally follows.

Driving   If you plan to rent a car, an international driver's license should be obtained prior to arrival. Some rental car companies require both a foreign license and an international driver's license. Many car rental agencies require that the lessee be at least 25 years of age; all require a major credit card.

Currency   United States money is based on the dollar. Bills come in six denominations: $1, $5, $10, $20, $50 and $100. Every dollar is divided into 100 cents. Coins are the penny (1 cent), nickel (5 cents), dime (10 cents) and quarter (25 cents).

You may not use foreign currency to purchase goods and services in the United States. Consider buying traveler's checks in dollar amounts. You may also use credit cards affiliated with an American company such as Interbank, Barclay Card, VISA, MasterCard and American Express.

Electricity and Electronics   Electric outlets use currents of 110 volts, 60 cycles. For appliances made for other electrical systems, you need a transformer or adapter. Travelers who use laptop computers for telecommunication should be aware that modem configurations for U.S. telephone systems may be different from their

European counterparts. Similarly, the U.S. format for videotapes is different from that in Europe; U.S. Park Service visitors centers and other stores that sell souvenir videos often have them available in European format.

Weights and Measurements The United States uses the English system of weights and measures. American units and their metric equivalents are as follows: 1 inch = 2.5 centimeters; 1 foot (12 inches) = 0.3 meter; 1 yard (3 feet) = 0.9 meter; 1 mile (5280 feet) = 1.6 kilometers; 1 ounce = 28 grams; 1 pound (16 ounces) = 0.45 kilogram; 1 quart (liquid) = 0.9 liter.

MAIL

If you're staying in a particular establishment during your visit, you can usually have personal mail sent there. Otherwise, for cardholders, **American Express** will hold letters for no charge at its Honolulu office for 30 days, and will provide forwarding services. If you decide to use their facilities, have mail addressed to American Express, Client Mail, 2424 Kalakaua Avenue, Honolulu, HI 96815. ~ 922-4718. If you don't use this service, your only other recourse is to have mail sent to a particular post office in care of general delivery.

Transportation

AIR

During the 19th century, sleek clipper ships sailed from the West Coast to Hawaii in about 11 days. Today, you'll be traveling by a less romantic but far swifter conveyance —the jet plane. Rather than days at sea, it will be about five hours in the air from California, nine hours from Chicago, or around 11 hours if you're coming from New York.

There's really nothing more rewarding than catching a plane to Hawaii. No fewer than seven major airlines—**United, Northwest, Hawaiian, Continental, American,** TWA and **Delta**—fly regular schedules to Honolulu.

Whichever carrier you choose, ask for the economy or excursion fare, and try to fly during the week; weekend flights are generally higher in price. To qualify for the lower price fares, it is sometimes necessary to book your flight two weeks in advance and to stay in the islands at least one week. Generally, however, the restrictions are minimal. Children under two years of age can fly for free, but they will not have a seat of their own. Each passenger is permitted two large pieces of luggage plus a carry-on bag. Shipping a bike or surfboard will cost extra.

There's one airport on Oahu and it's a behemoth. **Honolulu International Airport** is a Pacific crossroads, an essential link between North America and Asia. Honolulu International includes all the comforts of a major airport. You can check your bags or rent a locker; fuel up at a restaurant, coffee shop or cocktail lounge; shop at several stores; or shower.

If you have spare time, stop by the **Pacific Aerospace Museum,** a technology exhibition devoted to aviation and the islands. In one exhibit a six-inch-tall "holovision" pilot guides you around a 1930s-era prop plane, explaining how it flies. Or you can design your own plane, using a computer-assisted design monitor. Then take the flight simulator controls and "land" a jet at Honolulu International. There are also two theaters that recapture the dramatic history of aviation. Admission. ~ Honolulu International Airport, second floor; 839-0777.

GROUND TRANSPORT

To cover the eight or so miles into Waikiki, it's possible to hire a cab for approximately $20, plus a small charge for each bag. For $7, **Trans-Hawaiian Services** will take you to your Waikiki hotel or condominium. ~ 566-7333, 800-533-8765.

City buses #19 and #20 travel through Downtown Honolulu and Waikiki. This is the cheapest transportation, but you're only allowed to carry on baggage that fits on your lap. So, unless you're traveling very light, you'll have to use another conveyance.

GETTING BETWEEN ISLANDS

If you decide to venture off Oahu, you have a few options. Since cruise ships are the only commercial boats serving all six Hawaiian islands, most of the transportation is by plane. **Aloha Airlines** and **Hawaiian Airlines**, the state's major carriers, provide frequent interisland jet service. If you're looking for smooth, rapid, comfortable service, this is certainly it. You'll be buckled into your seat, offered a low-cost cocktail and whisked to your destination within about 20 minutes.

Without doubt, the best service aboard any interisland carrier is on Aloha Airlines. They have an excellent reputation for flying on time and offer a seven-day, unlimited travel pass for island-hopping travelers. I give them my top recommendation.

Now that you know how to fly quickly and comfortably, let me tell you about the most exciting way to get between islands. A few small airlines—such as **Aloha Island Air** and **Mahalo Air**—fly twin-engine propeller planes. These small airplanes travel at low altitudes and moderate speeds over the islands. Next to chartering a helicopter, they are one of the finest ways to see the islands from the air.

The service is very personalized; often the pilot will point out landmarks along the route, and sometimes he'll fly out of his way to show you points of particular interest. I often fly this way when I'm in the islands and highly recommend these small planes to anyone with a sense of adventure.

Let me describe a typical flight I took between Honolulu and Kona. So that I'd get a better view, the captain suggested that I sit up front in the copilot's seat. After taking off in a wide arc around Honolulu, we passed close enough to Diamond Head to gaze down into the crater, then headed across the Kaiwi Channel to Molokai. Since we had to pick up passengers at Molokai's lonely airstrip, the pilot gave us a tour of the island. We paralleled the island's rugged north face, where sharp cliffs laced with waterfalls drop thousands of feet to the sea. Then we swept in toward Maui for a view of Haleakala Crater, and continued past the Big Island's snowtipped volcanoes before touching down in Kona. All for the price of an airline ticket!

Rates for these twin-engine propeller planes are very competitive when compared with the interisland jets. Coupled with the fact that your ticket on the smaller carriers is worth a guided tour as well as a trip between islands, you really can't do better than booking your flights on these sturdy little planes.

Hawaii's grand oceanliner tradition is carried on today by **American Hawaii Cruises**. The S.S. *Independence* cruises the interisland waters, docking at Maui, the Big Island, Kauai and Pier 2 in Honolulu. The cruises are week-long affairs that evoke memories of the old steamship era. ~ 2 North Riverside Plaza, Chicago, IL 60606; 800-765-7000.

CAR RENTALS

Renting a car is as easy on Oahu as anywhere. Several rental agencies compete fiercely with one another in price and quality of service. So before renting, shop around: check the listings in this book, and also look for the special temporary offers that many rental companies sometimes feature.

There are several facts to remember when renting a car. First of all, a major credit card is essential. Also, many agencies don't rent at all to people under 25. Regardless of your age, many companies charge several dollars a day extra for insurance. The insurance is optional and expensive, and in many cases, unnecessary

A CIRCLE OF ALOHA

The lei. A symbol of Hawaii, along with grass skirts and shimmering palm trees. If you are fortunate enough to be met at the airport by someone you know, chances are you will be wreathed in fragrant blossoms and kissed on both cheeks. But if you come to the island as a stranger, give yourself this aromatic gift. At some point venture downtown to Maunakea Street where you will find a row of small shops selling plumeria, ginger or carnation leis. Lei-giving is a tradition that dates back to ancient times, when they were used as head wreaths as well as flower necklaces in religious ceremonies and were presented to the *alii*. And as in ancient times, the craft of lei-making is thriving today. You can still find leis that incorporate ferns, *pukeawe* (red berries), *lehua* blossoms and *maile* leaves into intricate works of art, some having hundreds of blossoms and made with *aloha*.

(many credit cards provide the same coverage when a rental is charged to the card). Find out if you credit card company offers this coverage. Your personal insurance policy may also provide for rental cars and, if necessary, have a clause added that will include rental car protection. Check on this before you leave home. But remember, whether you have insurance or not, you are liable for the first several thousand dollars in accident damage.

Rates fluctuate with the season; slack tourist seasons are great times for good deals. Also, three-day, weekly and monthly rates are almost always cheaper than daily rentals; cars with standard shifts are generally less than automatics; and compacts are more economical than the larger four-door models.

Of all the islands, Oahu offers the most rental agencies. At the airport, **Avis Rent A Car** (834-5564, 800-331-2212), **Budget Rent A Car** (836-1700, 800-527-0700), **Dollar Rent A Car** (831-2331, 800-800-4000), **National Interrent** (831-3800, 800-227-7368) and **Hertz Rent A Car** (831-3500, 800-654-3011) all have booths. Their convenient location helps to save time while minimizing the problem of picking up your car.

Though not at the airport, **Alamo Rent A Car** (833-4585, 800-327-9633) provides airport pick-up service.

There are many other Honolulu-based companies offering very low rates but providing limited pick-up service at the airport. I've never found the inconvenience worth the savings. There you are—newly arrived from the mainland, uncertain about your environment, anxious to check in at the hotel—and you're immediately confronted with the Catch-22 of getting to your car. Do you rent a vehicle in which to pick up your rental car? Take a bus? Hitchhike? What do you do with your bags meanwhile?

If your budget is important, consider one of the following cheaper but less convenient outfits: **Sears Rent A Car** (599-2205) or **VIP Car Rental** (922-4605).

If you prefer to go in high style, rent a Rolls Royce from **Cloud Nine** (524-7999, 800-524-7999) or a vintage car at **Cruisin' Classics Car Rentals** (923-6446, fax 926-6059).

JEEP RENTALS

I don't recommend renting a jeep. They're more expensive and less comfortable than automobiles, and won't get you to very many more interesting spots. In addition, the rental car collision insurance provided by most credit cards does not cover jeeps. Except in extremely wet weather when roads are muddy, all the places mentioned in this book, including the hidden locales, can be reached by car. However, if you choose to rent one, the following agencies offer them: **Adventure Rentals** (941-2222), **Dollar Rent A Car** (831-2330) and **VIP Car Rental** (922-4605).

It's a Big Ocean
Out There

For swimming, surfing, snorkeling and diving, there's no place quite like Oahu. With endless miles of white-sand beaches, the island attracts aquatic enthusiasts from all over the world. They come to enjoy Oahu's colorful coral reefs and matchless surf conditions.

Many water lovers, however, never realize how awesome the sea can be. Particularly on Oahu, where waves can reach 30-foot heights and currents flow unobstructed for thousands of miles, the ocean is sometimes as treacherous as it is spectacular. Dozens of people drown every year in Hawaii, many others are dragged from the crushing surf with broken backs, and countless numbers sustain minor cuts and bruises.

These accidents can be entirely avoided if you approach the ocean with a respect for its power as well as an appreciation of its beauty. All you have to do is heed a few simple guidelines. First, never turn your back on the sea. Waves come in sets: one group may be small and quite harmless, but the next set could be large enough to sweep you out to sea. Second, never swim alone.

Don't try to surf, or even bodysurf, until you're familiar with the sports' techniques and precautionary measures. Be extremely careful when the surf is high. If you get caught in a rip current, don't swim *against* it: swim *across* it, parallel to the shore. These currents, running from the shore out to sea, can often be spotted by their ragged-looking surface water and foamy edges.

Around coral reefs, wear something to protect your feet against coral cuts. Particularly good are the inexpensive Japanese *tabis*, or reef slippers. If you do sustain a coral cut, clean it with hydrogen peroxide, then apply an antiseptic or antibiotic substance. This is also good for octopus bites.

When stung by a Portuguese man-of-war or a jellyfish, mix unseasoned meat tenderizer with alcohol, leave it on the sting for ten or twenty minutes, then rinse it off with alcohol. The old Hawaiian remedies, which are reputedly quite effective, involve applying urine or green papaya.

If you step on the sharp, painful spines of a sea urchin, soak the affected area in very hot water for 15 to 90 minutes. Another remedy calls for applying urine or undiluted vinegar. If any of these preliminary treatments do not work, consult a doctor.

Oh, one last thing. The chances of encountering a shark are about as likely as sighting a UFO. But should you meet one of these ominous creatures, stay calm. He'll be no happier to see you than you are to confront him. Simply swim quietly to shore. By the time you make it back to terra firma, you'll have a hell of a story to tell.

MOPED RENTALS

In Waikiki, **Adventure Rentals** rents mopeds and motorcycles. ~ 1946 Ala Moana Boulevard. You can also try **Blue Sky Rentals**, located on the ground floor of the Inn On The Park Hotel. ~ 1920 Ala Moana Boulevard; 947-0101.

PUBLIC TRANSIT

Oahu has an excellent bus system that runs regularly to points all over the island and provides convenient service throughout Honolulu. Many of the beaches, hotels, restaurants and points of interest mentioned in this chapter are just a bus ride away. It's even possible to pop your money in the fare box and ride around the entire island.

TheBus carries more than 250,000 people daily, loading them into any of 700 vehicles that rumble along city streets and country roads from 4:50 a.m. until midnight. There are also express buses traveling major highways. Most buses are handicapped accessible and many have bike racks.

If you stay in Waikiki you'll inevitably be sardined into a #19 or #20 bus for the ride through Honolulu's tourist mecca. Many bus drivers are Hawaiian; I saw some hysterical scenes on this line when tourists waited anxiously for their stop to be called, only to realize they couldn't understand the driver's pidgin. Hysterical, that is, *after* those early days when *I* was the visitor with the furrowed brow.

But you're surely more interested in meeting local people than tourists, and you can easily do it on any of the buses outside Waikiki. They're less crowded and a lot more fun for people-watching.

For information on bus routes call **TheBus** at 848-5555. And remember, the only carry-on luggage permitted is baggage small enough to fit on your lap.

HITCHING

Thumbing is not as popular on Oahu as one might think, so the competition for rides is not too great. The heavy traffic also increases your chances considerably. Officially, you're supposed to hitch from bus stops only. While I've seen people hitching in many different spots, I'd still recommend standing at a bus stop. Not only will you be within the law, but you'll also be able to catch a bus if you can't hitch a ride.

AERIAL TOURS

The quickest way to see all Oahu has to offer is by taking to the air. In minutes you can experience the island's hidden waterfalls, secluded beaches and volcanic landmarks. Tranquil gliders and hovering whirlybirds all fly low and slow to make sure you see what you missed on the trip over from the mainland. You can also take extended flights that include the outer islands.

Rainbow Pacific Helicopters Ltd. offers tours of Waikiki and Honolulu, Hanauma Bay, the Koolau Mountains, Chinaman's Hat, Sacred Falls, Kahana Rainforest and the North Shore. They also take trips to the "Jurassic Park Valley," an area where parts of the movie were filmed. ~ 110 Kapalulu Place, Honolulu; 834-1111, 800-289-6412, fax 833-7406, e-mail rainpac@aloha.net.

To enjoy a one- or two-passenger glider trip, head out to **The Original Glider Rides** and talk to Mr. Bill. On your 20-minute trip you're likely to see fields of sugar cane, marine mammals, surfers working the North Shore and neighboring Kauai. You'll also enjoy peace and quiet while working your way down from 3000 feet. A videotape of the ride and your reactions makes a memorable souvenir. ~ Dillingham Airfield, Mokuleia; 677-3404.

Ready for goosebumps? Stroll through the past with a company called **Chicken Skin Tours**. Based in Honolulu and featuring master storyteller Glen Grant, they offer a number of walking tours. One guided walk takes you to the sinful saloons of Old Honolulu, another focuses on Mark Twain's favorite spots, and one of the most popular visits the haunted places (including Iolani Palace!) of Honolulu. ~ 943-0371.

With all the highrise hotels and plate-glass condominiums, Waikiki appears to have no history at all. But behind all that steel and brass beats an ancient heart. To help you discover its pulse, an outfit called **Passport Hawaii** conducts "A Journey to Old Waikiki." ~ 2634 South King Street; 943-0371.

The best way to visit Chinatown is on one of the walking tours sponsored by the **Chinese Chamber of Commerce**. The walking tour will carry you past temples, specialty stores and other intriguing spots around this diverse neighborhood. Fee. ~ 533-318

WALKING TOURS

▼▼▼▼▼▼▼▼▼▼▼▼▼▼▼▼▼▼▼▼▼
Addresses & Phone Numbers

OAHU

County Department of Parks and Recreation ~ Honolulu Municipal Building, 650 South King Street, Honolulu; 523-4525

Division of State Parks ~ 1151 Punchbowl Street, Room 310, Honolulu; 587-0300

Hawaii Visitors & Convention Bureau ~ 2270 Kalakaua Avenue, Room 801, Honolulu; 923-1811

Weather Report ~ 973-4380 for Honolulu; 973-4381 for entire island; 973-4383 for surfing weather

HONOLULU

Ambulance ~ 911

Books ~ Honolulu Book Shops, Ala Moana Center or 1001 Bishop Street; 941-2274 or 537-6224

Fire Department ~ 911

Fishing Supplies ~ K. Kaya Fishing Supplies, 901 Kekaulike; 538-1578

Hospital ~ Queen's Medical Center, 1301 Punchbowl; 538-9011

Laundromat ~ Waikiki Ena Road Laundry, 478-A Ena Road; 942-3451

Library ~ 478 South King Street; 586-3500

Pharmacy ~ Longs Drugs, Ala Moana Center, 1450 Ala Moana Boulevard; 941-4433

Photo Supply ~ Francis Camera Shop, Ala Moana Center, 1450 Ala Moana Boulevard; 973-4480

Police Department ~ 801 South Beretania Street; 529-3111 or 911 for emergencies

Post Office ~ 330 Saratoga Road; call 800-275-8777 for general postal information

WINDWARD COAST

Ambulance ~ 911

Fire Department ~ 911

Laundromat ~ Kailua Laundromat, Aulike Street, Kailua; 261-9201

Police Department ~ 801 South Beretania Street; 529-3111 or 911 for emergencies

NORTH SHORE

Ambulance ~ 911

Fire Department ~ 911

Police Department ~ 911

LEEWARD COAST

Ambulance ~ 911

Fire Department ~ 911

Laundromat ~ Waianae Speed Wash, 85-802 Farrington Highway; 696-9115

Police Department ~ 911

TWO

The Land
and Outdoor Adventures

With its luxurious parks, mountain trails and miles of white-sand beaches, Oahu is a paradise for campers, snorkelers and hikers. Because of Oahu's varied terrain and its' microenvironments, it's possible to experience all kinds of outdoor adventures. One day you'll hike through a steaming rainforest filled with tropical flowers; the next day you'll snorkel among darting reef fish then camp on a white-sand beach beneath towering ironwood trees.

Paradise means more than physical beauty, however. It also involves an easy life and a bountiful food supply. The easy living is up to you; just slow down from the frantic pace of mainland life and you'll discover that island existence can be relaxing. As for wild food—you'll find it hanging from trees, swimming in the ocean and clinging to coral reefs. Just be sure to use the proper techniques in taking from the environment and always keep Hawaii's delicate ecology in mind.

In this chapter, I'll detail some of the outdoor skills necessary to camp, hike and live naturally on Oahu. This is certainly not a comprehensive study of how to survive on a Pacific island; I'm just passing along a few facts I've learned while exploring Hawaii. I don't advise that you plan to live off the land. Oahu's environment is too fragile to support you full-time. Anyway, living that way is a hell of a lot of work! I'll just give a few hints on how to supplement your provisions with a newly caught fish or a fresh fruit salad. That way, not only will you save on food bills, you'll also get a much fuller taste of the islands.

Obviously, none of these techniques were developed by me personally. In fact, most of them date back centuries to the early days, when Polynesian explorers applied the survival skills they had learned in Tahiti and the Marquesas to the newly discovered islands of Hawaii. So as you set out to fish along a coral reef, hunt for shellfish in tidepools or gather seaweed at low tide, give a prayerful thanks to the generations of savvy islanders who have come before you.

▼▼▼▼▼▼▼▼▼▼
Geology

More than 25 million years ago a fissure opened along the Pacific floor. Beneath tons of sea water molten lava poured from the rift. This liquid basalt, oozing from a hot spot in the earth's center, created a crater along the ocean bottom. As the tectonic plate that comprises the ocean floor drifted over the earth's hot spot, numerous other craters appeared. Slowly, in the seemingly endless procession of geologic time, a chain of volcanic islands, stretching almost 2000 miles, emerged from the sea.

On the continents it was also a period of terrible upheaval. The Himalayas, Alps and Andes were rising, but these great chains would reach their peaks long before the Pacific mountains even touched sea level. Not until a few million years ago did these underwater volcanoes break the surface and become islands. By then, present-day plants and animals inhabited the earth, and apes were rapidly evolving into a new species.

For a couple of million more years, the mountains continued to grow. The forces of erosion cut into them, creating knife-edged cliffs and deep valleys. Then plants began germinating: mosses and ferns, springing from windblown spores, were probably first, followed by seed plants carried by migrating birds and on ocean currents. The steep-walled valleys provided natural greenhouses in which unique species evolved, while transoceanic winds swept insects and other life from the continents.

Some islands never survived this birth process: the ocean simply washed them away. The first islands that did endure, at the northwestern end of the Hawaiian chain, proved to be the smallest. Today these islands, with the exception of Midway, are barren uninhabited atolls. The volcanoes that rose last, far to the southeast, became the mountainous archipelago generally known as the Hawaiian Islands.

▼▼▼▼▼▼▼▼▼▼▼▼
Flora and Fauna

FLORA

Many of the plants you'll see on Oahu are not indigenous. In fact, much of the lush vegetation of this tropical island found its way here from locations all over the world. Sea winds, birds and seafaring settlers brought many of the seeds, plants, flowers and trees from the islands of the South Pacific, as well as from other, more distant regions. Over time, some plants adapted to the island's unique ecosystem and climate, creating strange new lineages and evolving into a completely new ecosystem. This process has long interested scientists, who call the Hawaiian Islands one of the best natural labs for studies of plant evolution.

Sugar cane arrived in Hawaii with the first Polynesian settlers, who appreciated its sweet juices. By the late 1800s, it was well established as a lucrative crop. The pineapple was first planted during the same century. A member of the bromeliad family, this spiky plant is actually a collection of beautiful pink, blue and purple flowers, each of which develops into fruitlets. The pineapple is a collection of these fruitlets, grown together into a single fruit that takes 14 to 17 months to mature. Sugar cane and pineapple are still the main crops in Hawaii, although competition from other countries and environmental problems caused by pesticides have taken their toll.

Visitors to Oahu will find the island a perpetual flower show. Sweetly scented plumeria, deep red, shiny anthurium, exotic ginger, showy birds of paradise, small lavender crown flowers, highly fragrant gardenias and the brightly hued hibiscus run riot on the island and add color and fragrance to the surrounding area. Scarlet and purple bougainvillea vines, and the aromatic lantana, with its dense clusters of flowers, are also found in abundance.

Although many people equate the tropics with the swaying palm tree, Oahu is home to a variety of exotic trees. The famed banyan tree, known for pillarlike aerial roots that grow vertically downward from the branches, spreads to form a natural canopy. When the roots touch the ground, they thicken, providing support for the tree's branches to continue expanding. The candlenut, or *kukui*, tree, originally brought to Hawaii from the South Pacific islands, is big, bushy and prized for its nuts, which can be used for oil or polished and strung together to make leis. With its cascades of bright yellow or pink flowers, the cassia tree earns its moniker—the shower tree. Covered with tiny pink blossoms, the canopied monkeypod tree has fernlike leaves that close up at night.

Found in a variety of shapes and sizes, the ubiquitous palm does indeed sway to the breezes on white-sand beaches, but it also comes in a short, stubby form featuring more frond than trunk. The fruit, or nuts, of these trees are prized for their oil, which can be utilized for making everything from margarine to soap. The wood (rattan for example) is often used for making furniture.

FRUITS AND VEGETABLES There's a lot more to Hawaii's tropical wonderland than gorgeous flowers and overgrown rainforests. The islands are also teeming with edible plants. Roots, fruits, vegetables, herbs and spices grow like weeds from the shoreline to the mountains. Following is a list of some of the more commonly found edibles.

Avocado: Covered with either a tough green or purple skin, this pear-shaped fruit sometimes weighs as much as three pounds. It grows on ten- to forty-foot-high trees, and ripens from June through November.

Bamboo: The bamboo plant is actually a grass with a sweet root that is edible and a long stem frequently used for making furniture. Often exceeding eight feet in height, bamboo is green until picked, when it turns a golden brown.

Banana: Polynesians use banana trees not only for food but also for clothing, roofing, medicines, dyes and even alcohol. The fruit, which grows upside down on broad-leaved trees, can be harvested as soon as the first banana in the bunch turns yellow.

Breadfruit: This large round fruit grows on trees that reach up to 60 feet in height. Breadfruit must be boiled, baked or fried.

Coconut: The coconut tree is probably the most important plant in the entire Pacific. Every part of the towering palm is used. Most people are concerned only with the hard brown nut, which yields delicious milk as well as a tasty meat. If the coconut is still green, the meat is a succulent jellylike substance. Otherwise, it's a hard but delicious white rind.

Oahu's island flower is the *ilima*, a small golden blossom.

Guava: A roundish yellow fruit that grows on a small shrub or tree, guavas are extremely abundant in the wild. They ripen between June and October.

Lychee nut: Found hanging in bunches from the lychee tree, this popular fruit is encased in red, prickly skin that peels off to reveal the sweet-tasting, translucent flesh.

Mango: Known as the king of fruits, the mango grows on tall shade trees. The oblong fruit ripens in the spring and summer.

Mountain apple: This sweet fruit grows in damp, shaded valleys at an elevation of about 1800 feet. The flowers resemble fluffy crimson balls; the fruit, which ripens from July to December, is also a rich red color.

Papaya: This delicious fruit, which is picked as it begins to turn yellow, grows on unbranched trees. The sweet flesh can be bright orange or coral pink in color. Summer is the peak harvesting season.

Passion fruit: Oval in shape, this tart yellow fruit grows to a length of about two or three inches. It's produced on a vine and ripens in summer or fall.

Taro: The tuberous root of this Hawaiian staple is pounded, then made into a grayish purple paste known as *poi*. One of the most nutritious foods, it has a rather bland taste. The plant has wide, shiny, thick leaves with reddish stems; the root is white with purple veins.

PAKALOLO For decades, Hawaii has been known for its sparkling beaches and lofty volcanoes. Agriculturally, the islands have grown famous by producing sugar cane and pineapples. But during the last several decades, the 50th state has become renowned for another crop, one which some deem a sacrament and others consider a sin.

In the islands it's commonly referred to as *pakalolo*. Mainlanders know it more familiarly by the locales in which it grows— Maui Wowie, Kona Gold, Puna Butter and Kauai Buds. Because of Hawaii's lush tropical environment, marijuana grows year-round and has become the state's number-one cash crop. Plants easily reach ten- or twelve-foot heights; colas as thick as bottle brushes drip with resin.

Now that marijuana is big business, ripoffs have become a harrowing problem in Hawaii. Growers often guard their crops with guns and booby traps. Because of this armed protection, it can be very dangerous to wander through someone's dope patch. It might be on public land far from the nearest road, but in terms of the explorer's personal safety, a marijuana plantation should be treated as the most private property imaginable. In the words of the islanders, it is strictly *kapu*.

On Oahu, it seems there is more wildlife in the water and air than on land. A scuba diver's paradise, the ocean is also a promised land for many other creatures. Coral, colorful fish and sea turtles are only part of this underwater community. Sadly, many of the island's coral reefs have been dying mysteriously in the last several years. No one is sure why, but many believe this is partially due to runoff from pesticides used in agriculture.

FAUNA

One of the few animals to live in the Hawaiian islands before the Polynesians' arrival, the Hawaiian monk seal has been hunted for its hide to the point of extinction. Now protected as an endangered species, this tropical seal is found mostly on the outer islands, although it is occasionally spotted on Oahu. Closely related to the elephant seal, the monk seal is not as agile or as fond of land as other seals.

Green sea turtles are common on all of the Hawaiian islands, although this was not always the case. Due to the popularity of their skins, they spent many years on the endangered species list, but are now making a comeback. Measuring three to four feet in diameter, these large reptiles frolic in saltwater only, and are often visible from the shore.

WHALES   Every year, humpback whales converge in the warm waters off the island to give birth to their calves. They begin their migration in Alaska and can be spotted in Hawaiian waters from November through May. The humpback, named for its practice of showing its dorsal fin when diving, is quite easy to spy. Measuring 45 feet and weighing over 40 tons, humpbacks feed in shallow waters, usually diving for periods of no longer than 15 minutes. They often sleep on the surface and breathe fairly frequently.

Humpbacks are quite playful, and are seen leaping, splashing and flapping their 15-foot tails over their backs. The best time for whale watching is from January to April. Unlike other whales, humpbacks have the ability to sing. Loud and powerful, their songs carry above and below the water for miles. The songs change every year, yet, incredibly, all the whales always seem to know the current one.

FISH   It'll come as no surprise to anyone that Oahu's waters literally brim with an extraordinary assortment of fish—over 400 different species, in fact.

The goatfish, with more than 50 species in its family world-wide, boasts at least ten in Oahu waters. This bottom dweller is recognized by a pair of whiskers, used as feelers for searching out food, that are attached to its lower jaw. The *moano* sports two stripes across its back and has shorter whiskers. The red-and-black banded goatfish has a multihued color scheme that also includes yellow and white markings; its light yellow whiskers are quite long. The head of the goatfish is considered poisonous and is not eaten.

Occasionally found on the sharper end of your line is the bone-fish, or *oio*. One of the best game fish in the area, its head extends past its mouth to form a somewhat transparent snout. The *awa*, or milkfish, is another common catch. This silvery, fork-tailed fish can grow longer than three feet and puts up a good fight.

A kaleidoscope of brilliantly colored specimens can be viewed around the reefs of Oahu; you'll feel like you're in a technicolor movie when snorkeling. Over 20 known species of butterfly fish are found in this area. Highlighted in yellow, orange, red, blue, black and white, they swim in groups of two and three. The long, tubular body of the needlefish, or *aha*, can reach up to 40 inches in length; this greenish, silvery species is nearly translucent. The masked angelfish flits around in deeper waters on the outer edge of reefs. The imperial angelfish is distinguishable by fantastic color patterns of dark blue hues. The Hawaiian fish with the longest name, the colorful *humuhumunukunukuapuaa*, is found in the shallow waters along the outer fringes of reefs.

Sharks, unlike fish, have skeletons made of cartilage; the hardest parts of their bodies are their teeth (once used as tools by the Hawaiians). If you spend a lot of time in the water, you may spot a shark. But not to worry; Hawaiian waters are just about the safest around. The harmless, commonly seen blacktipped and whitetipped reef sharks (named for the color of their fins) are as concerned about your activities as you are about theirs. The gray reef shark (gray back, white belly with a black tail) and tiger shark, however, are predatory and aggressive, but they are rarely encountered.

Another cartilaginous creature you might see in shallow water near the shoreline is the manta ray, a "winged" plankton feeder with two appendages on either side of its head that work to direct food into its mouth. The eagle ray, a bottom dweller featuring "wings" and a tail longer than its body, feeds in shallow coastal waters. When it's not feeding, it lies on the ocean floor and covers itself with a light layer of sand. Since some eagle rays have stingers, take precautions by shuffling the sand as you walk. Not only will you not be impaled, you will also be less likely to squash smaller, unsuspecting sea creatures.

While on Oahu, you'll inevitably see fish out of water as well—on your plate. The purple-blue-green-hued mahimahi, or dolphin fish, can reach six feet and 70 pounds. The *opakapaka* is another common dish and resides in the deeper, offshore waters beyond the reef. This small-scaled snapper is a reddish-olive color and can grow up to four feet long. Elongated with a sharply pointed head, the *ono* (also known as the wahoo) is a carnivorous, savage striped fish with dark blue and silver coloring. Perhaps the most ubiquitous fish is the ahi, or tuna, often used for sashimi.

BIRDS The island is also home to many rare and endangered birds. Like the flora, the birds in the Hawaiian islands are highly specialized. The state bird, the nene, or Hawaiian goose, is a cousin to the Canadian goose and mates for life. Unless you visit the Big Island or Haleakala, the only place you'll find a nene is at the Honolulu Zoo.

Also on the endangered species list, the Hawaiian hawk, or *io*, has had its status changed to "threatened." Existing exclusively on the Big Island, the regal *io* is found in a variety of habitats from forest to grassland, but is most often sighted on the slopes of Mauna Kea and Mauna Loa. On Oahu you'll have to view this critter at the zoo.

Known in Hawaiian mythology for its protective powers, the *pueo*, or Hawaiian owl, a brown-and-white-feathered bird is considered an endangered species on Oahu, and may be spotted in the mountainous areas of the island.

There *are* a few birds native to Hawaii that have thus far avoided the endangered species list. One of the most common birds is the yellow-green *amakihi*, but the red *iiwi*, more common on the Neighbor Islands is near extinction on Oahu, with maybe only five or so left on the island.

One common bird is the *iwa*, or frigate, a very large creature measuring three to four feet in length, with a wing span averaging seven feet. The males are solid black, while the females have a large white patch on their chest and tail. A predatory bird, they're easy to spot raiding the nesting colonies of other birds along the off-

SEA WORLD AT SEA

Take an early-morning voyage on a boat on the west coast and you might just encounter one of the ocean's friendliest and most acrobatic creatures. You might suddenly find yourself in the midst of a pod of spinner dolphins who will play tag with your craft and dance above the waves like a troupe of whirling dervishes. There's nothing quite like it. Other dolphins that may be sighted in Hawaiian waters are the bottlenose, Risso's, melon-headed, rough-toothed, pygmy killers, and spotted or striped dolphins.

shore rocks. If you see one, be careful not to point at it; legend has it that it's bad luck.

No doubt you will encounter the noisy black myna birds with their beady yellow eyes and shiny black feathers. They seem to be as numerous and sassy as the tourists on Waikiki's beach.

Other birds that make Oahu their home are the Hawaiian stilt and the Hawaiian coot—both water birds—along with the black noddy, American plover and wedge-tailed shearwater.

Not many wild four-footed creatures roam the island. Feral goats and pigs were brought here early on and have found a home in the island's forests. And some good news for people fearful of snakes: There is nary a serpent (or a sea serpent) on Oahu, although lizards such as skinks and geckos abound.

One can only hope that with the renewed interest in Hawaiian culture, and growing environmental awareness, Hawaii's plants and animals will continue to exist as they have for centuries.

Outdoor Adventures

CAMPING

Camping on Oahu usually means pitching a tent. There are a few secluded spots and hidden beaches, plus numerous county, state and federal parks where you can set up camp. However, before you set out on your camping trip, there are a few very important matters that I want to explain more fully. First, bring a campstove: firewood is scarce in most areas and soaking wet in others. You should also be careful to purify all of your drinking water. And be extremely cautious near streambeds as flash-flooding sometimes occurs, particularly on the windward coast. This is particularly true during the winter months, when heavy storms from the northeast lash the island.

Another problem that you're actually more likely to encounter are those nasty varmints that buzz your ear just as you're falling asleep—mosquitoes. Oahu contains neither snakes nor poison ivy, but it has plenty of these dive-bombing pests. Like me, you probably consider that it's always open season on the little bastards.

With most of the archipelago's other species, however, you'll have to be a careful conservationist. You'll be sharing the wilderness with pigs, goats, tropical birds, deer and mongooses, as well as a spectacular array of exotic and indigenous plants. They exist in one of the world's most delicate ecological balances. There are more endangered species in Hawaii than in all the rest of the United States. So keep in mind the maxim that the Hawaiians try to follow. *Ua mau ke ea o ka aina i ka pono:* The life of the land is preserved in righteousness.

Along with its traffic and crowds, Oahu has numerous parks. Unfortunately, these disparate elements overlap, and you may sometimes find you've escaped from Honolulu's urban jungle and landed in a swamp of weekend beachgoers. So it's best to plan outdoor adventures far in advance and to schedule them for weekdays if possible.

Currently, camping is allowed at 12 beach parks operated by the City and County of Honolulu. Six of these parks are on the island's windward side and four on the leeward side. Another two are on the North Shore. All in all there are a total of 251 campsites. The largest campground, Bellows Field Beach Park at Waimanalo on the Windward Coast, only allows camping at its 50 campsites on the weekends. Swanzy Beach Park at Kaaawa on the windward side is also a weekend-only campground. The others permit tent camping every night except Wednesday and Thursday. There are no trailer hookups.

Camping at **county parks** requires a permit. The free permits can be obtained from the Department of Parks and Recreation. ~ Honolulu Municipal Building, 650 South King Street, Honolulu, HI 96813; 523-4525. They are also available at any of the "satellite city halls" around the island.

State parks allow camping for five days and work on a first-come, first-served basis. The Division of State Parks issues the free permits. ~ 1151 Punchbowl Street, Room 131, Honolulu, HI 96813; 587-0300. You can also write in advance for permits.

There are four state parks on Oahu with camping facilities. **Malaekahana State Recreation Area** on the Windward Coast between Laie and Kahuku offers both tent camping and housekeeping cabins. Also on the Windward Coast, Oahu's largest state park **Kahana Valley State Park**, located between Kaaawa and Punaluu, has campsites. Tent camping is available at **Sand Island State Recreation Area** on Sand Island in Honolulu, as well as at **Keaiwa Heiau State Recreation Area** in the hills above Honolulu.

Remember when planning your trip, rainfall is heaviest on the Windward Coast, a little lighter on the North Shore and lightest of all on the Leeward Coast.

For camping equipment in Honolulu check with **Omar The Tent Man**. Omar rents and sells supplies. Closed Sunday. ~ 650-A Kakoi Street; 836-8785.

You might also want to obtain some hiking maps; they are available from **Hawaii Geographic Maps & Books**. The camping equipment you'll require is listed in the "Packing" section of the preceding chapter. ~ P.O. Box 1698, Honolulu, HI 96806; 538-3952.

The Bike Shop rents backpacks and two-person tents and has for sale a comprehensive line of camping equipment, from clothing and sleeping bags to tents and stoves. ~ 1149 South King Street; 596-0588.

McCully Bicycle and Sporting Goods also has a limited selection of camping equipment. ~ 2124 South King Street; 955-6329.

FISHING   While you're exploring the island, the sea will be your prime food source. Fishing on Oahu is good year-round, and the offshore waters are crowded with many varieties of edible fish. For deep-sea fishing you'll have to charter a boat, and freshwater angling requires a license; so I'll concentrate on surf-casting. It costs nothing to fish this way.

The easiest, most economical way to fish is with a hand-held line. Just get a 50- to 100-foot line, and attach a hook and a ten-ounce sinker. Wind the line loosely around a smooth block of wood, then remove the wood from the center. If your coil is free from snags, you'll be able to throw-cast it easily. You can either hold the line in your hand, feeling for a strike, or tie it to the frail end of a bamboo pole.

Beaches and rocky points are generally good places to surf-cast; the best times are during the incoming and outgoing tides. Popular baits include octopus, eel, lobster, crab, frozen shrimp and sea worms.

For freshwater angling head up into the Koolau Mountains to fish the **Nuuanu Reservoir** (open to the public one Sunday a month). Another possibility is the **Wahiawa Public Fishing Area**. Both of these reservoirs are good places to catch Chinese catfish.

DEEP-SEA FISHING   Many visitors to Hawaii don't think of Oahu as a place to deep-sea fish and instead wait until they get to the Neighbor Islands, but that may be a mistake. Oahu is the cheapest place in Hawaii to fish, with rates about 25 percent lower than, say, Maui.

The fish caught vary depending on the time of year, although it's mostly mahimahi, especially during the winter months. In the fall and summer you are likely to catch marlin, and in summer, ahi tuna as well. Although you're not guaranteed a catch, some record-breaking fish have been caught on boats operating out of Oahu. In 1970, an 1805-pound Pacific Blue Marlin, the largest fish ever caught anywhere in the world with a rod and reel, was the result of an Oahu-based fishing charter.

Although the boats are all charters, share charters are the norm, with a minimum of four passengers required. If there are not enough for a particular boat, the skipper may recommend a different boat or another day to go out. Keeping the fish you catch is not always part of the deal. If you would like to do so, negotiate with the boat owner or skipper beforehand.

Most of the island's fishing fleet dock at Kewalo Basin (Fisherman's Wharf) on Ala Moana Drive between Waikiki and downtown Honolulu.

Among the outfits you'll find **Kono Sports Fishing**, which fishes the Leeward Coast and the waters off Molokai. ~ Kewalo Basin, Honolulu; 536-7472. Departing on similar trips from Kewalo Basin

The
New
Travel

Travel today is becoming a personal art form. A destination no longer serves as just a place to relax: It's also a point of encounter. To many, this new wave in travel customs is labeled "adventure travel" and involves trekking glaciers or sweeping along in a hang glider; to others, it connotes nothing more daring than a restful spell in a secluded resort. Actually, it's a state of mind, a willingness not only to accept but seek out the uncommon and unique. It is also a chance to give, not just to take.

Few places in the world are more conducive to this imaginative new travel than Hawaii. Several organizations in the islands cater specifically to people who want to add local customs and unusual adventures to their vacation itineraries.

The **Nature Conservancy of Hawaii**, a nonprofit conservation organization, conducts two hikes and two work trips each month for members at the organization's Honouliuli Preserve in the southern Waianae Mountains of western Oahu. To request a yearly hiking schedule contact the organization by letter or fax. ~ 1116 Smith Street, Suite 201, Honolulu, HI 96817; 537-4508, fax 545-2019.

The **Hawaii Nature Center** offers hikes through Oahu's central mountains just about every weekend. It also offers talks by naturalists on such subjects as geology, birdlife and taro cultivation. There are hikes and activities for the little ones, too, with activities aimed for explorers as young as three years old. ~ 2131 Makiki Heights Drive, Honolulu, HI 96822; 955-0100, fax 955-0116.

The **Sierra Club** sponsors weekly hikes on Oahu, as well as trail building and other projects aimed at helping to preserve the island's natural heritage. The club has a recorded message line that lists weekly weekend outings. ~ 111 Bishop Street, Honolulu, HI 96813; 538-6616.

In existence since 1910, the **Hawaii Trail & Mountain Club** maintains a clubhouse for members in Waimanalo and sponsors hikes every weekend. Unlike the other environmental organizations listed here, this one is run entirely by volunteers and does not have an office. To become a member you must go on three hikes. ~ 674-1459, 377-5442.

is **Island Charters.** ~ 536-1555. Or consider **Sport Fishing**, which also ties up in Kewalo Basin. ~ 521-2087. **Maggie Joe** does day trips as well as overnight and multiday excursions. An overnight trip to Molokai or a five-day cruise to Kauai and Niihau are among the options. ~ 591-8888.

TORCHFISHING & SPEARFISHING   The old Hawaiians often fished at night by torchlight. They fashioned torches by inserting nuts from the *kukui* tree into the hollow end of a bamboo pole, then lighting the flammable nuts. When fish swam like moths to the flame, the Hawaiians speared, clubbed or netted them.

Today, it's easier to use a lantern and spear. (In fact, it's all *too* easy and tempting to take advantage of this willing prey: Take only edible fish and only what you will eat.) It's also handy to bring a facemask or a glass-bottomed box to aid in seeing underwater. The best time for torchfishing is a dark night when the sea is calm and the tide low.

During daylight hours, the best place to spearfish is along coral reefs and in areas where the bottom is a mixture of sand and rock. You can use a speargun or make your own spear with heavy rubber bands and a piece of metal. Then, equipped also with mask, fins and snorkel, you can explore underwater grottoes and spectacular coral formations while seeking your evening meal.

For information on seasons, licenses and official regulations, check with the Aquatic Resources Division of the State Department of Land and Natural Resources. This agency has offices on most of the major islands.

CRABBING   For the hungry adventurer, there are two important crab species in Hawaii—Kona crabs and Samoan crabs. The Kona variety are found in relatively deep water, and can usually be caught only from a boat. Samoan crabs inhabit sandy and muddy areas in bays and near river mouths. All you need to catch them is a net fastened to a round wire hoop and secured by a string. The net is lowered to the bottom; then, after a crab has gone for the bait, the entire contraption is raised to the surface.

SQUIDDING   Between June and December, squidding is another popular sport. Actually, the term is a misnomer: squid inhabit deep water and are

HOOK UP WITH A FRIEND

The ancient Hawaiians used pearl shells to attract the fish, and hooks, some made from human bones, to snare them. Your friends will probably be quite content to see you angling with store-bought artificial lures.

not usually hunted. What you'll really be after are octopuses. There are two varieties here, both of which are commonly found in water three or four feet deep: the *hee*, a greyish-brown animal that changes color like a chameleon, and the *puloa*, a red-colored mollusk with white stripes on its head.

Both are nocturnal and live in holes along coral reefs. At night by torchlight you can spot them sitting exposed on the bottom. During the day, they crawl inside the holes, covering the entrances with shells and loose coral.

The Hawaiians used to pick the octopus up, letting it cling to their chest and shoulders. When they were ready to bag their prize, they'd dispatch the creature by biting it between the eyes. You'll probably feel more comfortable spearing the beast.

SHELLFISH GATHERING

Other excellent food sources are the shellfish that inhabit coastal waters. Oysters and clams, which use their muscular feet to burrow into sand and soft mud, can be collected along the bottom of Oahu's bays. Lobsters, though illegal to spear, can be taken with short poles to which cable leaders and baited hooks are attached. You can also gather limpets, though I don't recommend it. These tiny black shellfish, locally known as *opihi*, cling tenaciously to rocks in areas of very rough surf. The Hawaiians gather them by leaping into the water after one set of waves breaks, then jumping out before the next set arrives. Being a coward myself, I simply order them in Hawaiian restaurants.

DIVING

One of the great myths about Oahu is that you need to go far off the beaten track to discover its secret treasures. The fact is that within half an hour of Waikiki are excellent snorkeling and diving opportunities. Only an hour away are excellent reefs easily reached by dive boats. From popular Hanauma Bay, just a short ride from the heart of Honolulu, to Kahe Point on the Leeward Coast, there are snorkeling and diving opportunities for beginners and certified pros alike.

Although the most popular snorkeling locale on the island is Hanauma Bay, and most people go there, other possible spots are Shark Cove on the North Shore and Electric Beach on Kahe Point on the northwest Coast. Or you can snorkel at Makua Beach, located between Makaha and Yokohama Bay on the Leeward Coast, and swim with the dolphins.

The best diving in Oahu depends on the season. In the summertime the north and west shores are best, but during winter the waves are too big to dive there. The North Shore's outstanding dive sites are Shark's Cove, known for its lava tubes, and Haleiwa, with its 100-foot sheer drop wall. There's also the Leeward Coast's Kahe Point, which has an artificial reef. During the winter months divers head for Magic Island, which is accessible by land from Ala Moana

One of Oahu's most exciting dive spots is Turtle Canyon, ...e-and-a-half miles offshore (accessed by boat), where you can swim with sea turtles.

Off the Leeward Coast is the *Mahi* shipwreck, which *Skin Diver* magazine ranked as the fifth best wreck dive in the world. There's also a shipwreck of sorts in front of Waikiki, where a YO257 World War II oil tanker has been brought in to create an artificial reef.

Because conditions vary, I strongly recommend seeking instruction and advice from local diving experts before setting out.

HONOLULU   Many shops rent and sell diving equipment and offer underwater tours. **South Seas Aquatics** features dives off a custom 38-foot dive boat. ~ 2155 Kalakaua Avenue, Suite 112, Honolulu, HI 96815; 922-0852, fax 922-0853.

Waikiki Diving Center takes divers to different sites around Oahu, depending on the time of year and the weather. The company offers three-day PADI and NAUI courses and sells, rents and repairs diving equipment. It will also take nondivers out on an inexpensive introductory scuba charter so they can see what the sport is all about. ~ 1734 Kalakaua Avenue, Honolulu; 955-5151, fax 955-6766.

Dan's Dive Shop offers two-tank dives daily. The first dive is usually the Waikiki shipwreck and the second Raibow Reef. ~ 660 Ala Moana Boulevard, Honolulu; 536-6181.

SOUTHEAST OAHU   **Aloha Dive Shop** runs courses for certified divers and students at Maunalua Bay in the southeast corner of the island. ~ Koko Marina Shopping Center, 7192 Kalanianaole Highway, Hawaii Kai; 395-5922.

LEEWARD COAST   **Hawaii Sea Adventures** heads to the west side of Oahu and dives the *Mahi* shipwreck. They feature lessons as well as half- and full-day trips and charters. ~ 98-718 Moanalua Road, Pearl City; 487-7515.

Bojac Aquatic has daily boat dives to such southside sites as the Pinnacles and Rainbow Reef, as well as the *Mahi* shipwreck off the west coast. It also conducts three-day and two-week PADI and NAUI courses. ~ 94-801 Farrington Highway; 671-0311.

WINDWARD COAST   **Windward Dive Center** offers classes as well as a few dive trips. ~ 789 Kailua Road, Kailua; 263-2311. At **Aaron's Dive Shop** you can choose between beach and boat dives, as well as special night trips. ~ 602 Kailua Road, Kailua; 261-1211.

NORTH SHORE   Depending on the season, the **Haleiwa Surf Center** teaches such sports as snorkeling, surfing, swimming, lifesaving, windsurfing and sailing. This county agency is also an excellent source of information on the island's water sports and facilities. ~ Haleiwa-Alii Beach Park, Haleiwa; 637-5051. **Surf 'n Sea** offers beach dives on the North Shore and Leeward Coast including the

Mahi shipwreck. ~ 62-595 Kamehameha Highway, Haleiwa; 637-9887.

Somewhere between snorkeling and scuba diving is Snuba, a relatively new watersport that's catching on in resort areas around the world. You don't need certification, and it's so safe even an eight-year-old can do it.

Snuba was created for those who would like to take snorkeling a step further but may not be quite ready for scuba diving. It's a shallow-water dive system that allows underwater breathing. Basically this is how it works. Swimmers wear a breathing device (the same one used in scuba diving) that is connected to a built-in scuba tank that floats on a raft. They also wear a weight belt, mask and fins. The air comes through a 20-foot tube connected to the raft, which follows the swimmer. Groups of six participants are taken out with a guide. They can dive up to 20 feet.

Snuba of Oahu offers snuba tours each day in Waikiki leaving from the Outrigger Reef Hotel. On Monday through Friday the company offers trips to Hanauma Bay and on Monday through Saturday to Maunalua Bay Activities Club in Hawaii Kai. Dives from the southwest portion of the island are the best. Daily trips leave from Ihilani Resort and involve a two-and-a-half hour sail out to sea; lunch is included. Common sightings include an array of fish, eels, dolphins and turtles. ~ 377 Keahole Street; 396-6163.

Surfing, a sport pioneered centuries ago by Hawaiian royalty, is synonymous with Oahu. Stars bring their boards from all over the world to join international competitions that take advantage of ideal surf and wind conditions. From the 30-foot winter rollers on the North Shore to beginner lessons off Waikiki, this is beach boy and girl territory. The Surf News Network operates **Surfline**, a call-in recorded message information service that updates surf information for surfers and windsurfers several times a day. ~ 596-7873.

WAIKIKI If you'd like to surf Waikiki, you can rent a board from **Prime Time Rentals** on Fort De Russy Beach. ~ 949-8952. At the **Aloha Beach Service**, in front of the Sheraton Moana Surfrider Hotel, offers lessons and rents long boards. ~ 922-3111. **Waikiki Beach Services** offers both private and group lessons at the Outrigger Reef Hotel. ~ 2169 Kalia Road; 924-4941.

A number of stores located in different parts of the island also rent boards. Near downtown, go to **Local Motion** for surfboard rentals. ~ 1714 Kapiolani Boulevard, Honolulu; 955-7873. In the Diamond Head area, **Downing Hawaii** rents boards. ~ 3021 Waialae Avenue, Honolulu; 737-9696.

NORTH SHORE A resource for both the participatory and spectator aspects of surfing is the **Haleiwa Surf Center**. Surf lessons

ormally run September through early May. Haleiwa-Alii Beach
ark, Haleiwa; 637-5051. In the same area surfing lessons and ren-
..ls are also available from **Surf and Sea**. ~ 62-595 Kamehameha
Highway, Haleiwa; 637-9887.

**WIND-
SURFING**

Windsurfing is becoming almost as popular as surfing these days,
and few places are better to try this sport than on Oahu. If you're
just starting out or are at an intermediate level, the bedroom community of Kailua on the Windward Coast, about a half-hour drive
from Honolulu, is the place to go. This is the best place in Hawaii
for all but the most advanced sailors. There's a protective reef and
no breakers, and on-shore trades provide just the right winds for
the sport year-round. The quiet town has also become a sort of
windsurfing resort, with scores of bed-and-breakfasts offering accommodations at reasonable rates.

WINDWARD COAST **Kailua Sailboard and Kayak Company** will
teach you the tricks of the trade or help you brush up on your technique. You can also rent sail boards, boogie boards, long boards
and snorkeling equipment here. ~ 130 Kailua Road, Kailua; 262-
2555. In the same area, **Naish Hawaii** offers lessons and rentals.
This company manufactures its own boards and also operates a
shop filled with the latest in sailboarding apparel and accessories
and long boards. ~ 155-A Hamakua Drive, Kailua; 261-6067. Try
Windsurfing Hawaii for sail boards. ~ 155-A Hamakua Drive,
Kailua; 261-3539.

NORTH SHORE For classes and information check out the **Haleiwa Surf Center**. Lessons are generally given from May through
early September. ~ Haleiwa-Alii Beach Park, Haleiwa; 637-5051.

SAILING

One of the best ways to enjoy Oahu is aboard a sailboat. From
brief cruises off Honolulu to a day-long charter along the North
Shore, this is the perfect antidote to the tourist crowds. It's also sur-
prisingly affordable.

Te Kaveka, a sleek 44-foot catamaran, takes up to 18 people
out along the Koolina coast past Nanakuli to Maili Point. Not only
will you enjoy two hours of wind-in-your-face-sun-on-your-back
sailing, but you will get to snorkel in one of Oahu's top spots. ~
Wind-n-Sea Hawaii, Koolina; 679-0111.

Honolulu Sailing Company and the beach stands in front of
Hilton Hawaiian Village in Waikiki sponsor cruises, interisland sail-
ing, whale-watching trips and weddings at sea. ~ 47-335 Lulani
Street; 239-3900.

If you're eager to charter your own yacht, contact **The Yacht
Connection**. The company charters all sizes of vessels ranging from
fishing boats to luxury yachts. ~ 1750 Kalakaua Avenue, Suite
3138, Honolulu; 523-1383.

Above Heaven's Gate operates charter group cruises to the Diamond Head reef area aboard a 56-foot teakwood pirate ship. You can also take a guided Hobie-cat tour off the Windward Coast to undiscovered islands most tourists miss (by appointment only). Along the way you'll enjoy Waimanalo, Lanikai and Kailua Bay. You can also learn how to sail this swift 16-foot craft. They also do weddings at sea and in exotic locations. ~ 41-1010 Laumilo Street, Waimanalo Bay; 259-5429, 800-800-2933, fax 259-5633, e-mail howie@hawaiiweddings.com.

Those staying around Haleiwa may be interested in sailing with **North Shore Catamaran Charters**, which has daily trips aboard its 40-foot catamaran that carries up to 25 passengers. From the end of December through April, there are three-hour whale-watching trips, from May to September, four-hour snorkel/picnic cruises, and sunset sails twice a week throughout the year. ~ 59740 Alapio Road, Haleiwa; 638-8279.

KAYAKING

A sport well suited for Oahu, kayaking is an ideal way to explore the island's protected bays, islands and inland rivers. It seems that kayakers are popping up everywhere, particularly around the southeast coast of the island and up the Waimea River. To rent or purchase kayaks and equipment, or to sign up for lessons and tours, consider **Go Bananas** just outside Waikiki. ~ 799 Kapahulu Avenue; 737-9514. For kayak rentals contact **Kailua Sailboard and Kayak Company**. ~ 130 Kailua Road, Kailua; 262-2555. **Twogood Kayak Hawaii** also rents kayaks. ~ 345 Hahani Street, Kailua; 262-5656.

If you'd like to go on a group kayak expedition, sign on with **Kayak Oahu Adventures** for one of its one- to one-and-a-half-hour Diamond Head paddling tours or two-hour snorkeling trips. You may want to try whitewater kayaking—it's kind of like surfing—but in a kayak. The company also runs trips up the Waimea River. ~ 1311 Kapiolani Boulevard, Honolulu; 593-4415.

WATER-SKIING

Near Koko Head, **Suyderhoud Water Ski Center** offers instruction every day. A beginning class is 30 minutes, but you can also ski for 15 or 45 minutes or an hour. ~ Koko Marina Shopping Center, 1792 Kalaneanaole Highway, Honolulu; 395-3773.

PARA-SAILING

Vacations offer a time for new adventures, to try a sport you've never attempted before, like parasailing. **Aloha Parasail** offers ten-minute flights. You'll share a boat with five other fliers, so the entire trip takes about two hours from the time you leave your hotel and return. You must weigh between 100 to 275 pounds. (Those weighing less can go tandem.) ~ P.O. Box 90846, Honolulu 96835; 521-2446.

Big Sky Parasail will also pick you up at your hotel for a flight above Hanauma Bay. Afterward you can go snorkeling or diving—they'll provide you with snorkeling and diving equipment. Big Sky's weight restrictions are 80 to 320 pounds. ~ Koko Marina Shopping Center, 1792 Kalaneanaole Highway, Honolulu; 396-9224.

SKYDIVING & HANG GLIDING

You can learn to skydive and participate in a tandem dive with Skydive Hawaii at Dillingham Airfield on the North Shore. Upon arrival you'll watch a video and participate in a 20-minute training session. A tandem master trains students how to put on the equipment, what to do in the plane, how to get out and how to deploy the parachute. Once 13,000 feet in the air, the excitement begins. You'll free fall at about 120 mph for about one minute, then open the parachute at 5500 feet for a five-minute ride at a smooth 12 mph after that. ~ 68-760 Farrington Highway; 637-9700.

Another skydiving operation at Dillingham Field is Pacific International Skydiving Center. ~ 68-760 Farrington Highway; 637-7472.

North Shore Hang Gliding offers daily tandem hang gliding instruction at Dillingham Field. Call the company, and they'll also give you information on hang gliding in the area. ~ P.O. Box 640, Waialua 96791; 637-3178.

RIDING STABLES

Located on the Windward Coast across from Chinaman's Hat, Kualoa Ranch leads one- and two-hour weekend rides in Kaaawa Valley. They also offer many other activities including a trip to Secret Island and snorkeling tours. Don't forget your swimsuit. ~ 49-560 Kamehameha Highway, Kaaawa; 237-8515.

The Turtle Bay Hilton on the North Shore has riding programs for the general public. They offer 45-minute guided tours for beginning riders, as well as 45-minute rides for advanced equestrians. These, and a one-and-one-half hour evening ride, all take place on the grounds of the hotel, with trails along the beach and through a lovely wooded area. ~ 293-8811.

Happy Trails Ranch on the North Shore conducts one- to two-hour trail rides through a rainforest valley and pastureland. Riders stop at tropical orchards to sample whatever fruit is in season. The ranch also has peacocks, showbird chickens, a wild boar and six species of ducks. Children will love this place, and they can ride if they are six years or older. ~ P.O. Box 461, Kahuku; 638-7433, fax 638-5975.

GOLF

Even before Tiger Woods, golf has been a very popular sport among visitors in Hawaii, and no other island has more golf courses than Oahu. With more than 30 to choose from, there's one to suit every level of play. And the scenery is spectacular.

HONOLULU   For a round of golf in Honolulu, try the Ala Wai Golf Course, Hawaii's first municipal course. The *Guiness Book of*

World Records named it the busiest in the world. ~ 404 Kapahulu Avenue; 732-6426. **Hawaii Kai Golf Course** is a popular spot with both tourists and *kamaainas*. ~ 8902 Kalanianaole Highway; 395-2358.

WINDWARD COAST   The lush **Olomana Golf Links** has an 18-hole course. ~ 41-1801 Kalanianaole Highway, Waimanalo; 259-7926. For an inexpensive round of golf visit the **Bay View Golf Links**. ~ 45-285 Kaneohe Bay Drive, Kaneohe; 247-0451. Located below the Nuuanu Pali Lookout, the **Pali Golf Course** affords sweeping views of the rugged Koolaus and the windward coastline. ~ 45-050 Kamehameha Highway, Kaneohe; 266-7612. If you want to play a casual game, try the nine-hole **Kahuku Golf Course**. ~ Kahuku; 293-5842. The **Koolau Golf Course**, with a slope rating of 71.7, has been declared the toughest course in America by the United States Golf Association. ~ Kianaole Road, Kaneohe; 247-8873.

NORTH SHORE   The **Links at Kuilima**, on the grounds of the Turtle Bay Hilton Golf and Tennis Resort, was created around an existing 100-acre wetland preserve, which serves as home to several endangered Hawaiian birds. The 18-hole course was designed by golf professional Arnold Palmer. There's also a 9-hole course. ~ Kahuku; 293-8811.

LEEWARD COAST AND CENTRAL OAHU   Set amid fields of sugarcane and pineapple along the Leilehua Plateau in the center of Oahu, the **Hawaii Country Club** is a bit rundown, but offers some challenging holes. ~ 94-1211 Kunia Road, Wahiawa; 622-1744. The **Mililani Golf Club**, though not particularly demanding, provides lovely views of the Koolau and Waianae ranges. ~ 95-176 Kuahelani Avenue, Mililani; 623-2254. The flat **Ted Makalena Golf Course** is not well maintained, but is still popular with local golfers. ~ 93-059 Waipio Point Access Road, Waipahu; 296-7888.

At the **Ko Olina Golf Club** on the leeward coast, golfers must drive their carts under a waterfall to get to the 12th hole of this

SHORELINE HARVEST

There are still some people who don't think of seaweed as food, but it's very popular among Japanese, and it once served as an integral part of the Hawaiian diet. It's extremely nutritious, easy to gather and very plentiful. Rocky shores are the best places to find the edible species of seaweed. Some of them float in to shore and can be picked up; other species cling stubbornly to rocks and must be freed with a knife; still others grow in sand or mud. Low tide is the best time to collect seaweed: more plants are exposed, and some can be taken without even getting wet.

championship course. They will also enjoy the series of lakes, brooks and waterfalls that meanders through the 18-hole course. ~ 92-1220 Aliinui Drive, Kapolei; 676-5309.

Especially beautiful is the **Sheraton Makaha Golf Club** in the Makaha Valley, where sheer volcanic cliffs tower 1500 feet above lush greens, and golfers share the course with birds and peacocks. ~ 84-626 Makaha Valley Road, Makaha; 695-9544, 695-9511.

TENNIS

Many of Oahu resorts offer complete tennis facilities. But don't despair if your hotel lacks nets. There are dozens of public tennis courts in 47 locations around the island. These courts are easily accessible, and it's a great way to meet local players. You may even be able to pick up a game.

Honolulu's public courts can be crowded, especially on weekends and in the evening after work, but don't despair. All courts have a 45-minute rule. If someone is waiting to play, those on the court have to quit after 45 minutes, so you never have to wait too long. Most of the courts are also lighted, allowing you to hang out at the beach until after sunset and play tennis in the cool of the evening.

In the Waikiki area, try **Kapiolani Park**. ~ Kalakaua Avenue. **Diamond Head Tennis Center** is another option in the area. ~ Paki Avenue. There are courts across from Ala Moana Center at **Ala Moana Regional Park**. ~ Ala Moana Boulevard.

In Greater Honolulu you can serve and volley at **Keehi Lagoon**. ~ Off the Nimitz Highway, Honolulu. Or opt for a set in the lush Manoa Valley at **Manoa Valley District Park**. ~ 2721 Kaaipu Avenue, Manoa.

For your tennis needs on the Windward Coast, try **Kailua District Park**. ~ 21 South Kainalu Drive, Kailua. Or visit **Kaneohe District Park**. ~ 45-660 Keaahala Road, Kaneohe.

Sunset Beach Neighborhood Park, with two lighted courts, is an option on the North Shore. ~ 59-360 Kamehameha Highway, Haleiwa.

Lighted courts are also available at **Waianae District Park** on the Leeward Coast. ~ 85-601 Farrington Highway, Waianae.

Call the County Department of Parks and Recreation for more information on public courts. ~ 971-7150. The Hawaii Visitors & Convention Bureau has information on private courts. ~ 923-1811.

BIKING

Oahu is blessed with excellent roads, well-paved and usually flat, and cursed with heavy traffic. About three-quarters of Hawaii's population lives here, and it sometimes seems like every person owns a car.

Honolulu can be a cyclist's nightmare, but outside the city the traffic is somewhat lighter. And Oahu drivers, accustomed to tourists driving mopeds, are relatively conscious of bicyclists.

If you'd really like to get away from it all, try mountain bik[...] Oahu's most popular mountain bike trail is **Mauna Wili** on [...] windward side. It starts from the Pali lookout and goes all the way to Waimanalo.

Keep in mind that the Windward Coast is the wet side, the North Shore is slightly drier and the south and west coasts are the driest of all. And remember, rip-offs are a frequent fact of life on Oahu. Leaving your bike unlocked is asking for a long walk back.

If you'd like a little two-wheeled company, check out the **Hawaii Bicycling League**, which regularly sponsors bike rides. ~ Box 4403, Honolulu, HI 96812; phone/fax 735-5756.

Bike Rentals In Waikiki, **Coconut Cruisers** rents beach cruisers and mountain bikes. ~ 2301 Kalakaua Avenue; 924-1644. Also in Waikiki, **Adventure Rentals** rents mountain bikes. ~ 1946 Ala Moana Boulevard; 941-2222. **Blue Sky Rentals** has mountain, road and tandem bikes. ~ 1920 Ala Moana Boulevard; 947-0101. **Island Triathlon & Bike** rents mountain bikes, but they only have a few. With the rental comes a helmet and complete repair kit. ~ 569 Kapahulu Avenue; 732-7227.

Bike Repairs In addition to doing repair work, **Eki Cyclery** sells accessories and mountain bikes. ~ 1603 Dillingham Boulevard, Honolulu; 847-2005. With mountain, road and triathlon bikes for sale, **The Bike Shop** also does repair work. ~ 1149 South King Street, Honolulu; 596-0588. In central Oahu, try **Waipahu Bicycle** for repairs. ~ 94-320 Waipahu Depot Street, Waipahu; 671-4091.

HIKING

There are numerous hiking trails within easy driving distance of Honolulu. I have listed these as well as trails in the Windward Coast and North Shore areas. Unfortunately, many Oahu treks require special permission from the state, the armed services or private owners. But you should find that the hikes suggested here, none of which require official sanction, will provide you with ample adventure.

To hike with a group or to obtain further information on hiking Oahu, contact the **Sierra Club**. ~ P.O. Box 2577, Honolulu, HI 96803; 538-6616, fax 537-9019. Or you can stop by their office (233 Merchant Street), but call ahead. Another agency that also sponsors regular weekend hikes is the **Hawaii Trail and Mountain Club**. ~ P.O. Box 2238, Honolulu, HI 96804. The **Hawaii Nature Center** offers guided hikes every Saturday morning. Call ahead to make a reservation. ~ 2131 Makiki Heights Drive; 955-0100.

All distances listed for hiking trails are one way unless otherwise noted.

GREATER HONOLULU If you're staying in Waikiki, the most easily accessible hike is the short jaunt up **Diamond Head** crater. There's a sweeping view of Honolulu from atop this famous landmark. The trail begins inside the crater, so take Diamond Head

Road around to the inland side of Diamond Head, then follow the tunnel leading into the crater.

In the Koolau Mountains above Diamond Head there is a trail that climbs almost 2000 feet and affords excellent panoramas of the Windward Coast. To get to the **Lanipo Trail** (3 miles), take Waialae Avenue off of Route H-1. Then turn up Wilhelmina Road and follow until it reaches Maunalani Circle and the trailhead.

For spectacular vistas overlooking the lush Palolo and Manoa Valleys, you can hike **Waahila Ridge Trail** (2 miles). To get there, take St. Louis Heights Drive (near the University of Hawaii campus) and then follow connecting roads up to Waahila Ridge State Recreation Area.

The following trails can be combined for longer hikes. Contact the **Hawaii Nature Center** for free maps and trail information. ~ 2131 Makiki Heights Drive, Honolulu; 955-0100. **Manoa Falls Trail** (0.8 mile) goes through Manoa Valley. This is a pleasant jaunt that follows Waihi Stream through a densely vegetated area to a charming waterfall. **Manoa Cliffs Trail** (3 miles) a pleasant family hike, follows a precipice along the west side of Manoa Valley. And **Puu Ohia Trail** (2 miles), which crosses Manoa Cliffs Trail, provides splendid views of the Manoa and Nuuanu valleys. Both trails begin from Tantalus Drive in the hills above Honolulu. **Makiki Valley Trail** (1.1 miles) begins near Tantalus Drive. Composed of three interlinking trails, this loop passes stands of eucalyptus and bamboo trees and offers some postcard views of Honolulu. Another loop trail, **Judd Memorial** (1.3 miles), crosses Nuuanu Stream and traverses bamboo, eucalyptus and Norfolk pine groves en route to the Jackass Ginger Pool. To get there, take the Pali Highway (Route 61) several miles north from Honolulu. Turn onto Nuuanu Pali Drive and follow it about a mile to Reservoir Number Two spillway.

In the mountains above Pearl Harbor, at Keaiwa Heiau State Recreation Area, you will find the **Aiea Loop Trail** (4.8 miles). Set

WALK SOFTLY AND SAFELY

Most trails you'll be hiking are composed of volcanic rock. Since this is a very crumbly substance, be extremely cautious when climbing any rock faces. In fact, you should avoid steep climbs if possible. It's advisable to wear long pants when hiking in order to protect your legs from rock outcroppings, insects and spiny plants. Stay on the trails: Oahu's dense undergrowth makes it very easy to get lost. If you get lost at night, stay where you are. Because of the low latitude, night descends rapidly here; there's practically no twilight. Once darkness falls, it can be very dangerous to move around.

in a heavily forested area, this hike passes the wreckage of a World War II cargo plane. It provides an excellent chance to see some of the native Hawaiian trees—*lehua*, *ohia* and *koa*—used by local woodworkers. (For directions to Keaiwa Heiau State Recreation Area, see the "Greater Honolulu Beaches & Parks" section in this book.)

Another hike is along **Waimano Trail** (7 miles), which climbs 1600 feet to an astonishing vista point above Oahu's Windward Coast. There are swimming holes en route to the vista point. To get there, take Kamehameha Highway (Route 90) west to Waimano Home Road (Route 730). Turn right and go two-and-a-half miles to a point along the road where you'll see a building on the right and an irrigation ditch on the left. The trail follows the ditch.

SOUTHEAST OAHU   There are several excellent hikes along this shore. The first few are within ten miles of Waikiki, near **Hanauma Bay**. From the beach at Hanauma you can hike two miles along the coast and cliffs to the Halona Blowhole. This trek passes the Toilet Bowl, a unique tidepool with a hole in the bottom that causes it to fill and then flush with the wave action. Waves sometimes wash the rocks along this path, so be prepared to get wet (and be careful!).

At the intersection where the short road leading down toward Hanauma Bay branches from Kalanianaole Highway (Route 72), there are two other trails. **Koko Head Trail** (1 mile), a hike to the top of a volcanic cone, starts on the ocean side of the highway. This trek features some startling views of Hanauma Bay, Diamond Head and the Koolau Range. Another hike, along **Koko Crater Trail** (1 mile), leads from the highway up to a 1208-foot peak. The views from this crow's nest are equally spectacular.

WINDWARD COAST   There are several other particularly pretty hikes much farther north, near the village of Hauula. **Sacred Falls Trail** (2.2 miles) gently ascends through a canyon and arrives at a waterfall and swimming hole. The trailhead for this popular trek is near Kamehameha Highway (Route 83) just south of Hauula.

Then, in Hauula, if you turn off of Kamehameha Highway and head inland for about a quarter-mile up Hauula Homestead Road, you'll come to Maakua Road. Walk up Maakua Road, which leads into the woods. About 300 yards after entering the woods, the road forks. Maakua Gulch Trail branches to the left. If you continue straight ahead you'll be on Hauula Trail, but if you veer left onto Maakua Gulch Trail, you'll encounter yet another trail branching off to the left in about 150 yards. This is Papali Trail (also known as Maakua Trail).

Maakua Gulch Trail (3 miles), en route to a small waterfall, traverses a rugged canyon with extremely steep walls. Part of the trail lies along the stream bed, so be ready to get wet. **Hauula Trail**

(2.5 miles) ascends along two ridges and provides fine vistas of the Koolau Range and the Windward Coast. **Papali Trail** (2.5 miles) drops into Papali Gulch, then climbs high along a ridge from which you can view the surrounding countryside.

NORTH SHORE AND LEEWARD COAST   You can approach the trail to **Kaena Point** either from the North Shore or the Leeward Coast. It's a dry, rock-strewn path that leads to Oahu's northwest tip. There are tidepools and swimming spots en route, plus spectacular views of a rugged, uninhabited coastline. To get to the trailhead, just drive to the end of the paved portion of Route 930 on the North Shore or Route 93 on the Leeward Coast. Then follow the jeep trail out to Kaena Point. Either way, it's about a two-mile trek.

THREE

History and Culture

POLYNESIAN ARRIVAL   The island of Hawaii, the Big Island, was the last land mass created in the dramatic geologic upheaval that formed the Hawaiian islands. But it was the first Hawaiian island to be inhabited by humans. Perhaps as early as the third century, Polynesians sailing from the Marquesas Islands, and then later from Tahiti, landed near Hawaii's southern tip. The boats were formidable structures, catamaran-like vessels with a cabin built on the platform between the wooden hulls. The sails were woven from coconut fibers. Some of the vessels were a hundred feet long and could do 20 knots, making the trip to Hawaii in a month.

The Polynesians had originally come from the coast of Asia about 3000 years before. They had migrated through Indonesia, then pressed inexorably eastward, leapfrogging across archipelagoes until they finally reached the last chain, the most remote—Hawaii.

These Pacific migrants were undoubtedly the greatest sailors of their day, and stand among the finest in history. When close to land they could smell it, taste it in the seawater, see it in a lagoon's turquoise reflection on the clouds above an island. They knew 150 stars. From the color of the water they determined ocean depths and current directions. They had no charts, no compasses, no sextants; sailing directions were simply recorded in legends and chants. Yet Polynesians discovered the Pacific, from Indonesia to Easter Island, from New Zealand to Hawaii. They made the Vikings and Phoenicians look like landlubbers.

CAPTAIN COOK   They were high islands, rising in the northeast as the sun broke across the Pacific. First one, then a second and, finally, as the tall-masted ships drifted west, a third island loomed before them. Landfall! The British crew was ecstatic. It meant fresh water, tropical fruits, solid ground on which to set their boots and a chance to carouse with the native women. For their captain, James Cook, it was another in an amazing career of discoveries. The man whom many call history's greatest explorer was about to land in one of the last spots on earth to be discovered by the West.

49

He would name the place for his patron, the British earl who became famous by pressing a meal between two crusts of bread. The Sandwich Islands. Later they would be called Owhyhee, and eventually, as the Western tongue glided around the uncharted edges of a foreign language, Hawaii.

It was January 1778, a time when the British Empire was still basking in a sun that never set. The Pacific had been opened to Western powers over two centuries before, when a Portuguese sailor named Magellan crossed it. Since then, the British, French, Dutch and Spanish had tracked through in search of future colonies.

They happened upon Samoa, Fiji, Tahiti and the other islands that spread across this third of the globe, but somehow they had never sighted Hawaii. Even when Cook finally spied it, he little realized how important a find he had made. Hawaii, quite literally, was a jewel in the ocean, rich in fragrant sandalwood, ripe for agricultural exploitation and crowded with sea life. But it was the archipelago's isolation that would prove to be its greatest resource. Strategically situated between Asia and North America, it was the only place for thousands of miles to which whalers, merchants and bluejackets could repair for provisions and rest.

Cook was 49 years old when he shattered Hawaii's quiescence. The Englishman hadn't expected to find islands north of Tahiti. Quite frankly, he wasn't even trying. It was his third Pacific voyage and Cook was hunting bigger game, the fabled Northwest Passage that would link this ocean with the Atlantic.

But these mountainous islands were still an interesting find. He could see by the canoes venturing out to meet his ships that the lands were inhabited; when he finally put ashore on Kauai, Cook discovered a Polynesian society. He saw irrigated fields, domestic animals and high-towered temples. The women were bare-breasted, the men wore loincloths. As his crew bartered for pigs, fowls and bananas, he learned that the natives knew about metal and coveted iron like gold.

If iron was gold to these "Indians," then Cook was a god. He soon realized that his arrival had somehow been miraculously timed, coinciding with the Makahiki festival, a wild party celebrating the roving deity Lono whose return the Hawaiians had awaited for years. Cook was a strange white man sailing monstrous ships—obviously he was Lono. The Hawaiians gave him gifts, fell in his path and rose only at his insistence.

But even among religious crowds, fame is often fickle. After leaving Hawaii, Cook sailed north to the Arctic Sea, where he failed to discover the Northwest Passage. He returned the next year to Kealakekua Bay on the Big Island, arriving at the tail end of another exhausting Makahiki festival. By then the Hawaiians had tired of his constant demands for provisions and were suffering from a new disease that was obviously carried by Lono's archangelic crew—syphilis. This Lono was proving something of a free-loader.

Tensions ran high. The Hawaiians stole a boat. Cook retaliated with gunfire. A scuffle broke out on the beach and in a sudden violent outburst, which surprised the islanders as much as the interlopers, the Hawaiians discovered that their god could bleed. The world's finest mariner lay face down in foot-deep water, stabbed and bludgeoned to death.

Cook's end marked the beginning of an era. He had put the Pacific on the map, his map, probing its expanses and defining its fringes. In Hawaii he ended a thousand years of solitude. The archipelago's geographic isolation, which has always played a crucial role in Hawaii's development, had finally failed to protect it, and a second theme had come into play—the islands' vulnerability. Together with the region's "backwardness," these conditions would now mold Hawaii's history. All in turn would be shaped by another factor, one which James Cook had added to Hawaii's historic equation: the West.

KAMEHAMEHA AND KAAHUMANU The next man whose star would rise above Hawaii was present at Cook's death. Some say he struck the Englishman, others that he took a lock of the great leader's hair and used its residual power, its *mana*, to become king of all Hawaii.

Kamehameha was a tall, muscular, unattractive man with a furrowed face, a lesser chief on the powerful island of Hawaii. When he began his career of conquest a few years after Cook's death, he was a mere upstart, an ambitious, arrogant young chief. But he fought with a general's skill and a warrior's cunning, often plunging into the midst of a melee. He had an astute sense of technology, an intuition that these new Western metals and firearms could make him a king.

In Kamehameha's early years, the Hawaiian islands were composed of many fiefdoms. Several kings or great chiefs, continually warring among themselves, ruled individual islands. At times, a few kings would carve up one island or a lone king might seize several. Never had one monarch controlled all the islands.

But fresh players had entered the field: Westerners with ample firepower and awesome ships. During the decade following Cook,

SAILORS EXTRAORDINAIRE

Centuries before Columbus happened upon the New World, and during a time when European mariners were rarely venturing outside the Mediterranean Sea, entire families of Polynesians were crossing 2500 miles of untracked ocean in hand-carved canoes.

only a handful had arrived, mostly Englishmen and Americans, and they had not yet won the influence they soon would wield. However, even a few foreigners were enough to upset the balance of power. They sold weapons and hardware to the great chiefs, making several of them more powerful than any of the others had ever been. War was imminent.

While British sailors were discovering Hawaii, the English army was battling a ragtag band of revolutionaries for control of the American colonies.

Kamehameha stood in the center of the hurricane. Like any leader suddenly caught up in the terrible momentum of history, he never quite realized where he was going or how fast he was moving. And he cared little that he was being carried in part by Westerners who would eventually want something for the ride. Kamehameha was no fool. If political expedience meant Western intrusion, then so be it. He had enemies among chiefs on the other islands; he needed the guns.

When two white men came into his camp in 1790, he had the military advisers to complement a fast expanding arsenal. Within months he cannoaded Maui. In 1792, Kamehameha seized the Big Island by inviting his main rival to a peaceful parley, then slaying the hapless chief. By 1795, he had consolidated his control of Maui, grasped Molokai and Lanai, and begun reaching greedily toward Oahu. He struck rapidly, landing near Waikiki and sweeping inland, forcing his enemies to their deaths over the precipitous cliffs of the Nuuanu Pali.

The warrior had become a conqueror, controlling all the islands except Kauai, which he finally gained in 1810 by peaceful negotiation. Kamehameha proved to be as able a bureaucrat as he had been a general. He became a benevolent despot who, with the aid of an ever-increasing number of Western advisers, expanded Hawaii's commerce, brought peace to the islands and moved his people inexorably toward the modern age.

He came to be called Kamehameha the Great, and history first cast him as the George Washington of Hawaii, a wise and resolute leader who gathered a wartorn archipelago into a kingdom. Kamehameha I. But with the revisionist history of the 1960s and 1970s, as Third World people questioned both the Western version of events and the virtues of progress, Kamehameha began to resemble Benedict Arnold. He was seen as an opportunist, a megalomaniac who permitted the Western powers their initial foothold in Hawaii. He used their technology and then, in the manner of great men who depend on stronger allies, was eventually used by them.

As long a shadow as Kamehameha cast across the islands, the event that most dramatically transformed Hawaiian society occurred after his death in 1819. The kingdom had passed to Kamehameha's son Liholiho, but Kamehameha's favorite wife, Kaahumanu, usurped the power. Liholiho was a prodigal son, dissolute, lacking self-certainty, a drunk. Kaahumanu was a woman for all seasons, a canny politician who combined brilliance with boldness, the feminist of her day. She had infuriated Kamehameha by eating forbidden foods and sleeping with other chiefs, even when he placed a taboo on her body and executed her lovers. She drank liquor, ran away, proved completely uncontrollable and won Kamehameha's love.

It was only natural that when he died, she would take his *mana*, or so she reckoned. Kaahumanu gravitated toward power with the drive of someone whom fate has unwisely denied. She carved her own destiny, announcing that Kamehameha's wish had been to give her a governmental voice. There would be a new post and she would fill it, becoming in a sense Hawaii's first prime minister.

And if the power, then the motion. Kaahumanu immediately marched against Hawaii's belief system, trying to topple the old idols. For years she had bristled under a polytheistic religion regulated by taboos, or *kapus*, which severely restricted women's rights. Now Kaahumanu urged the new king, Liholiho, to break a very strict *kapu* by sharing a meal with women.

Since the act might help consolidate Liholiho's position, it had a certain appeal to the king. Anyway, the *kapus* were weakening: these white men, coming now in ever greater numbers, defied them with impunity. Liholiho vacillated, went on a two-day drunk before gaining courage, then finally sat down to eat. It was a last supper, shattering an ancient creed and opening the way for a radically new divinity. As Kaahumanu had willed, the old order collapsed, taking away a vital part of island life and leaving the Hawaiians more exposed than ever to foreign influence.

Already Western practices were gaining hold. Commerce from Honolulu, Lahaina and other ports was booming. There was a fortune to be made dealing sandalwood to China-bound merchants, and the chiefs were forcing the common people to strip Hawaii's forests. The grueling labor might make the chiefs rich, but it gained the commoners little more than a barren landscape. Western diseases struck virulently. The Polynesians in Hawaii, who numbered 300,000 in Cook's time, were extremely susceptible. By 1866, their population had dwindled to less than 60,000. It was a difficult time for the Hawaiian people.

MISSIONARIES AND MERCHANTS   Hawaii was not long without religion. The same year that Kaahumanu shattered tradition, a group of New England missionaries boarded the brig *Thaddeus* for a voyage around Cape Horn. It was a young company—many were in their twenties or thirties—and included a doctor, a printer and several teachers. They were all strict Calvinists, fearful that the second coming was at hand and possessed of a mission. They were bound for a strange land called Hawaii, 18,000 miles away.

Hawaii, of course, was a lost paradise, a hellhole of sin and savagery where men slept with several wives and women neglected to wear dresses. To the missionaries, it mattered little that the Hawaiians had lived this way for centuries. The churchmen would save these heathens from hell's everlasting fire whether they liked it or not.

The delegation arrived in Kailua on the Big Island in 1820 and then spread out, establishing important missions in Honolulu and Lahaina. Soon they were building schools and churches, conducting services in Hawaiian and converting the natives to Christianity.

The missionaries rapidly became an integral part of Hawaii, despite the fact that they were a walking contradiction to everything Hawaiian. They were a contentious, self-righteous, fanatical people whose arrogance toward the Hawaiians blinded them to the beauty and wisdom of island lifestyles. Where the natives lived in thatch homes open to the soothing trade winds, the missionaries built airless clapboard houses with New England–style fireplaces. While the Polynesians swam and surfed frequently, the new arrivals, living near the world's finest beaches, stank from not bathing. In a region where the thermometer rarely drops much below 70°, they wore long-sleeved woolens, ankle-length dresses and clawhammer coats. At dinner they preferred salt pork to fresh beef, dried meat to fresh fish. They considered coconuts an abomination and were loath to eat bananas.

And yet the missionaries were a brave people, selfless and God-fearing. Their dangerous voyage from the Atlantic had brought them into a very alien land. Many would die from disease and overwork; most would never see their homeland again. Bigoted though they were, the Calvinists committed their lives to the Hawaiian people. They developed the Hawaiian alphabet, rendered Hawaiian into a written language and, of course, translated the Bible. Theirs was the first printing press west of the Rockies. They introduced Western medicine throughout the islands and created such an effective school system that, by the mid-19th century, 80 percent of the Hawaiian population was literate. Unlike almost all the other white people who came to Hawaii, they not only took from the islanders, they also gave.

But to a missionary, *giving* means ripping away everything repugnant to God and substituting it with Christianity. They would have to destroy Hawaiian culture in order to save it. Though instructed by their church elders not to meddle in island politics, the missionaries soon realized that heavenly wars had to be fought on earthly battlefields. Politics it would be. After all, wasn't government just another expression of God's bounty?

They allied with Kaahumanu and found it increasingly difficult to separate church from state. Kaahumanu converted to Christianity, while the missionaries became government advisers and helped pass laws protecting the sanctity of the Sabbath. Disgusting practices such as hula dancing were prohibited.

Politics can be a dangerous world for a man of the cloth. The missionaries were soon pitted against other foreigners who were quite willing to let the clerics sing hymns, but were damned opposed to permitting them a voice in government. Hawaii in the 1820s had become a favorite way station for the whaling fleet. As the sandalwood forests were decimated, the island merchants began looking for other industries. By the 1840s, when over 500 ships a year anchored in Hawaiian ports, whaling had become the islands' economic lifeblood.

During the heyday of the whaling industry, more American ships visited Hawaii than any other port in the world.

Like the missionaries, the whalers were Yankees, shipping out from bustling New England ports. But they were a hell of a different cut of Yankee. These were rough, crude, boisterous men who loved rum and music, and thought a lot more of fornicating with island women than saving them. After the churchmen forced the passage of laws prohibiting prostitution, the sailors rioted along the waterfront and fired cannons at the mission homes. When the smoke cleared, the whalers still had their women.

Religion simply could not compete with commerce, and other Westerners were continuously stimulating more business in the islands. By the 1840s, as Hawaii adopted a parliamentary form of government, American and British fortune hunters were replacing missionaries as government advisers. It was a time when anyone, regardless of ability or morality, could travel to the islands and become a political powerhouse literally overnight. A consumptive American, fleeing the mainland for reasons of health, became chief justice of the Hawaiian Supreme Court while still in his twenties. Another lawyer, shadowed from the East Coast by a checkered past, became attorney general two weeks after arriving.

The situation was no different internationally. Hawaii was subject to the whims and terrors of gunboat diplomacy. The archipelago was solitary and exposed, and Western powers were beginning to eye it covetously. In 1843, a maverick British naval officer actually annexed Hawaii to the Crown, but the London government later countermanded his actions. Then, in the early 1850s, the threat of American annexation arose. Restless Californians, fresh from the gold fields and hungry for revolution, plotted unsuccessfully in Honolulu. Even the French periodically sent gunboats in to protect their small Catholic minority.

Finally, the three powers officially stated that they wanted to maintain Hawaii's national integrity. But independence seemed increasingly unlikely. European countries had already begun claiming other Pacific islands, and with the influx of Yankee missionaries and whalers, Hawaii was being steadily drawn into the American orbit.

THE SUGAR PLANTERS   There is an old Hawaiian saying that describes the 19th century: The missionaries came to do good, and they did very well. Actually the early evangelists, few of whom profited from their work, lived out only half the maxim. Their sons would give the saying its full meaning.

This second generation, quite willing to sacrifice glory for gain, fit neatly into the commercial society that had rendered their fathers irrelevant. They were shrewd, farsighted young Christians who had grown up in Hawaii and knew both the islands' pitfalls and potentials. They realized that the missionaries had never quite found Hawaii's pulse, and they watched uneasily as whaling became the lifeblood of the islands. Certainly it brought wealth, but whaling was too tenuous—there was always a threat that it might dry up entirely. A one-industry economy would never do; the mission boys wanted more. Agriculture was the obvious answer, and eventually they determined to bind their providence to a plant that grew wild in the islands—sugar cane.

The first sugar plantation was started on Kauai in 1835, but not until the 1870s did the new industry blossom. By then, the Civil War had wreaked havoc with the whaling fleet, and a devastating winter in the Arctic whaling grounds practically destroyed it. The mission boys, who prophesied the storm, weathered it quite comfortably. They had already begun fomenting an agricultural revolution.

Agriculture, of course, means land, and in the 19th century practically all Hawaii's acreage was held by the king and the chiefs. So in 1850, the mission sons, together with other white entrepreneurs, pushed through the Great Mahele, one of the slickest real estate laws in history. Rationalizing that it would grant chiefs the liberty to sell land to Hawaiian commoners and white men, the mission sons established a western system of private property.

The Hawaiians, who had shared their chiefs' lands communally for centuries, had absolutely no concept of deeds and leases. What resulted was the old $24-worth-of-beads story. The benevolent Westerners wound up with the land, while the lucky Hawaiians got practically nothing. Large tracts were purchased for cases of whiskey; others went for the cost of a hollow promise. The entire island of Niihau, which is still owned by the same family, sold for $10,000. It was a bloodless coup, staged more than 40 years before the revolution that would topple Hawaii's monarchy. In a sense it made the 1893 uprising anticlimactic. By then Hawaii's future would already be determined: white interlopers would own four times as much land as Hawaiian commoners.

Following the Great Mahele, the mission boys, along with other businessmen, were ready to become sugar planters. The *mana* once again was passing into new hands. Obviously, there was money to be made in cane, a lot of it, and now that they had land, all they needed was labor. The Hawaiians would never do. Cook might have recognized them as industrious, hardworking people, but the sugar planters considered them shiftless. Disease was killing them off anyway, and the Hawaiians who survived seemed to lose the will to live. Many made appointments with death, stating that in a week they would die; seven days later they were dead.

Foreign labor was the only answer. In 1850, the Masters and Servants Act was passed, establishing an immigration board to import plantation workers. Cheap Asian labor would be brought over. It was a crucial decision, one that would ramify forever through Hawaiian history and change the very substance of island society. Eventually these Asian workers transformed Hawaii from a chain of Polynesian islands into one of the world's most varied and dynamic locales, a meeting place of East and West.

Between 1850 and 1930, 180,000 Japanese, 125,000 Filipinos, 50,000 Chinese, and 20,000 Portuguese immigrated to Hawaii.

The Chinese were the first to come, arriving in 1852 and soon outnumbering the white population. Initially, with their long pigtails and uncommon habits, the Chinese were a joke around the islands. They were poor people from southern China whose lives were directed by clan loyalty. They built schools and worked hard so that one day they could return to their native villages in glory. They were ambitious, industrious and—ultimately—successful.

Too successful, according to the sugar planters, who found it almost impossible to keep the coolies down on the farm. The Chinese came to Hawaii under labor contracts, which forced them to work for five years. After their indentureship, rather than reenlisting as the sugar bosses had planned, the Chinese moved to the city and became merchants. Worse yet, they married Hawaiian women and were assimilated into the society.

These coolies, the planters decided, were too uppity, too ready to fill social roles that were really the business of white men. So in the 1880s, they began importing Portuguese. But the Portuguese thought they already *were* white men, while any self-respecting American or Englishman of the time knew they weren't.

The Portuguese spelled trouble, and in 1886 the sugar planters turned to Japan, with its restricted land mass and burgeoning population. The new immigrants were peasants from Japan's southern islands, raised in an authoritarian, hierarchical culture in which the father was a family dictator and the family was strictly defined by its social status. Like the Chinese, they built schools to protect their heritage and dreamed of returning home someday; but unlike their Asian neighbors, they only married other Japanese. They sent home for "picture brides," worshipped their ancestors and Emperor and paid ultimate loyalty to Japan, not Hawaii.

The Japanese, it soon became evident, were too proud to work long hours for low pay. Plantation conditions were atrocious; workers were housed in hovels and frequently beaten. The Japanese simply did not adapt. Worst of all, they not only bitched, they organized, striking in 1909.

So in 1910, the sugar planters turned to the Philippines for labor. For two decades the Filipinos arrived, seeking their fortunes and leaving their wives behind. They worked not only with sugar cane but also with pineapples, which were becoming a big business in the 20th century. They were a boisterous, fun-loving people, hated by the immigrants who preceded them and used by the whites who hired them. The Filipinos were given the most menial jobs, the worst working conditions and the shoddiest housing. In time, another side of their character began to show—a despondency, a hopeless sense of their own plight, their inability to raise passage money back home. They became the untouchables of Hawaii.

REVOLUTIONARIES AND ROYALISTS   Sugar, by the late 19th century, was king. It had become the center of island economy, the principal fact of life for most islanders. Like the earlier whaling industry, it was drawing Hawaii ever closer to the American sphere. The sugar planters were selling the bulk of their crops in California; having already signed several tariff treaties to protect their American market, they were eager to further strengthen mainland ties. Besides, many sugar planters were second-, third- and fourth-generation descendants of the New England missionaries; they had a natural affinity for the United States.

There was, however, one group that shared neither their love for sugar nor their ties to America. To the Hawaiian people, David Kalakaua was king, and America was the nemesis that had long threatened their independence. The whites might own the land, but the Hawaiians, through their monarch, still held substantial political power. During Kalakaua's rule in the 1870s and 1880s, anti-colonialism was rampant.

The sugar planters were growing impatient. Kalakaua was proving very antagonistic; his nationalist drumbeating was becoming louder in their ears. How could the sugar merchants convince the United States to annex Hawaii when all these silly Hawaiian royalists were running around pretending to be the Pacific's answer to the British Isles? They had tolerated this long enough. The Hawaiians were obviously unfit to rule, and the planters soon joined with other businessmen to form a secret revolutionary organization. Backed by a force of well-armed followers, they pushed through the "Bayonet Constitution" of 1887, a self-serving document that weakened the king and strengthened the white landowners. If Hawaii was to remain a monarchy, it would have a Magna Carta.

But Hawaii would not be a monarchy long. Once revolution is in the air, it's often difficult to clear the smoke. By 1893, Kalakaua was dead and his sister, Liliuokalani, had succeeded to the throne. She was an audacious leader, proud of her heritage, quick to defend it and prone to let immediate passions carry her onto dangerous ground. At a time when she should have hung fire, she charged, proclaiming publicly that she would abrogate the new constitution and reestablish a strong monarchy. The revolutionaries had the excuse they needed. They struck in January, seized government buildings and, with four boatloads of American marines and the support of the American minister, secured Honolulu. Liliuokalani surrendered.

Hawaii's first president was Sanford Dole, a missionary's son whose name eventually became synonymous with pineapples.

It was a highly illegal coup; legitimate government had been stolen from the Hawaiian people. But given an island chain as isolated and vulnerable as Hawaii, the revolutionaries reasoned, how much did it really matter? It would be weeks before word reached Washington of what a few Americans had done without official sanction, then several more months before a new American president, Grover Cleveland, denounced the renegade action. By then the revolutionaries would already be forming a republic.

Not even revolution could rock Hawaii into the modern age. For years, an unstable monarchy had reigned; now an oligarchy composed of the revolution's leaders would rule. Officially, Hawaii was a democracy; in truth, the Chinese and Japanese were hindered from voting, and the Hawaiians were encouraged not to bother. Hawaii, reckoned its new leaders, was simply not ready for democracy. Even when the islands were finally annexed by the United States in 1898 and granted territorial status, they remained a colony.

More than ever before, the sugar planters, alias revolutionaries, held sway. By the early 20th century, they had linked their plantations into a cartel, the Big Five. It was a tidy monopoly composed of five companies that owned not only the sugar and pineapple industries, but the docks, shipping companies and many of the stores, as well. Most of these holdings, happily, were the property of a few interlocking, intermarrying mission families—the Doles, Thurstons, Alexanders, Baldwins, Castles, Cookes and others— who had found heaven right here on earth. They golfed together and dined together, sent their daughters to Wellesley and their sons to Yale. All were proud of their roots, and as blindly paternalistic as their forefathers. It was their destiny to control Hawaii, and they made very certain, by refusing to sell land or provide services, that mainland firms did not gain a foothold in their domain.

What was good for the Big Five was good for Hawaii. Competition was obviously not good for Hawaii. Although the Chinese and Japanese were establishing successful businesses in Honolulu and some Chinese were even growing rich, they posed no immediate threat to the Big Five. And the Hawaiians had never been good at capitalism. By the early 20th century, they had become one of the world's most urbanized groups. But rather than competing with white businessmen in Honolulu, unemployed Hawaiians were forced to live in hovels and packing crates, cooking their poi on stoves fashioned from empty oil cans.

Political competition was also unhealthy. Hawaii was ruled by the Big Five, so naturally it should be run by the Republican Party. After all, the mission families were Republicans. Back on the mainland, the Democrats had always been cool to the sugar planters, and it was a Republican president, William McKinley, who eventually annexed Hawaii. The Republicans, quite simply, were good for business.

The Big Five set out very deliberately to overwhelm any political opposition. When the Hawaiians created a home-rule party around the turn of the century, the Big Five shrewdly co-opted it by running a beloved descendant of Hawaii's royal family as the Republican candidate. On the plantations they pitted one ethnic group against another to prevent the Asian workers from organizing. Then, when labor unions finally formed, the Big Five attacked them savagely. In 1924, police killed 16 strikers on Kauai. Fourteen years later, in an incident known as the "Hilo massacre," the police wounded 50 picketers.

The Big Five crushed the Democratic Party by intimidation. Polling booths were rigged. It was dangerous to vote Democratic— workers could lose their jobs, and if they were plantation workers, that meant losing their houses, as well. Conducting Democratic meetings on the plantations was about as easy as holding a hula dance in an old missionary church. The Democrats went underground.

Those were halcyon days for both the Big Five and the Republican Party. In 1900, only five percent of Hawaii's population was white. The rest was comprised of races that rarely benefitted from Republican policies. But for the next several decades, even during the Depression, the Big Five kept the Republicans in power.

While the New Deal swept the mainland, Hawaii clung to its colonial heritage. The islands were still a generation behind the rest of the United States—the Big Five enjoyed it that way. There was nothing like the status quo when you were already in power. Other factors that had long shaped Hawaii's history also played into the hands of the Big Five. The islands' vulnerability, which had always favored the rule of a small elite, permitted the Big Five to establish an awesome cartel. Hawaii's isolation, its distance from the mainland, helped protect their monopoly.

THE JAPANESE AND THE MODERN WORLD   All that ended on December 7, 1941. On what would afterwards be known as the "Day of Infamy," a flotilla of six aircraft carriers carrying over 400 planes unleashed a devastating assault on Pearl Harbor. Attacking the Pacific Fleet on a Sunday morning, when most of the American ships were unwisely anchored side by side, the Japanese sank or badly damaged six battleships, three destroyers and several other vessels. Over 2400 Americans were killed.

The Japanese bombers that attacked Pearl Harbor sent shock waves through Hawaii that are still rumbling today. World War II changed all the rules of the game, upsetting the conditions that had determined island history for centuries.

Ironically, no group in Hawaii would feel the shift more thoroughly than the Japanese. On the mainland, Japanese-Americans were rounded up and herded into relocation camps. But in Hawaii that was impossible; there were simply too many, and they comprised too large a part of the labor force.

When Japan's Emperor declared war on the United States in 1941, 160,000 Japanese-Americans were living in Hawaii, fully one-third of the islands' population.

Many were second-generation Japanese, *nisei*, who had been educated in American schools and assimilated into Western society. Unlike their immigrant parents, the *issei*, they felt few ties to Japan. Their loyalties lay with America, and when war broke out they determined to prove it. They joined the U.S. armed forces and formed a regiment, the 442nd, which became the most frequently decorated outfit of the war. The Japanese were heroes, and when the war ended many heroes came home to the United States and ran for political office. Men like Dwight Eisenhower, Daniel Inouye, John Kennedy and Spark Matsunaga began winning elections.

By the time the 442nd returned to the home front, Hawaii was changing dramatically. The Democrats were coming to power. Leftist labor unions won crucial strikes in 1941 and 1946. Jack Burns, an former cop who dressed in tattered clothes and drove around Honolulu in a beat-up car, was creating a new Democratic coalition.

Burns, who would eventually become governor, recognized the potential power of Hawaii's ethnic groups. Money was flowing into the islands—first military expenditures and then tourist dollars, and non-whites were rapidly becoming a new middle class. The Filipinos still constituted a large part of the plantation force, and the Hawaiians remained disenchanted, but the Japanese and Chinese were moving up fast. Together they comprised a majority of Hawaii's voters.

Burns organized them, creating a multiracial movement and thrusting the Japanese forward as candidates. By 1954, the Democrats controlled the legislature, with the Japanese filling one out of every two seats in the capital. Then, when Hawaii attained statehood five years later, the voters elected the first Japanese ever to serve in Congress. Today one of the state's U.S. senators and a congressman are Japanese. On every level of government, from municipal to federal, the Japanese predominate. They have arrived. The *mana*, that legendary power coveted by the Hawaiian chiefs and then lost to the sugar barons, has passed once again—to a people who came as immigrant farm-workers and stayed to become the leaders of the 50th state.

The Japanese and the Democrats were on the move, but in the period from World War II until the present day, everything was in motion. Hawaii was in upheaval. Jet travel and a population boom shattered the islands' solitude. While in 1939 about 500 people flew to Hawaii, now more than six million land every year. The military population escalated as Oahu became a key base not only during World War II but throughout the Cold War and the Vietnam War, as well. Hawaii's overall population exploded from about a half-million just after World War II to over one million at the present time.

No longer did the islands lag behind the mainland; they rapidly acquired the dubious quality of modernity. Hawaii became America's 50th state in 1959, Honolulu grew into a bustling highrise city, and condominiums mushroomed along Maui's beaches. Outside investors swallowed up two of the Big Five corporations, and several partners in the old monopoly began conducting most of their business outside Hawaii. Everything became too big and moved too fast for Hawaii to be entirely vulnerable to a small interest group. Now, like the rest of the world, it would be prey to multinational corporations. By the 1980s, it would also be of significant interest to investors from Japan. In a few short years they succeeded in buying up a majority of the state's luxury resorts, including every major beachfront hotel in Waikiki, sending real estate prices into an upward spiral that did not level off until the early 1990s.

One element that has not plateaued during the current decade is the Native Hawaiian movement. Nativist sentiments were spurred in January 1993 by the 100th anniversary of the American overthrow of the Hawaiian monarchy. Over 15,000 people turned out to mark the illegal coup. Later that year, President Clinton signed a statement issued by Congress formally apologizing to the Hawaiian people. Then in 1994, the United States Navy returned the island of Kahoolawe to the state of Hawaii. Long a rallying symbol for the Native Hawaiian movement, the unoccupied island had been used for decades as a naval bombing target. By 1996, efforts to clean away bomb debris and make the island habitable were well under way.

Today, with its own indigenous people's movement, average house prices over $300,000 and an inflation factor that saw prices rise over 200% in 20 years, Hawaii has finally arrived. It is so much a part of the United States that one segment of the population is advocating secession. An island chain that slept for centuries has been awakened by the forces of change and is in turn beginning to disrupt the complacency of the forces that have long kept it dormant.

Culture

Hawaii, according to Polynesian legend, was discovered by Hawaii-loa, an adventurous sailor who often disappeared on long fishing trips. On one voyage, urged along by his navigator, Hawaii-loa sailed toward the planet Jupiter. He crossed the "many-colored ocean," passed over the "deep-colored sea," and eventually came upon "flaming Hawaii," a mountainous island chain that spewed smoke and lava.

History is less romantic. The Polynesians who found Hawaii were probably driven from their home islands by war or some similar calamity. They traveled in groups, not as lone rangers, and shared their canoes with dogs, pigs and chickens, with which they planned to stock new lands. Agricultural plants such as coconuts, yams, taro, sugar cane, bananas and breadfruit were also stowed on board.

Most important, they transported their culture, an intricate system of beliefs and practices developed in the South Seas. After undergoing the stresses and demands of pioneer life, this traditional lifestyle was transformed into a new and uniquely Hawaiian culture.

It was based on a caste system that placed the *alii* or chiefs at the top and the slaves, *kauwas*, on the bottom. Between these two groups were the priests, *kahunas* and the common people or *makaainanas*. The chiefs, much like feudal lords, controlled all the land and collected taxes from the commoners who farmed it.

Life centered around the *kapu*, a complex group of regulations that dictated what was sacred or profane. For example, women were not permitted to eat pork or bananas; commoners had to prostrate themselves in the presence of a chief. These strictures were vital to Hawaiian religion; *kapu* breakers were directly violating the will of the gods and could be executed for their actions. And there were a lot of gods to watch out for, many quite vindictive. The four central gods were *Kane*, the creator; *Lono*, the god of agriculture; *Ku*, the war god; and *Kanaloa*, lord of the underworld. They had been born from the sky father and earth mother, and had in turn created many lesser gods and demigods who controlled various aspects of nature.

It was, in the uncompromising terminology of the West, a stone-age civilization. Though the Hawaiians lacked metal tools, the wheel and a writing system, they managed to include within their short inventory of cultural goods everything necessary to sustain a large population on a chain of small islands. They fashioned fish nets from coconut fibers, made hooks out of bone, shell and ivory, and raised fish in rock-bound ponds. The men used irrigation in their farming. The women made clothing by pounding mulberry bark into a soft cloth called *tapa*, dyeing elaborate patterns into the fabric. They built peak-roofed thatch huts from native *pili* grass and *lauhala* leaves. The men fought wars with spears, slings, clubs and daggers! The women used mortars and pestles to pound the roots of the taro plant into poi, the islanders' staple food.

The West labeled these early Hawaiians "noble savages." Actually, they often lacked nobility. The Hawaiians were cannibals who sometimes practiced human sacrifice and often used human bait to fish for sharks. They constantly warred among themselves and would mercilessly pursue a retreating army, murdering as many of the vanquished soldiers as possible.

But they weren't savages either. The Hawaiians developed a rich oral tradition of genealogical chants and created beautiful lilting songs to accompany their hula dancing. Their musicians mastered several instruments including the *ukeke* (a single-stringed device resembling a bow), an *ohe* or nose flute, conch shells, rattles and drums made from gourds, coconut shells or logs. Their craftsmen produced the world's finest featherwork, weaving thousands of tiny feathers into golden cloaks and ceremonial helmets. The Hawaiians helped develop the sport of surfing. They also swam, boxed, bowled and devised an intriguing game called *konane*, a cross between checkers and the Japanese game of go. They built hiking trails from coral and lava, and created an elemental art form in the images— petroglyphs—that they carved into rocks along the trails.

They also achieved something far more outstanding than their varied arts and crafts, something which the West, with its awesome knowledge and advanced technology, has never duplicated. The Hawaiians created a balance with nature. They practiced conservation, establishing closed seasons on certain fish species and carefully guarding their plant and animal resources. They led a simple life, without the complexities the outside world would eventually thrust upon them. It was a good life: food was plentiful, people were healthy and the population increased. For a thousand years, the Hawaiians lived in delicate harmony with the elements. It was not until the West entered the realm, transforming everything, that the fragile balance was destroyed. But that is another story entirely.

PEOPLE   Because of its unique history and isolated geography, Hawaii is truly a cultural melting pot. It's one of the few states in the union in which caucasians are a minority group. Whites, or *haoles* as they're called in the islands, comprise only about 23 percent of Hawaii's 1.1 million population. Japanese constitute 20 percent, Filipinos 10 percent, Hawaiians and part-Hawaiians account for 19 percent, Chinese about 5 percent and other racial groups 23 percent.

It's a very young, vital society. More than half the community is under thirty-five and over one-third of the people were born of racially mixed parents.

One trait characterizing many of these people is Hawaii's famous spirit of *aloha*, a genuine friendliness, an openness to strangers, a willingness to give freely. Undoubtedly, it is one of the finest qualities any people has ever demonstrated. *Aloha* originated with the Polynesians and played an important role in ancient Hawaiian civilization.

CUISINE

Nowhere is the influence of Hawaii's melting pot population stronger than in the kitchen. While in the islands, you'll probably eat not only with a fork, but with chopsticks and fingers, as well. You'll sample a wonderfully varied cuisine. In addition to standard American fare, hundreds of restaurants serve Hawaiian, Japanese, Chinese, Korean, Portuguese and Filipino dishes. There are also fresh fruits aplenty—pineapples, papayas, mangoes, bananas and tangerines—plus native fish such as mahimahi, marlin and snapper.

The prime Hawaiian dish is poi, made from crushed taro root and served as a pasty purple liquid. It's pretty bland fare, but it does make a good side dish with roast pork or tripe stew. You should also try *laulau*, a combination of fish, pork and taro leaves wrapped in a *ti* leaf and steamed. And don't neglect to taste baked *ulu* (breadfruit) and *opihi* (limpets). Among the other Hawaiian culinary traditions are *kalua* pig, a shredded pork dish baked in an *imu* (underground oven); *lomilomi* salmon, which is salted and mixed with onions and tomatoes; and chicken *laulau*, prepared in taro leaves and coconut milk.

A good way to try all these dishes at one sitting is to attend a luau. I've always found the tourist luaus too commercial, but you might watch the newspapers for one of the special luaus sponsored by civic organizations.

A SLICE OF THE PIE

In ancient Hawaii, each island was divided like a pie into wedge-shaped plots, ahupuaas, which extended from the ocean to the mountain peaks. In that way, every chief's domain contained fishing spots, village sites, arable valleys and everything else necessary for the survival of his subjects.

Japanese dishes include sushi, sukiyaki, teriyaki and tempura, plus an island favorite—sashimi, or raw fish. On most any menu, including McDonald's, you'll find *saimin*, a noodle soup filled with meat, vegetables and *kamaboko* (fishcake).

Three out of every four Hawaii residents live on the island of Oahu, and almost half reside in Honolulu.

You can count on the Koreans for *kim chi*, a spicy salad of pickled cabbage and *kun koki*, barbecued meat prepared with soy and sesame oil. The Portuguese serve up some delicious sweets including *malasadas* (donuts minus the holes) and *pao doce*, or sweet bread. For Filipino fare, I recommend *adobo*, a pork or chicken dish spiced with garlic and vinegar, and *pochero*, a meat entrée cooked with bananas and several vegetables. In addition to a host of dinner dishes, the Chinese have contributed some less common treats such as *manapua* (a steamed bun filled with barbecued pork) and oxtail soup. They also introduced crack seed to the islands. Made from dried and preserved fruit, it provides a treat as sweet as candy.

As the Hawaiians say, *"Hele mai ai."* Come and eat!

LANGUAGE The language common to all Hawaii is English, but because of its diverse cultural heritage, the archipelago also supports several other tongues. Foremost among these are Hawaiian and pidgin. Hawaiian, closely related to other Polynesian languages, is one of the most fluid and melodious languages in the world. It's composed of only twelve letters: five vowels—*a, e, i, o, u* and seven consonants—*h, k, l, m, n, p, w.*

At first glance, the language appears formidable: how the hell do you pronounce *humuhumunukunukuapuaa*? But actually it's quite simple. After you've mastered a few rules of pronunciation, you can take on any word in the language.

The first thing to remember is that every syllable ends with a vowel, and the next to last syllable receives the accent.

The next rule to keep in mind is that all the letters in Hawaiian are pronounced. Consonants are pronounced the same as in English (except for the *w*, which is pronounced as a *v* when it introduces the last syllable of a word—as in *ewa* or *awa*. Vowels are pronounced the same as in Latin or Spanish: *a* as in *among*, *e* as in *they*, *i* as in *machine*, *o* as in *no* and *u* as in *too*. Hawaiian has four vowel combinations or diphthongs: *au*, pronounced *ow*, *ae* and *ai*, which sound like *eye*, and *ei*, pronounced *ay*.

By now, you're probably wondering what I could possibly have meant when I said Hawaiian was simple. I think the glossary that follows will simplify everything while helping you pronounce common words and place names. Just go through the list, starting with words like aloha and luau that you already know. After you've practiced pronouncing familiar words, the rules will become second nature; you'll practically be a *kamaaina*.

Just when you start to speak with a swagger, cocky about having learned a new language, some young Hawaiian will start talking at you in a tongue that breaks all the rules you've so carefully mastered. That's pidgin. It started in the 19th century as a lingua franca among Hawaii's many races. Pidgin speakers mix English and Hawaiian with several other tongues to produce a spicy creole. It's a fascinating language with its own vocabulary, a unique syntax and a rising inflection that's hard to mimic.

Pidgin is definitely the hip way to talk in Hawaii. A lot of young Hawaiians use it among themselves as a private language. At times they may start talking pidgin to you, acting as though they don't speak English; then if they decide you're okay, they'll break into English. When that happens, you be one *da kine brah*.

So *brah*, I take *da kine* pidgin words, put 'em together with Hawaiian, make one big list. Savvy?

aa (**ah**-ah)—a type of rough lava
ae (eye)—yes
aikane (eye-**kah**-nay)—friend
akamai (ah-**kah**-my)—wise
alii (ah-**lee**-ee)—chief
aloha (ah-**lo**-ha)—hello; greetings; love
aole (ah-**oh**-lay)—no
auwe (ow-**way**)—ouch!
brah (bra)—friend; brother; bro'
bumby (**bum**-bye)—after a while; by and by
dah makule guys (da mah-**kuh**-lay guys)—senior citizens
da kine (da kyne)—whatdyacallit; thingamajig; that way
diamondhead—in an easterly direction
duh uddah time (duh **uh**-duh time)—once before
ewa (**eh**-vah)—in a westerly direction
hale (**hah**-lay)—house
haole (**how**-lee)—Caucasian; white person
hapa (**hah**-pa)—half
hapa-haole (**hah**-pa **how**-lee)—half-Caucasian
heiau (hey-ee-**ow**)—temple
hele on (**hey**-lay own)—hip; with it
holo holo (**ho**-low **ho**-low)—to visit
howzit? (hows-it)—how you doing? what's happening?
hukilau (who-key-lau)—community fishing party
hula (**who**-la)—Hawaiian dance
imu (**ee**-moo)—underground oven
ipo (**ee**-po)—sweetheart
jag up (jag up)—drunk
kahuna (kah-**who**-nah)—priest
kai (kye)—ocean
kaka-roach (**kah**-kah roach)—ripoff; theft

kamaaina (kah-mah-**eye**-nah)—a longtime island resident

kane (**kah**-nay)—man

kapu (**kah**-poo)—taboo; forbidden

kaukau (cow-cow)—food

keiki (**kay**-key)—child

kiawe (key-**ah**-vay)—mesquite tree

kokua (ko-**coo**-ah)—help

kona winds (**ko**-nah winds)—winds that blow against the trades

lanai (lah-**nye**)—porch; also island name

lauhala (lau-**hah**-lah) or *hala* (**hah**-lah)—a tree whose leaves are used in weaving

lei (lay)—flower garland

lolo (low-low)—stupid

lomilomi (**low**-me-**low**-me)—massage; also raw salmon

luau (**loo**-ow)—feast

mahalo (mah-**hah**-low)—thank you

mahalo nui loa (mah-**ha**-low **new**-ee **low**-ah)—thank you very much

mahu (**mah**-who)—gay; homosexual

makai (mah-**kye**)—toward the sea

malihini (mah-lee-**hee**-nee)—newcomer; stranger

mauka (**mau**-kah)—toward the mountains

nani (**nah**-nee)—beautiful

ohana (oh-**hah**-nah)—family

okole (oh-**ko**-lay)—rear; ass

okolemaluna (oh-ko-lay-mah-**loo**-nah)—a toast: bottoms up!

ono (**oh**-no)—tastes good

pahoehoe (pah-**hoy**-hoy)—ropy lava

pakalolo (pah-kah-**low**-low)—marijuana

pakiki head (pah-**key**-key head)—stubborn

pali (**pah**-lee)—cliff

paniolo (pah-nee-**oh**-low)—cowboy

pau (pow)—finished; done

pilikia (pee-lee-**key**-ah)—trouble

puka (**poo**-kah)—hole

pupus (**poo**-poos)—hors d'oeuvres

shaka (**shah**-kah)—great; perfect

swell head—angry

tapa (**tap**-ah)—tree bark which is used as a fabric

wahine (wah-**hee**-nay)—woman

wikiwiki (**wee**-key-**wee**-key)—quickly; in a hurry

you get stink ear—you don't listen well

MUSIC

Music has long been an integral part of Hawaiian life. Most families keep musical instruments in their homes, gathering to play at impromptu living room or backyard jam sessions. Hawaiian folk tunes are passed down from generation to generation. In the earliest days, it was the sound of rhythm instruments and chants that filled the air. Drums were fashioned from hollowed-out gourds, coconut shells and breadfruit logs, then covered with sharkskin. Gourds and coconuts, adorned with tapa cloth and feathers, were also filled with shells or pebbles to produce a rattling sound. Other instruments included the nose flute, a piece of bamboo similar to a mouth flute, but played by exhaling through the nostril; the bamboo organ; and *puili*, pieces of bamboo split into strips, which were struck rhythmically against the body.

Western musical scales and instruments were introduced by explorers and missionaries. As ancient Hawaiian music involved a completely different musical system, Hawaiians had to completely re-adapt. Actually, western music caught on quickly, and the hymns brought by missionaries fostered a popular musical style—the *himeni* or Hawaiian church music.

Hawaii has been the birthplace of several different musical instruments and styles. The ukulele, modeled on a Portuguese guitar, quickly became the most popular Hawaiian instrument. Its small size made it easy to carry, and with just four strings, it was simple to play. During the early 1900s, the steel guitar was exported to the mainland. Common in country-and-western music today, it was invented by a young man who experimented by sliding a steel bar across guitar strings.

The slack-key style of guitar playing also comes from Hawaii. In tuning, the six strings are loosened and then played in a variety of ways, from plucking or slapping the strings to sliding along them. A number of different tunings exist, and many have been passed down through families for generations.

During the late 19th century, *"hapa-*haole" songs became the rage. The ukelele was instrumental in contributing to this Hawaiian fad. Written primarily in English with pseudo-Hawaiian themes, songs like "Tiny Bubbles" and "Lovely Hula Hands" were later introduced to the world via Hollywood.

The Hawaiian craze continued on the mainland with radio and television shows such as "Hawaii Calls" and "The Harry Owens Show." In the 1950s, little mainland girls donned plastic hula skirts and danced along with Hilo Hattie and Ray Kinney.

NO OOMPAH-PAH! MO' BETTAH BRAH!

Strangely enough, a Prussian bandmaster named Henry Berger had a major influence on contemporary Hawaiian music. Brought over in the 19th century by King Kalakaua to lead the Royal Hawaiian Band, Berger helped Hawaiians make the transition to western instruments.

It was not until the 1970s that both the hula and music of old Hawaii made a comeback. Groups such as the Sons of Hawaii and the Makaha Sons of Niihau, along with Auntie Genoa Keawe and the late Gabby Pahinui, became popular. Before long, a new form of Hawaiian music was being heard, a combination of ancient chants and contemporary sounds, performed by such islanders as Henry Kapono, Kalapana, Olomana, the Beamer Brothers, the Peter Moon Band and the Brothers Cazimero.

Today many of these groups, along with other notables such as Hapa, the Kaau Crater Boys, Brother Nolan, Willie K. and Butch Helemano, bring both innovation to the Hawaiian music scene and contribute to the preservation of an ancient tradition.

HULA

Along with palm trees, the hula—swaying hips, grass skirts, colorful leis—is linked forever in people's minds with the Hawaiian Islands. This western idea of hula is very different from what the dance has traditionally meant to native Hawaiians.

Hula is an old dance form, its origin shrouded in mystery. The ancient hula, *kahiko*, was more concerned with religion and spirituality than entertainment. Originally performed only by men, it was used in rituals to communicate with a deity—a connection to nature and the gods. Accompanied by drums and chants, *kahiko* expressed the islands' culture, mythology and history in hand and body movements. It later evolved from a strictly religious rite to a method of communicating stories and legends. Over the years, women were allowed to study the rituals and eventually became the primary dancers.

When westerners arrived, the *kahiko* hula began another transformation. Explorers and sailors were more interested in its erotic element, ignoring the cultural significance. Missionaries simply found it scandalous and set out to destroy the tradition. They dressed Hawaiians in western garb and outlawed the *kahiko* hula.

The hula tradition was resurrected by King David Kalakaua. Known by the moniker "Merrie Monarch," Kalakaua loved music and dance. For his coronation in 1883, he called together the kingdom's best dancers to perform the chants and hulas once again. He was also instrumental in the development of the contemporary hula, the *auwana* hula, which added new steps and movements and was accompanied by ukeleles and guitars rather than drums.

By the 1920s, modern hula had been popularized by Hollywood, westernized and introduced as kitschy tropicana. Real grass skirts gave way to cellophane versions, plastic leis replaced fragrant island garlands, and exaggerated gyrations supplanted the hypnotic movements of the traditional dance.

Fortunately, with the resurgence of Hawaiian pride in recent decades, Polynesian culture has been reclaimed and *kahiko* hula and chants have made a welcome comeback.

FOUR

Waikiki

To understand the geography of Waikiki you need only know about Waikiki Beach. And to understand Waikiki Beach, you must know two things. The first is that major hotels line the beach, practically from one end to the other, and are used as landmarks by visitors and local residents alike. The other fact to remember is that to visitors Waikiki Beach is a single sandy ribbon two miles long, but to local folks it represents many beaches in one. When you park your beach towel here, consider that every few strides will carry you into another realm of Waikiki's culture and history.

Waikiki is where Hawaiian tourism began, and its reputation as a retreat dates back centuries. It is believed that the area was a favorite recreation site for the long-ago kings of Oahu and Maui, and a holy place as well. The site of the Royal Hawaiian Hotel was previously a *heiau pookanaka*, or sacrificial temple, and strictly off limits to the common people.

When Hawaii's royalty established Honolulu as their capital in the mid-1800s, Waikiki continued as a getaway, thanks to sunny shores and well-formed waves, just right for their favorite sport of surfing. The royal family would often invite well-known visitors such as Robert Louis Stevenson and Jack London to join them at their Waikiki retreat. And it gradually gained a reputation with not-so-well-known haoles as well. By the late 1800s, guesthouses were springing up along the strand. The first hotel, the Moana, was built at the turn of the century, as was a tram line from downtown Honolulu that brought visitors and townspeople to enjoy the beach and surf at Waikiki.

The area might have remained an isolated getaway surrounded by swamps if it weren't for the dredging of the Ala Wai canal in the 1920s. The swamps were drained and filled with coral from the canal, laying the foundation for what would some-day be one of the world's most famous resort areas. But not quite yet.

First there had to be tourists—and a way to bring them to Honolulu. Matson Navigation built the 650-passenger *Mololo* in 1925, and the glory days of Hawaiian tourism began. Matson also developed the Royal Hawaiian Hotel to the tune of

$2 million, an astronomical sum at the time. But the investment paid off, and Waikiki began to compete with Europe as a vacation destination for the well-heeled.

More hotels were built, and during World War II, GIs on leave soaked up the sun on Waikiki's shores, further establishing its reputation. Then in the jet age that followed, it became a highrise resort area. A motley collection of hotels, squeezed together in the small space that is Waikiki, stands as an architectural monument to the neighborhood's history and gives each section of Waikiki a different flavor.

This fabled peninsula extends two miles from the Ala Wai Yacht Harbor to Diamond Head and measures a half-mile in width from the Ala Wai Canal to the Pacific. Kalakaua Avenue, the main drag, is packed elbow to elbow with throngs of visitors. Paralleling the ocean, this broad boulevard is all at once noisy, annoying, exciting, cosmopolitan and fascinating. It buzzes with activity from sunrise, when the joggers take to the sidewalks, to late at night, when vacationers are returning to their hotels or just strolling by to check out the scene. Today, visitors from Japan, Korea and Australia, arriving in ever-increasing numbers, add to the international atmosphere. Sometimes the streets of Waikiki are as entertaining as a nightclub show. Or so it seems.

But the main appeal is still the district's white-sand corridor. Dotting the beach are picnic areas, restrooms, showers, concession stands and beach equipment rentals. Most of the beach is protected by coral reefs and sea walls, so the swimming is excellent, the snorkeling fair. This is also a prime area for surfing. Two- to four-foot waves, good for beginners and still challenging to experienced surfers, are common here.

The western flank of Waikiki Beach sits near the **Ilikai Hotel**. Here you will find a pretty lagoon fringed by palm trees. ~ 1777 Ala Moana Boulevard.

The curving strand nearby, fronting Hilton Hawaiian Village at 2005 Kalia Road, is called **Kahanamoku Beach**. Named for Hawaii's great surfer, Duke Kahanamoku, it features numerous facilities. Beach stands rent everything from towels, chairs and air mattresses to snorkel sets, surfboards and Hobie-cat sailboats.

Also here is Port Hilton, the pier from which the resort complex launches catamaran cruises. One of these boats will take you to what may be the only hidden attraction around Waikiki, the **Atlantis Submarine**, a 48-passenger sub located just off the coast that carries visitors to the bottom for a close-up look at an artificial reef, complete with sunken ships and airplanes, created to bring back marine life to the area. Admission. ~ 973-9811, 800-548-6262.

Fort De Russy Beach, owned by the military but open to the public, features the area's widest swath of white sand. It is also

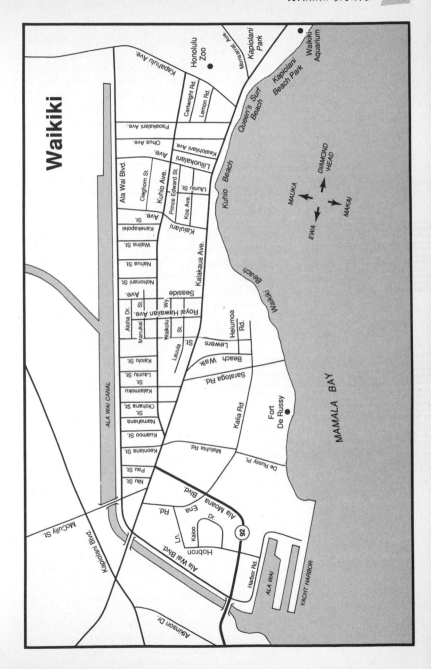

Waikiki

beautifully backdropped by a grove of palm trees. There are rest-rooms, picnic tables and barbecues, plus tennis, squash and volley-ball courts.

The nearby **U.S. Army Museum of Hawaii** has every weapon from Hawaiian shark teeth blades to modern-day instruments of destruction. You can also trace the United States' unending series of military campaigns from the uniforms (ours and theirs) on ex-hibit here. Closed Monday. ~ Kalia Road; 438-2821.

Past Fort De Russy Beach stretches a palisade of highrise ho-tels. Lining the beachfront, they provide numerous facilities for thirsty sunbathers or adventuresome athletes. Continue on and you will pass the Sheraton strip, a lengthy stretch of Waikiki Beach fronted entirely by Sheraton hotels. This section marks Waikiki's center of action. The first hotel is the **Sheraton Waikiki**. A highrise structure built with two curving wings, it resembles a giant bird roosting on the beach. ~ 2255 Kalakaua Avenue.

The hotels here are so famous that the nearby strand is named **Royal-Moana Beach**. Stretching between the Royal Ha-waiian and Moana hotels, it has been a sun-soaked gathering place for decades. That's because these two grand dames are Waikiki's oldest hotels. The **Royal Hawaiian Hotel** is Hawaii's "Pink Palace," a Spanish Moorish–style caravansary painted shocking pink. Built in 1927, it is a labyrinth of gardens, colonnades and balconies; the old place is certainly Waikiki's most interesting edi-fice. ~ 2259 Kalakaua Avenue; 923-7311.

The woodframe **Sheraton Moana Surfrider Hotel**, built in 1901, was Waikiki's first resort. Its vaulted ceilings, tree-shaded court-yard and spacious accommodations reflect the days when Hawaii was a retreat for the rich. This beach is also the site of one of Wai-kiki's most renowned surfing spots, Canoe's Surf. ~ 2365 Kalakaua Avenue; 922-3111.

Just beyond the Moana Hotel at 2453 Kalakaua Avenue is **Ku-hio Beach Park**, which runs along Kalakaua Avenue from Kaiulani to Kapahulu avenues. In addition to a broad sandy beach, there are numerous facilities here—picnic areas, beach equipment rentals, showers, restrooms and lifeguards on duty. The shady pavilions in this public park also attract local folks who come to play cards and chess. Needless to say, this convenient beach is often quite crowded. Diners like it because of its proximity to many Waikiki budget restaurants; parents favor the beach for its protective sea wall, which provides a secure area where kids can swim; and people-watchers find it an ideal place to check out the crowds of tourists and local residents.

HIDDEN ►   Hidden behind St. Augustine Catholic Church sits the tiny **Da-mien Museum**, a tribute to Father Damien, the Belgian priest best known for his work in Kalapaupa, the leper colony on Molokai. Father Damien established churches throughout the islands, but his dedication to those suffering from Hanson's Disease (leprosy) is what made him a Hawaiian hero. The exhibits include his glasses, chalice and other unassuming belongings, as well as his prayer book and vestments. Photos depicting his final years on Molokai, where he, too, died of the disease, paint an evocative portrait of this selfless man. Closed weekends. ~ 130 Ohua Avenue; 923-2690.

The strand just beyond is called **Queen's Surf**. Here also are pic-nic areas, shady pavilions, restroom facilities and showers. Something of a Bohemian quarter, this pretty plot draws gays, local artists and a wide array of intriguing characters. On the weekends, conga drummers may be pounding out rhythms along the beach while other people gather to soak in the scene.

◄ *HIDDEN*

Kapiolani Park next door extends across 140 acres on both sides of Kalakaua Avenue. Hawaii's oldest park, this tree-studded playland dates back more than 100 years. Perhaps more than anything else, it has come to serve as a jogger's paradise. From dawn 'til dark, runners of all ages, colors, sizes and shapes beat a path around its perimeter. But Kapiolani offers something to just about anyone. There are tennis courts, softball and soccer fields, an archery area, and much more. To fully explore the park, you must visit each of its features in turn.

First is the **Waikiki Aquarium**, the place where you can finally discover what a *humuhumunukunukuapuaa*, that impossibly named fish, really looks like. (Don't be surprised if the name proves to be longer than the fish.) Within the aquarium's glass walls, you'll see more than 350 different species of fish originating from Hawaiian and South Pacific waters. Ranging from rainbow-hued tropical fish to blacktip reef sharks, they constitute a broad range of underwater species. Then there are Hawaiian monk seals (an endangered

✔ **CHECK THESE OUT**

- Visit the **Waikiki Aquarium** so you can tell your friends you saw a *humuhumunukunukuapuaa* fish. *page 75*
- Discover why the locals call the **Royal Hawaiian**—a Spanish-Moorish fantasy on Waikiki Beach—the "Pink Palace." *page 82*
- Sit under a lovely hau tree by the beach and enjoy a leisurely breakfast at the **Hau Tree Lanai**, where birds greet you with their tropical songs. *page 86*
- Join the crowds at the **International Market Place**, where scores of tiny shops and stands sell an incredible array of souvenirs. *page 88*
- Join the local beach boys and learn to surf at the **Aloha Beach Service** in front of the Sheraton Moana Surfrider Hotel. *page 39*

species) and other intriguing creatures. A biodiversity exhibit features a rotating display of species not native to Hawaii. Admission. ~ 2777 Kalakaua Avenue; 923-9741.

HIDDEN ►   The **Queen Kapiolani Garden** is planted across the park at the corner of Monsarrat and Paki avenues. With its colorful flowerbeds and shady pavilion, this is a pretty place to stroll and picnic.

There's one event that takes place in Kapiolani Park that has become an institution—the **Kodak Hula Show**, staged in the bleachers near the Waikiki Shell and Monsarrat Avenue. This free, hour-long presentation features ukulele music and hula dancers in ti-leaf skirts. The ukuleles plunk, the dancers sway and the tourists snap pictures (presumably using Kodak cameras and film). It is one of those attractions that is so hokey it is actually interesting. Some people come just to watch the tourists with their sunburned faces and matching aloha shirts. In any case, every Tuesday through Thursday at 10 a.m. you will encounter swarms of people lining the bleachers. ~ 627-3300.

The park's most outstanding feature is the **Honolulu Zoo**. Like city zoos everywhere, this tropical facility has a resident population of elephants, giraffes, ostriches, zebras, hippos, catacals, Sumatran tigers, black-mane lions, alligators and so on. But it also includes animals more common to the islands, creatures like the nene (a rare Hawaiian goose), Vietnamese pot-bellied pig and wild sheep. Perhaps most interesting of all, there is an outstanding collection of tropical birds. Admission. ~ 971-7171.

Just beyond Kapiolani Park stretches beautiful and tranquil **Sans Souci Beach**, which extends from the **Natatorium** (a now-closed saltwater swimming pool) to the New Otani Kaimana Beach Hotel. ~ 2863 Kalakaua Avenue.

Sans Souci is certainly not a hard place to find, as one of the world's most famous landmarks rises just behind it. More than any other place in the islands, **Diamond Head** is the trademark of Hawaii. A 760-foot crater, it is the work of a volcano that has been dead for about 100,000 years. To the Hawaiians it was known as *Leahi*. They saw in its sloping hillsides the face of an ahi, or yellow-fin tuna. Then, in the 19th century, sailors mistook its volcanic

CATCH A WAVE

All along Waikiki Beach, concessions offer rides on **outrigger canoes**. They are long, sleek fiberglass crafts resembling ancient Polynesian canoes. Each seats four to six passengers, plus a captain. For several dollars you can join the crew on a low-key wave-riding excursion that will have you paddling as hard and fast as you can to catch waves and ride them far from the shore.

glass rocks for rare gems and gave the promontory its present name. Formed 350,000 years ago, this natural landmark was a sacred place to the ancient Hawaiians. A *heiau* once graced its slopes and King Kamehameha is said to have worshiped here, offering a human sacrifice to the Polynesian war god.

It is possible to drive into the gaping maw of this old dragon. Just take Kalakaua Avenue until it meets Diamond Head Road, then follow the latter around to the inland site of the crater. From there a tunnel leads inside. Once within, there is a three-quarter-mile trail climbing to the rim of the crater. From here you can gaze along Oahu's southeast corner and back across the splendid little quarter called Waikiki.

LODGING

While it may no longer be the simple country retreat it was at the century's turn, Waikiki does have one advantage: believe it or not, it's a great place to find low-rent hotels. A lot of the cozy old hostelries have been torn down and replaced with highrises, but a few have escaped the urban assault. Some of those skyscrapers, too, are cheaper than you might think. So let's take a look at some of the better bargains Waikiki has to offer. One thing to consider when staying in Waikiki is that it is not exactly quiet. Early morning garbage trucks and late-night party-goers make considerable street noise. Streets on the outskirts (Saratoga Road) are less noisy than those in the heart of things—such as Lewers and Beach Walk.

The **Malihini Hotel** will give you a feel for Honolulu's earlier, lowrise era. An attractive complex that spreads out instead of up, this 30-unit hotel is just a short stroll from the beach. Though pretty on the outside, its sparse furnishings, scant decoration and cinderblock walls give a vacant feel to the place. But the studios are spacious and come equipped with kitchenettes. The one-bedroom apartments have air conditioning and will sleep up to five people. ~ 217 Saratoga Road; 923-9644. BUDGET.

Rising higher from the ground, while still keeping costs low, is the **Royal Grove Hotel**, a six-story, 87-unit establishment. If you can get past the garish pink exterior here, you'll find the rooms more tastefully designed. All are carpeted and comfortably furnished, and some are decorated in simple but appealing styles. There are televisions and telephones in many of the higher-priced rooms upstairs, plus an almond-shaped pool and spacious lobby downstairs. Rents vary according to which wing of this sprawling building your bags are parked in. Some rooms even have kitchenettes and air conditioning, so it's hard to go wrong here. ~ 151 Uluniu Avenue; 923-7691, fax 922-7508. BUDGET TO MODERATE.

If you'd like to stay directly across the street from the beach, check into the **Waikiki Circle Hotel**. This 14-story hotel-in-the-round has air-conditioned rooms at reasonable rates. Many have an ocean view, which is the main advantage here. ~ 2464 Kalakaua Avenue; 923-1571, 800-922-7866, fax 926-8024. DELUXE.

An inexpensive place for both men and women in Waikiki is the **YMCA Central Branch**. It's handily situated across the street from Ala Moana Center and a block from the beach. And you're welcome to use the gym, pool, saunas, television room and coffee shop. You can also expect the usual Y ambience—long sterile hallways leading to an endless series of identical, cramped, uncarpeted rooms. You will pay several dollars more for a private bathroom, but low prices help make up for the lack of amenities. ~ 401 Atkinson Drive; 941-3344, fax 941-8821. BUDGET.

Interclub Waikiki is a sparkling clean hostel close to the beach, featuring dormitory and private rooms alike. Numbering 140 beds, it features a TV lounge complete with checkerboard, dart board and plenty of plump furniture. There is a laundry but no kitchen facilities. ~ 2413 Kuhio Avenue; 924-2636, fax 922-3993. BUDGET.

The walls are still cinderblock, but some recent remodeling should perk up the **Waikiki Prince Hotel**. Many of the rooms are equipped with kitchenettes. ~ 2431 Prince Edward Street; 922-1544, fax 924-3712. BUDGET.

Budget travelers should also consider a stay at **Hostelling International—Waikiki**. This helpful facility features dormitory-style accommodations and private studio units available for couples. The latter are plain cinder block rooms with private baths and mini-refrigerators. Open to both men and women, the hostel provides bedding, a common kitchen and creates a family-style atmosphere conducive to meeting other travelers. ~ 2417 Prince Edward Street; 926-8313, fax 922-3798. BUDGET.

There are two places in the moderate-price category that I particularly recommend. All are small, intimate and close to the beach. First is the **Hale Pua Nui**, a congenial home away from home. There are 22 studio apartments here, each spacious, well-furnished and cross-ventilated. The rooms are quaintly decorated, carpeted and equipped with kitchenettes, cable television and air conditioning. The personalized service you receive from the management makes the Hale Pua Nui an ideal vacation spot. ~ 228 Beach Walk; 923-9693, fax 923-9678. MODERATE.

The second is **Kai Aloha Apartment Hotel**, just around the corner. Here intimacy is combined with modern convenience; each room has air conditioning, an all-electric kitchen, radio, telephone with voice mail, cable television and carpeting. Studio apartments have lovely rattan furniture and are attractively decorated with old drawings and paintings. The one-bedroom apartments will comfortably sleep four people. Daily maid service. ~ 235 Saratoga Road; 923-6723, fax 922-7592. MODERATE.

A lowrise hotel tucked away in the shadow of vaulting condos, **The Breakers** is truly a find. Dating to the 1950s, this Waikiki original consists of 66 rooms and 15 suites surrounding a pool and landscaped patio. Shoji doors add to the ambience while kitchenettes in every room and a location one block from the beach round out the features. ~ 250 Beach Walk; 923-3181, 800-426-0494, fax 923-7174. DELUXE.

Beach Walk is one street in Waikiki that specializes in hotel bargains. In addition to the Hale Pua Nui and The Breakers, you'll find the **Hawaiiana Hotel**. Another intimate, low-slung facility, it offers a garden courtyard arrangement with rooms surrounding either of the hotel's two pools. Many of the rooms have a private lanai; all have wicker armoires, a full kitchen and pastel decor. ~ 260 Beach Walk; 923-3811, 800-535-0085, fax 926-5728, fax 800-633-5085. MODERATE TO DELUXE.

> Tourists are relative newcomers to Hawaii: Not a single hotel in Waikiki was built before the 20th century.

If you're willing to sacrifice intimacy, you may find that the **Outrigger Coral Seas Hotel** is the best deal in Waikiki. This seven-story hostelry is located just a hundred yards from the beach. They are appealing accommodations with air conditioning, telephones, wall-to-wall carpeting and small lanais. In some units you can add a mini-kitchenette to the list of extras. There's a pool at another Outrigger hotel next door that guests may use. If you want, just for the hell of it, to directly experience the Waikiki tourist scene, this is the place. The Outrigger Coral Seas Hotel is at the heart of the action. ~ 250 Lewers Street; 923-3881, 800-462-6262, fax 800-622-4852. MODERATE.

Also in the center of Waikiki is the nearby **Edgewater Hotel**. Located a stone's skip from the beach, this 184-unit colossus offers excellent accommodations at low prices. Each room comes with carpeting, telephone, TV, cable movies, refrigerator and shared lanai; many rooms also have a kitchenette. The decor is bland but the furniture comfy. Downstairs is an open-air lobby with adjoining restaurant and pool. ~ 2168 Kalia Road; 922-6424, 800-462-6262. MODERATE TO DELUXE.

A small boutique hotel right across the street from the beach, the **Aston Waikiki Beachside Hotel** is the kind of place where the receptionist already knows your name when you first walk in the door. It's as if they were waiting for you. The rooms are small but attractively done in coordinated coral colors with Chinese screen paintings and furnishings. The rooms in front have a balcony with two chairs and a table, so guests can watch the parade of surfers and sun worshipers below. This place is popular with business travelers and couples. ~ 2452 Kalakaua Avenue; 931-2100, fax 931-2129. DELUXE TO ULTRA-DELUXE.

The **Honolulu Prince Hotel** was once a college dormitory. Today it's a ten-story hotel with a comfortable lobby. The standard rooms are small and blandly decorated; some are equipped with full kitchens. Located near the beach, this hotel also features one- and two-bedroom apartments available. ~ 415 Nahua Street; 922-1616, 800- 321-2558, fax 922-6223. MODERATE TO DELUXE.

White Sands Waikiki Resort is more expensive but also more fashionable. This is a modern, attractive complex of three low-slung buildings surrounding a garden and swimming pool. The rooms come with all-electric kitchenette, telephone, color TV and air conditioning. ~ 431 Nohonani Street; 923-7336, 800-634-6981, fax 702-736-2263. DELUXE.

Dominating the mid-range hotel scene in Waikiki are the Out-rigger hotels. It seems like everywhere you turn in this tourist enclave another one looms above: There are almost two dozen. While prices range across the entire spectrum, one facility that offers a special value is the **Outrigger Village**. Located on a busy street a block from the beach, it offers rooms with or without kitchenettes at reasonable cost. You can expect street noise, and the lobby caters more to vendors than guests, but there is a pool. ~ 240 Lewers Street; 923-3881, 800-462-6262, fax 922-2330. MODERATE.

White louvered windows and bright floral-print bedspreads give the **Outrigger East** a resort feel, even though it's a highrise city hotel two blocks from the beach. Many rooms are equipped with kitchenettes, including stove and oven, refrigerator, toaster, sink and coffeemaker, and there's an inexpensive coffee shop on the premises. ~ 2375 Kuhio Avenue; 369-7777, 800-688-7444, fax 926-4334. DELUXE.

The **Coconut Plaza**, a ten-story highrise, has some accommodations with kitchenettes; all guest rooms have refrigerators and microwaves. Decorated in Mexican tile and furnished with wicker, the rooms are attractively appointed. The lobby adds elements of elegance in the form of an open-air lounge and pool. Breakfast included. ~ 450 Lewers Street; 923-8828, 800-882-9696, fax 923-3473. DELUXE.

The **Ewa Hotel** has 90 rooms. Tucked away on a back street one block from the beach, this pastel-and-rattan establishment has a spiffy 1980s aura about it. Close to Kapiolani Park and offering kitchenettes in many rooms, it is particularly convenient for families. ~ 2555 Cartwright Road; 922-1677, 800-359-8639, fax 923-8538. MODERATE.

About the same size is the **Waikiki Hana Hotel**, a 73-room place that offers a restaurant and small lobby. Quiet (for Waikiki), friendly and comfortable, its rooms are brightly decorated and trimly appointed with air conditioning and color televisions. Some have kitchenettes and lanais. ~ 2424 Koa Avenue; 926-8841, 800-367-5004, fax 924-3770. MODERATE TO DELUXE.

One of the island's few gay-run hotels, **Hotel Honolulu** rests on a quiet side street just off Kuhio Avenue. It's a three-story deco post-modern structure that has been beautifully landscaped and finely decorated. Guest rooms are bright, carpeted wall-to-wall and equipped with tile bathrooms, stall showers and kitchen facilities. Each is decorated along a different theme: Japanese, English, Chinese, Hollywood, Safari and so on. There's also a rooftop garden sundeck to round off this well-run facility. ~ 376 Kaiolu Street; 926-2766, 800-426-2766, fax 922-3326. MODERATE TO DELUXE.

If the **Outrigger Waikiki Surf Hotel** has no space in its central facility, they can probably fit you into one of their two other buildings. All are located in central Waikiki. The guest rooms are adequately, if unimaginatively, decorated and come with TV, air conditioning, telephone and lanai. ~ 2200 Kuhio Avenue; 923-7671, 800-688-7444, fax 921-4959. MODERATE.

What better combination can you ask for than a place that is both a hotel *and* a hostel? At the **Island Hostel/Hotel**, located inside the Hawaiian Colony building, you can book a room with private bath or join fellow travelers in a coed dorm room. Both include kitchen privileges. ~ 1946 Ala Moana Boulevard; 942-8748. BUDGET.

Holiday Inn Waikiki, another good bargain, is easy walking distance from both Ala Moana Center and the beach. For the price, accommodations at this 17-story caravansary are relatively plush. Each room has air conditioning, television, telephone, decorations, carpeting, a shower-tub combination, a small refrigerator, in-room coffee and an in-room safe. The room I saw was quite spacious and contained a king-size bed. ~ 1830 Ala Moana Boulevard; 955-1111, 800-465-4329, fax 947-1799. MODERATE TO DELUXE.

Also consider the **Mark Waikiki Grand Hotel**, across the street from lush Kapiolani Park. The standard rooms in this ten-story building are comfortable, pleasant places to park your bags. Downstairs there's a windswept lobby. ~ 134 Kapahulu Avenue; 923-1511, 800-535-0085, fax 922-2421. DELUXE.

Near the Mark Waikiki Grand Hotel is the **Polynesian Hostel Beach Club**. Bunks are set up in former hotel rooms which means that each room has its own refrigerator and bathroom and only sleeps four to five people. Laundry facilities and a full kitchen are available for guests, but the real highlight is the top-floor sundeck

▸◆◆◆◄

STAY AT SOMEBODY ELSE'S PLACE!

If you're planning on staying in Honolulu for a week or more and would like to do so in the comfort of someone else's fully furnished apartment, **Waikiki Vacation Rentals** offers studios in addition to one- and two-bedroom condos. The months of December, January and February are often booked two to three months in advance, so call ahead for availability. ~ 1580 Makaloa Street, Suite 770; 946-9371, 800-543-5663, fax 943-6934. BUDGET TO ULTRA-DELUXE.

with its view of Kapiolani Park, Diamond Head and the beach. ~ 2584 Lemon Road; 922-1340, fax 923-4146. BUDGET.

The **Queen Kapiolani Hotel** is a 314-room facility that rises 19 stories above nearby Kapiolani Park. There's a spacious lobby, three floors of public rooms, several shops and a swimming pool here. The guest rooms are plainly decorated and modest in size. Located one block from the beach. ~ 150 Kapahulu Avenue; 922-1941, 800-367-5004, fax 596-0158. DELUXE.

There are also two attractive facilities on the edge of Waikiki that are removed from the crowds. The **New Otani Kaimana Beach Hotel** rests beside beautiful Sans Souci Beach in the shadow of Diamond Head. Its two restaurants and oceanside bar lend the feel of a big hotel, but the friendly staff and standard rooms create a family atmosphere. ~ 2863 Kalakaua Avenue; 923-1555, 800-356-8264, fax 922-9404. DELUXE TO ULTRA-DELUXE.

HIDDEN ►

Another hotel, equally secluded, has been nicely refurbished. Located even closer to the fabled crater, the **Diamond Head Beach Hotel** is an ultra-contemporary establishment. The rooms are done in soft pastel tones and adorned with quilted beds and potted plants. Located on the ocean, this 13-story facility is one of the most chic resting places around. Continental breakfast is served to the guests and some rooms come with a kitchen. ~ 2947 Kalakaua Avenue; 922-1928, 800-367-2317, fax 924-1982. ULTRA-DELUXE.

There are two hotels right on the beach at Waikiki that capture the sense of old Hawaii. Waikiki was little more than a thatch-hut village when its first deluxe hotel went up in 1901. Today the **Sheraton Moana Surfrider Hotel** retains the aura of those early days in its Colonial architecture and Victorian decor. Insist on a room in the main building with its traditional appointments and turn-of-the-century ambience. Downstairs are restaurants, bars, a lobby filled with wicker furniture, and an ancient banyan tree beneath which Robert Louis Stevenson once wrote. ~ 2365 Kalakaua Avenue; 922-3111, 800-325-3535, fax 923-5984. ULTRA-DELUXE.

Just down the beach resides the grand dame of Hawaiian hotels. Built in 1927 and affectionately known as "The Pink Palace," the **Royal Hawaiian** is an elegant, Spanish Moorish–style building complete with colonnaded walkways and manicured grounds. This castle-away-from-home is decorated in French provincial fashion and features a fabulous lobby bedecked with chandeliers. Adjacent to the original building is a 17-story tower that brings the room count to 675. Worth visiting even if you never check in. ~ 2259 Kalakaua Avenue; 923-7311, 800-325-3535, fax 931-7840. ULTRA-DELUXE.

If you'd prefer to go native and stay in a private home, contact one of the bed-and-breakfast referral numbers. These include **Bed and Breakfast Honolulu** (595-7533, 800-288-4666, fax 595-2030), **Pacific Hawaii Bed and Breakfast** (phone/fax 486-8838, 800-999-

6026) or **Bed and Breakfast Hawaii** (822-7771, 800-733-1632, fax 822-2723). ~ MODERATE TO DELUXE.

CONDOS

The **Royal Kuhio**, a good bet for families, is a 389-unit highrise two blocks from Waikiki Beach. One-bedroom units feature fully equipped kitchens and balconies with ocean or mountain views. Prices start at $95. ~ 2240 Kuhio Avenue; 923-0555, 800-927-0555, fax 923-0720.

Kaulana Kai Resort at Waikiki has 90 comfortable units with kitchenettes and private lanais. The suites, which include a full living room, are a good value for families. Studios run $99 to $120 and suites run $160 to $250. ~ 2425 Kuhio Avenue; 922-7777, 800-367-5666, fax 922-9473.

At the **Aston Waikiki Beach Tower** all 90 suites and penthouses feature contemporary furniture, wetbars, kitchens and beautiful lanais. The kids will enjoy the game room, pool and paddle tennis court. One-bedroom units begin at $450. Suites for up to six guests start at $550. This is Waikiki's finest condominium. ~ 2470 Kalakaua Avenue; 926-6400, 800-922-7866, fax 926-7380.

At **Patrick Winston's Hawaiian King Rentals**, one-bedroom apartments rent for $65 to $119 for one to four people. All suites are comfortably furnished with rattan furniture and feature lanais and full and complete kitchens. Eight of the eleven units have washers and dryers. One block from the beach. ~ 417 Nohonani Street, Suite 409; 924-3332 phone/fax, 800-545-1948; e-mail hawnking@iau.com.

Aston Waikiki Shore offers 90 studios as well as one- and two-bedroom units. These condos feature complete kitchens, washer/dryers and great views. Studios run $150 to $165. One bedroom units are $210 to $235. Two-bedroom units accommodating up to six cost $295 to $335. ~ 2161 Kalia Road; 926-4733, 800-367-2353, fax 922-2902.

Waikiki Lanais is located on a quiet street near the Ala Wai Canal and has 160 one- and two-bedroom units, each with a good-sized living room and kitchen. One-bedroom accommodations start at $159. Two-bedroom condos, sleeping up to six, begin at $199. ~ 2452 Tusitala Street; 923-0994, 800-535-0085, fax 922-2421.

The **Pacific Monarch** has studio apartments from $140 to $160 offering kitchenettes and balconies, and one-bedroom units are $145 to $175 for up to four. There is a rooftop pool, jacuzzi and sauna, and the beach is just two blocks away. ~ 2427 Kuhio Avenue; 923-9805, 800-922-7866, fax 924-3220.

At **Waikiki Banyan** one-bedroom units are $180 to $215 for one to four people. These highrise ocean and mountain view units have full kitchens, rattan furniture and lanais. One block from the beach. ~ 201 Ohua Avenue; 922-0555, 800-366-7765, fax 922-0906.

Several services rent condominiums on Oahu. They include **Condo Rentals of Waikiki** at 413 Seaside Avenue (923-0555, 800-927-0555, fax 922-0720) and **Marc Resorts** at 2155 Kalakaua Avenue (926-5900, 800-535-0085, fax 922-9421).

DINING

This tourist mecca is crowded with restaurants. Since the competition is so stiff, the cafés here are cheaper than anywhere else on the islands. There are numerous American restaurants serving moderately good food at modest prices, so diners looking for standard fare will have no problem. But as you're probably seeking something more exotic, I'll also list some interesting Asian, Hawaiian, health food and other offbeat restaurants.

To find an affordable meal on Kalakaua Avenue, the oceanfront strip, try the bottom floor of the **Waikiki Shopping Plaza**. Here about a dozen ethnic and American restaurants offer takeout food as well as full course sitdown dinners. ~ 2250 Kalakaua Avenue. BUDGET.

Near the center of the action on busy Lewers Street, about 50 macadam-paved yards from the beach, is **The J. R.'s**. This glorified takeout stand has balcony seating overlooking the street. Downstairs you place your order for incredibly cheap breakfast specials, sandwiches and plate lunches, and dinners. ~ 226 Lewers Street; 971-3593. BUDGET.

Jungle Waikiki is a hot nightclub later on, but at lunch and dinner, it's a well-regarded, excellently priced restaurant. Using all fresh ingredients, they prepare chicken dijon, skewered shrimp, fettuccine primavera, penne with meat sauce and fresh fish. ~ 311 Lewers Street; 922-7808. BUDGET.

Up on the third floor of the Royal Hawaiian Shopping Center you'll happen upon **Spaghetti! Spaghetti!** At lunch or dinner there's an all-you-can-eat spaghetti buffet and salad bar. The spread includes several different types of pastas as well as an array of sauces. A great place to pack away those carbohydrates. ~ 2201 Kalakaua Avenue; 922-7724. BUDGET TO MODERATE.

On a balcony in the International Market Place, **Coconut Willy's Bar & Grill** has a dinner menu that includes a teriyaki steak and shrimp platter, fish and chips, and mahimahi. There are also hamburgers, sandwiches and salads. Set beside the banyan tree that dominates the market, the place has a funky appeal. ~ 2330 Kalakaua Avenue; 923-9454. MODERATE.

For a just-before-midnight snack—they close at 12:00—or to satisfy cravings for a hot bowl of noddle soup, you're never too far from an **Ezogiku**. Rub shoulders with Japanese tourists at the counter in one of these hole-in-the-wall eateries serving ramen in a variety of styles, including curry, pork and wonton. There are three locations to choose from in Waikiki. ~ 2420 Koa Avenue, 922-

2473; 2546 Lemon Road, 923-2013; 2146 Kalakaua Avenue, 926-8616. BUDGET.

Over on Kuhio Avenue, just a block in from the beach strip, there's a cluster of good, inexpensive restaurants. This area is the heart of Waikiki's gay scene. At the heart of the heart is **Treats**, formerly Hamburger Mary's, a sidewalk café fringed with potted plants. The adjoining bar is gay, but Treats attracts gays and straights alike. They come to this combination deli/coffeehouse for reuben and vegetarian sandwiches, bagels with lox and cream cheese, soups and salads. ~ 2109 Kuhio Avenue; 923-0669. MODERATE.

Next door to Treats is **Bananas**, a Thai sidewalk café that is related to Keo's, the city's best-known Thai restaurant. Here you can dine on curries, noodle dishes and other Southeast Asian entrées. The brick-paved patio is open and informal, adorned with umbrellas and tropical plants. Dinner only. ~ 2139 Kuhio Avenue; 922-6262. MODERATE.

At **Hernando's Hideaway** you can munch on nachos at the bar or settle on the patio and order from a full Mexican menu. There are enchiladas, tostadas and burritos. ~ 2139 Kuhio Avenue; 922-7758. BUDGET.

Perry's Smorgy, with its two locations—at the Outrigger Coral Seas Hotel and on Kuhio Avenue—has an inexpensive buffet at dinner, lunch and breakfast. With an extensive salad bar, plus a host of meat and fish platters, this all-you-can-eat emporium is hard to beat. I'd suggest the Outrigger branch; it's right on the waterfront. ~ 250 Lewers Street, 922-8814; 2380 Kuhio Avenue, 926-0184. BUDGET.

A great place for breakfast, the **Waikiki Broiler** has inexpensive specials every morning. Dining is outdoors under thatched umbrellas or in a small dining room. It's on a busy corner so the atmosphere is not exactly idyllic, but it's hard to match the prices—at dinner you can enjoy steak, shrimp, scallop and chicken entrées. ~ 200 Lewers Street; 923-8836. MODERATE.

The International Food Court, tucked into the northwest corner of the International Market Place, features a cluster of food stands and a patio for dining beneath a banyan tree. Here you'll find **Bautista's Filipino Kitchen** (923-7220), where the specialties include noodles, beef stew, mixed vegetables and menudo with green fish. **Peking Garden** (926-6060) has traditional Chinese dishes including beef and broccoli, chicken chop suey and eggplant with chicken. For Japanese food, go to **Choi's Kitchen** (923-5614), where *saimin* and chicken teriyaki are popular dishes. ~ 2330 Kalakaua Avenue. BUDGET.

The **Shore Bird Beach Broiler** is a beachfront dining room that's a great place to enjoy a reasonably priced dinner and an ocean view. This is a cook-your-own-food facility that offers steak kabob, fresh fish, teriyaki chicken and barbecued ribs. One of the best bargains on Waikiki Beach, the Shore Bird is inevitably crowded, so try to dine early. ~ Reef Hotel, 2169 Kalia Road; 922-2887. MODERATE.

For oceanfront dining, **The Beachside Café** is true to its name. With indoor and patio dining and a big buffet bar, it's a standard-fare American restaurant lacking in imagination but filled with beautiful views. Open for breakfast, lunch and dinner, the café serves steak, hamburgers and egg dishes. Ask for a table outside. ~ Sheraton Moana Surfrider Hotel, 2365 Kalakaua Avenue; 922-3111. MODERATE TO DELUXE.

♦♦♦♦♦♦♦♦♦♦♦♦♦♦♦♦♦♦♦

During the last decade, Waikiki has changed from a ticky tacky shopping enclave to an upscale international marketplace.

Apart from the bustle of Waikiki but still right on the beach is the **Hau Tree Lanai**. Here beneath the interwoven branches of twin *hau* trees you can enjoy patio dining with a view that extends across Waikiki to the distant mountains. I particularly favor the place for breakfast (the French toast is delicious), but they also have a lunch and dinner menu that ranges from steamed vegetables to curried chicken to fresh island fish. In the evening the place is illuminated by torches, and soft breezes wisp off the water, adding to the enchantment. ~ 2863 Kalakaua Avenue; 923-1555. DELUXE.

The food is pretty standard fare at the Sheraton Waikiki's **Ocean Terrace** but the view deserves five stars. Set poolside next to the beach in one of the state's largest hotels, this open-air dining room provides a welcome means to dine on the water. Popular for breakfast, lunch and dinner, the Ocean Terrace's evening menu includes filet mignon, lobster, teriyaki steak, linguine with clams and mahimahi. ~ 2255 Kalakaua Avenue; 922-4422. DELUXE.

If you decide to go to **Nick's Fishmarket**, plan on eating seafood. You have never seen such a list of fresh fish dishes. Not that much of it will seem familiar, but there is mahimahi, *opakapaka* and *ulua*. Or if you prefer to dine on something you recognize, how about shrimp scampi, abalone, lobster or scallops? Very chic; highly recommended. ~ 2070 Kalakaua Avenue; 955-6333. ULTRA-DELUXE.

Dishes like sautéed *opakapaka* garnished with shiitake and asparagus risotto, medallions of veal with linguine, and herb-crusted rack of lamb with ratatouille make **Bali-By-The-Sea** a special favorite. Plush seating, nautical lamps, fresh flowers and soft ocean breezes add to the charm of this elegant restaurant. Dress code. Closed (most) Sundays. ~ Hilton Hawaiian Village, 2005 Kalia Road; 949-4321. ULTRA-DELUXE.

The cuisine at **Acqua** is Mediterranean/Pacific and the ambience dovetails with it neatly. Everything is pastels and primary colors with bright contemporary artwork and an ocean view to match. The menu features several pasta dishes and a host of "main attractions." That means you can order paella, prawn fettuccine au gratin or chicken risotto; or go for something more sophisticated such as phyllo-wrapped mahimahi, pepper-crusted steak, plum chicken, bouillabaisse or veal osso buco. Dinner only. ~ Hawaiian Regent Hotel, 2552 Kalakaua Avenue; 924-0123. MODERATE TO DELUXE.

It's not surprising that Waikiki's most fashionable hotel, the Halekulani, contains one of the district's finest restaurants. Situated on an open-air balcony overlooking the ocean, **La Mer** has a reputation for elegant dining in intimate surroundings. French-inspired dishes include rack of lamb marinated in thyme and garlic and filet of Barbary duck crusted with goat cheese. Add the filigree woodwork and sumptuous surroundings and La Mer is one of the island's most attractive waterfront dining rooms. Dinner only. ~ 2199 Kalia Road; 923-2311. ULTRA-DELUXE.

Downstairs from La Mer is **Orchids**, serving a mix of Hawaiian and Continental cuisine like roasted duckling with wild rice and lamb Provençal. Orchids is open for breakfast, lunch and dinner. ~ 2199 Kalia Road; 923-2311. DELUXE TO ULTRA-DELUXE.

GROCERIES

The best grocery store in Waikiki is also the biggest. Prices at **The Food Pantry** are inflated, but not as much as elsewhere in this tourist enclave. ~ 2370 Kuhio Avenue; 923-9831.

ABC **Discount Stores**, a chain of sundry shops with branches all around Waikiki, are convenient, but have a very limited stock and even higher prices.

If you are willing and able to shop outside Waikiki, you'll generally fare much better price-wise. Try the **Foodland** supermarket in the Ala Moana Center just outside Waikiki. Cheaper than Waikiki groceries, it's still more expensive than Greater Honolulu stores. ~ 1450 Ala Moana Boulevard; 949-5044.

Also in the Ala Moana Center, **Vim and Vigor** has a standard stock of food items, as well as a juice bar and lunch counter. ~ 1450 Ala Moana Boulevard; 955-3600.

SHOPPING

This tourist mecca is a great place to look but not to buy. Browsing the busy shops is like studying a catalog of Hawaiian handicrafts. It's all here. You'll find everything but bargains. With a few noteworthy exceptions, the prices include the unofficial tourist surcharges that merchants worldwide levy against visitors. Windowshop Waikiki, but plan on spending your shopping dollars elsewhere.

One Waikiki shopping area I do recommend is **Duke's Lane**. This alleyway, running from Kalakaua Avenue to Kuhio Avenue near the International Market Place, may be the best place in all Hawaii to buy jade jewelry. Either side of the lane is flanked by mobile stands selling rings, necklaces, earrings, stick pins, bracelets and more. It's a prime place to barter for tiger's eyes, opals and mother-of-pearl pieces.

The main shopping scene is in the malls. **Waikiki Shopping Plaza** has six floors of stores and restaurants. ~ 2250 Kalakaua Avenue. Here are jewelers, sundries and boutiques, plus specialty shops like **Waldenbooks**, with an excellent line of magazines as well as paperbacks and bestsellers. ~ 922-4154.

The nearby **Royal Hawaiian Shopping Center** spans Kalakaua Avenue from Lewers Street all the way to the Royal Hawaiian Hotel. Along this four-tiered marathon course, you can purchase jewelry, cameras or ice cream. There are boutiques, sporting goods stores, surf shops, art galleries, craft shops and practically everything else conceivable—all at the very center of Waikiki. ~ Kalakaua Avenue.

Then there's **King's Village**, a mock Victorian town that suggests how Britain might have looked had the 19th-century English invented polyethylene. The motif may be trying to appear antiquated, but the prices are unfortunately quite contemporary. ~ 131 Kaiulani Avenue at Kalakaua Avenue.

International Market Place is my favorite browsing spot. With tiny shops and vending stands spotted around the sprawling grounds, it's a relief from the claustrophobic shopping complexes. There's an old banyan spreading across the market, plus thatched treehouses, a carp pond, brick sidewalks and woodfront stores. You won't find many bargains, but the sightseeing is priceless. ~ 2330 Kalakaua Avenue.

The **Waikiki Trade Center** is another strikingly attractive mall. With an air of Milanese splendor about it, this glass-and-steel complex is a maze of mirrors. In addition to the stained-glass windows and twinkling lights, there are several worthwhile shops. ~ Kuhio and Seaside avenues.

Some of Hawaii's smartest shops are located in the **Atrium Shops** at the Hyatt Regency Waikiki. This triple-tiered arcade is *the* place to look when you are seeking the very best. Glamour and style are passwords around here. There are fine-art shops, designer apparel stores, gem shops and much more. ~ 2424 Kalakaua Avenue.

Hilton Hawaiian Village contains the **Rainbow Bazaar**, an array of shops spread around the grounds of Hawaii's largest resort complex. This plaza contains a number of stores specializing in island fashions, plus gift shops and import emporia. The shopping center has been designed in Oriental style, with curving tile roofs and brilliantly painted roof beams. You can stroll along an Asian arcade, past lofty banyan trees and flowering gardens, to stores filled with rare art and Far Eastern antiquities. ~ 2005 Kalia Road.

Actually it's the other 20 percent that predominates at **80% Straight Inc.** This gay men's shop has cards, clothes, videos and gift items. Located on the 2100 block of Kuhio Avenue, it's in the heart of Waikiki's gay district. ~ 2139 Kuhio Avenue; 923-9996.

Aloha
Patrol

You'll spot them strolling down the streets of Waikiki every night and at the North Shore beaches during the day. They wear navy blue T-shirts with Aloha Patrol emblazoned across the front in bold yellow letters. They're members of the "Aloha Patrol," and they're here to help you.

Crime ranks at the top of the list of problems facing Honolulu residents. Whenever you meet the locals they're likely to talk about the rise in robberies and car break-ins. If you rent a car in Hawaii the company will warn you not to leave valuables inside, and you'll be reminded at the parks and the beaches by signs stating the same thing. Although your chances of being ripped off are probably pretty slim, as a tourist you are a prime target, so it's something to be wary of.

Tired of having crime tarnish their island's reputation, the citizens of Oahu have taken action. In late 1996, they formed the first Aloha Patrol to be a citizen's watchgroup and the eyes and ears of the police in Waikiki, as well as to be the spirit of aloha for guests. Early the next year, they expanded their work to the North Shore.

There are more than 200 volunteers in the program, with residents from all over the island participating. Members range in age from 20 to over 80 and have a wide variety of jobs and professions. The one thing they all have in common, however, is the goal to make Oahu a better place to live and visit.

In Waikiki, the Aloha Patrol members meet each night at a local hotel, then walk the streets from 7 p.m. until 11 p.m., answering questions, giving directions, telling people about themselves and the Aloha Patrol and, if they see any problems, alerting the police by two-way radio. On the North Shore, they patrol the beach parking lots each afternoon to prevent car break-ins. And it seems to work. Since the program began, there have been no robberies in the afternoons at the patrolled beaches and visitors to Honolulu can be assured that the streets of Waikiki are safer because of the folks in their navy blue T-shirts.

Just a couple doors down, **Down Under Honolulu** has the widest array of men's underwear in creation (or at least in Honolulu). ~ 2139-F Kuhio Avenue; 922-9229.

Following a similar theme but covering the rest of the body is **Physique**. This men's clothing store has T-shirts, slacks and a limited assortment of other apparel items. ~ 2139-A Kuhio Avenue; 921-7297.

Extending from Kuhio Avenue to Kalaimoku Street, **Old Waikiki Market** is an open-air, low-rent "mall." Here vendors sell souvenirs, T-shirts and assorted gewgaws from thatch-roofed kiosks. ~ 2139 Kuhio Avenue.

HIDDEN ►

Looking for a vintage silk shirt? Those famous Hawaiian styles, like the one Montgomery Clift sported in *From Here to Eternity*, are among the alluring items at **Bailey's Antiques and Aloha Shirts**. If an original silky is beyond your means, they also have a collection of reproductions. ~ 517 Kapahulu Avenue; 734-7628.

NIGHTLIFE Hawaii has a strong musical tradition, kept alive by excellent groups performing their own compositions as well as old Polynesian songs. I'm not talking about the "Blue Hawaii"–"Tiny Bubbles"–"Beyond the Reef" medleys that draw tourists in droves, but *real* Hawaiian music as performed by Hapa, the Brothers Cazimero, Keola and Kapono Beamer, Marlene Sai, Melveen Leed and others.

Over at **Nick's Fishmarket**, the hot sounds of a dance band draw flocks of locals and visitors alike Friday and Saturday night. ~ 2070 Kalakaua Avenue; 955-6333.

On Friday and Saturday night, a contemporary Hawaiian duo stars at the **Paradise Lounge**. A pianist performs on Wednesday night. Choose between table or lounge seating in this carpeted club, which is decorated with Hawaiian landscapes painted by local artists. ~ 2005 Kalia Road; 949-4321.

The **Esprit Nightclub** is a congenial spot situated right on Waikiki Beach. This cozy club features a house band that plays music from different eras Tuesday through Saturday, features special guests on Sunday and Monday and offers spectacular ocean

ISLAND SOUL

If you spend any time in Honolulu, don't neglect to check out the authentic sounds of the local talent. Many of these musicians—Keola and Kapono Beamer and the Brothers Cazimero—will probably be playing at a local club. Consult the daily newspapers, or, if you want to hear these groups before paying to see them, listen to KCCN at 1420 on the radio dial. This all-Hawaiian station is the home of island soul.

views every night of the week. ~ Sheraton Waikiki Hotel, 2255 Kalakaua Avenue; 922-4422.

Tired of the old nine-to-five grind? For a change of pace try **Scruples,** where the schedule is eight to four—8 p.m. to 4 a.m. that is. Promising "dance and romance," this popular night spot features dancing to Top-40 tunes. Cover and minimum. ~ 2310 Kuhio Avenue; 923-9530.

The **Maharaja Restaurant,** an establishment as formal and upscale as its name implies, offers dancing to Top-40 deejay music. Cover and dress code. ~ Waikiki Trade Center, 2255 Kuhio Avenue; 922-3030.

The Cellar specializes in dancing, with Top-40 tunes spun by a deejay Wednesday through Sunday. It's a top spot for a hot night. Cover. ~ 205 Lewers Street; 923-9952.

Nearby, **Waikiki Broiler** has a live band playing Hawaiian or reggae music nightly. ~ 200 Lewers Street at Kalia Road; 923-8836.

Jungle Waikiki features a nightly dance party with a variety of musical styles. Cover. ~ 311 Lewers Street; 922-7808.

Eurasia Night Club and Sports Bar has a deejay playing hip-hop and retro sounds Wednesday through Saturday night. Call for the daily musical menu. There's a light show, dancefloor and dartboards. Live bands perform Sunday, Monday and Tuesday night. Cover. ~ Hawaiian Regent Hotel, 2552 Kalakaua Avenue; 921-5335.

Acqua offers live Latin music Thursday, Friday and Saturday night in a plush setting. With an ocean view and relaxing ambience, this lounge in the Hawaiian Regent Hotel is part of a light, airy, Mediterranean restaurant. ~ 2552 Kalakaua Avenue; 924-0123.

Coconut Willy's Bar & Grill, situated on a balcony in the International Market Place, has a live band that starts in the afternoon and continues on into the night. It may be local music or country. Delightful setting. ~ 2330 Kalakaua Avenue; 923-9454.

Locals head for **Duke's Canoe Club** to hear Hawaiian and contemporary musicians perform nightly. You'll hear slack-key and steel guitars on a balcony overlooking the Pacific. ~ 2335 Kalakaua Avenue; 922-2268.

◄ HIDDEN

For live sounds, cruise into **Wave Waikiki** and catch local bands that perform on Tuesday night. There is also a deejay playing alternative dance music nightly. Cover after 10 p.m. ~ 1877 Kalakaua Avenue; 941-0424.

With room for 300 of your closest friends, **Moose McGillycuddy's Pub and Café** is a prime place to dance to live bands. Deejays also spin Top-40 music. Known for its weird pictures, this establishment is easily spotted. Just look for the only building on Lewers Street sporting a stuffed moose head. Weekend cover. ~ 310 Lewers Street; 923-0751.

The sound is a mix of '80s alternative, funk classics and industrial dance music at **Rendezvous**. This place is billed as Honolulu's "hot mod dance party." But remember, no baseball caps and no sagging pants. ~ 478 Ena Road; 942-5282.

GAY SCENE   The gay scene, which traditionally centered around several clubs on Waikiki's Kuhio Avenue, has spread west to Eaton Square, near the corner of Eaton and Hobron streets, not far away. Both areas are popular, although Kuhio still boasts the most clubs.

On Kuhio, **Treats** is a U-shaped bar with a side patio. With recorded music and television, it's a major spot for drinking and carousing. Formerly known as Hamburger Mary's, it has been drawing crowds for years. ~ 2109 Kuhio Avenue; 923-0669.

Next door, **Trixx** is a patio-style bar with deejay music and dancing nightly. On Thursday through Saturday night from 11 p.m. to 1 a.m., they feature dancers. Together with Treats, which is actually part of the same complex, it is the capital of gay nightlife not only in Waikiki, but throughout Hawaii. Cover. ~ 2109 Kuhio Avenue; 923-0669.

Club goers hang in and out at **Angles Waikiki**, where a bar in the center of the room provides a place to socialize as does the lanai outside. There are pool tables and videos, as well as a dancefloor. Every Wednesday, crowds compete for cash prizes in the Best Chest/Best Buns contest, and Sensually Certified, an all-male revue, entertains on Thursday and Sunday nights. ~ 2256 Kuhio Avenue; 926-9766.

Fusion Waikiki is another gay club open until 4 a.m. This three-floor hot spot features dancing to progressive deejay music. There are male strip shows four nights a week. Cover. ~ 2260 Kuhio Avenue; 924-2422.

Eaton Square houses **Windows**. Stylish yet casual in its decor, this gay bar, popular with men and women, is adorned with sensual prints. The featured entertainment consists of darts, pool and relaxation. ~ 444 Hobron Lane; 946-4442.

HIDDEN ►   Tucked away in the back of Eaton Square, **P-10A**, a 24-hour private coffee bar, gives gay guys an alternative place to meet. It's an alcohol- and smoke-free relaxing retreat, serving coffee and tea. For entertainment there are video games, a pool table, x-rated movies and, most importantly, conversation in this low-key, quiet hangout. Although it's a private club, it costs no more than a night at a bar. Cover. ~ Eaton Square, Hobron and Eaton streets; 942-8536.

Michelangelo is a cozy club with dancing, karaoke, contests and special events. Monday is music trivia night. Tuesday is underwear night, a fashion parade of the wackiest and weirdest. There's a strip show on Wednesday, Friday and Saturday nights. ~ Eaton Square, Hobron and Eaton streets; 951-0008.

At **1739 Kalakaua,** if you don't like the music in one room, you can just walk into the next. There's a main club room and a lounge, each with its own deejay playing different types of tunes. The walls are a virtual art gallery decorated with the works of a different artist each month. (They are for sale.) On Wednesday catch GUESS (Gorgeous, Unique, Extravagant, Sassy, Sensational), a floorshow featuring Hawaii's finest female impersonators. Cover Thursday through Sunday. ~ 1739 Kalakaua Avenue; 949-1739.

At a private showing in the **Douglas Simonson Studio** you can view this internationally known artist's paintings and drawings of male nudes. Call for an appointment and directions. ~ 737-6275.

WAIKIKI BEACH Famous all over the world, the strand in Waikiki is actually several beaches in one. **Kahanamoku Beach, Fort De Russy Beach, Royal-Moana Beach, Kuhio Beach Park** and **Queen's Surf** form an unbroken string that runs from the Ala Wai Canal to Diamond Head Crater. Together they comprise Waikiki Beach. Since going to the beach in this busy enclave also means exploring Waikiki itself, I have placed the beach descriptions in the sightseeing section on the preceding pages.

BEACHES & PARKS

FIVE

Downtown Honolulu

While the Neighbor Islands and rural Oahu still move at a leisurely, laid-back pace, downtown Honolulu marches to a different drummer. As the political and commercial heart of Hawaii and the center of the only major metropolis in all of Polynesia, it plays a role far more vital than its compact size would seem to warrant.

The state, county and city government offices can all be found here, as can the headquarters of the companies that control Hawaii and whose influence reaches well beyond its shores to both the U.S. mainland and Asia. Honolulu's importance as a city has a long history, one that is partially told in its many historic buildings.

The development of Honolulu received a major boost when King Kamehameha III moved his capital from Lahaina to Honolulu in the 1840s. Although the missionaries had already established themselves in the area, it was at about this time that they began to build the church and houses that can still be seen today. As sugar developed as an agricultural industry and a cash economy took hold, the companies that were created to handle this business chose Honolulu as their headquarters.

A walk through the downtown area is a journey into the city's history. Begin at the old mission houses, now the Mission Houses Museum, and stroll past Kawaihao Church and Iolani Palace. Continue on to Merchant Street, with its 19th- and early-20th-century brick buildings, which once housed the city's financial district and headquarters for the "Big Five" companies that controlled Hawaii's economy. Wander through Chinatown past crowded restaurants adorned with ducks hanging in the windows and herbal medicine shops lined with jars and drawers of leaves, twigs, bark and flowers.

Walk down by the waterfront, where Matson Line luxury steamers delivered the first tourists and gave birth to another industry, one which still keeps Hawaii's economy thriving today. And finally, ride the elevator to the top of the Aloha Tower for a bird's-eye view of the highrise office buildings that define downtown Honolulu today.

A fitting place to begin your tour is among the oldest homes in the islands. The buildings at the **Mission Houses Museum** seem to be borrowed from a New England landscape, and in a sense they were. The Frame House, a trim white wooden structure, was cut on the East Coast and shipped around the Horn to Hawaii. That was back in 1821, when this Yankee-style building was used to house missionary families.

Like the nearby Chamberlain Depository and other structures here, the Frame House represents one of the missionaries' earliest centers in Hawaii. It was in 1819 that Congregationalists arrived in the islands; they immediately set out to build and proselytize. In 1831, they constructed the Chamberlain Depository from coral and used it as a storehouse. The neighborhood's Coral House, built of the same durable material ten years later, was used by the first press ever to print in the Hawaiian language. The Mission Houses complex tells much about the missionaries, who converted Hawaiian into a written language, then proceeded to rewrite the entire history of the islands. The museum is run by the Hawaiian Mission Children's Society. Closed Sunday and Monday. Admission. ~ 553 South King Street; 531-0481.

Opposite, at South King and Punchbowl streets, is the **Kawaihao Church**. This imposing edifice required 14,000 coral blocks for its construction. Completed in 1842, it has been called the Westminster Abbey of Hawaii, because coronations and funerals for Hawaiian kings and queens were once conducted here. Services are still performed in Hawaiian and English every Sunday at 10:30 a.m.; attending them is not only a way to view the church interior, but also provides a unique cultural perspective on contemporary Hawaiian life. Also note that the tomb of King Lunalilo rises in front of the church, and behind the church lies the cemetery where early missionaries and converted Hawaiians were buried.

Across South King Street, that brick structure with the stately white pillars is the **Mission Memorial Building**, constructed in 1916 to honor those same early church leaders. The nearby Renaissance-style building with the tile roof is **Honolulu Hale**, the City Hall. You might want to venture into the central courtyard, an open-air plaza surrounded by stone columns.

As you continue along South King Street in a westerly direction toward the center of Honolulu, **Iolani Palace** will appear on your right. Built for King Kalakaua in 1882, this stunning Renaissance-style mansion served as a royal residence until Queen Liliuokalani was overthrown in 1893. Later the ill-starred monarch was imprisoned here; eventually, after Hawaii became a territory of the United States, the palace was used as the capitol building. Today it represents the only royal palace in the United States. Guided tours lead you along the *koa* staircases and past the magnificent chandeliers and Corinthian columns that lend a touch of European grandeur to this splendid building.

Also located on the palace grounds are the **Iolani Barracks,** where the Royal Household Guards were stationed, and the **Coronation Pavilion** upon which the "Champagne King" was crowned. You can tour the palace grounds for free, but there is an admission charge for the building. Reservations are strongly advised; children under five are not allowed. Tours are given Wednesday through Saturday. Closed Sunday, Monday and Tuesday. ~ South King and Richards streets; 522-0832.

Directly across the street rises the **Kamehameha Statue,** honoring Hawaii's first king. A huge gilt-and-bronze figure cast in Italy, it is draped with flower leis on special occasions. The spear-carrying warrior wears a feather cape and helmet. Behind him stands **Aliiolani Hale,** better known as the Judiciary Building. Back in the days of the monarchy, it served as the House of Parliament.

Behind Iolani Palace is the **State Capitol Building.** Unlike the surrounding structures, this is an ultramodern building, completed in 1969. Encircled by flared pillars that resemble palm trees, the capitol represents a variety of themes. Near the entrance there's a statue of Father Damien, the leper martyr of Molokai Island. The House and Senate chambers are designed in a cone shape to resemble volcanoes, and the open-air courtyard is a commentary on the state's balmy weather. Tours of the capitol building and the legislature are given Monday through Friday. ~ Bounded by South Beretania, Richards and Punchbowl streets; 586-0178, 586-0146, fax 586-0212.

For a tour of Honolulu's waterfront, head down Richards Street from the State Capitol Building toward Pier 7 on Ala Moana Boulevard, where the imposing and historic **Falls of Clyde** lies berthed. A completely restored century-old sailing ship, the *Falls of Clyde* is reputedly the only fully rigged four-masted ship in the world. In the old days it was used to carry sugar and oil across the Pacific. Honolulu was then a harbor filled with tall-masted ships, so crowded at the dock that they bumped one another's gunwales. Part of this proud fleet, the *Falls of Clyde* was built in Scotland and sailed halfway round the world.

For a single admission charge you can tour this marvelous piece of floating history and view the *Hokulea,* a double-hulled canoe that has sailed several times to Tahiti. A 60-foot replica of an ancient Polynesian craft, it follows the traditional designs of the boats used by the early Tahitians. On several historic voyages during the past two decades this fragile craft has been sailed between Hawaii and French Polynesia by Hawaiian navigators. Using no modern instruments, navigating by stars and wave patterns, they traced the course of their ancestors. Also part of this **Hawaii Maritime Center**

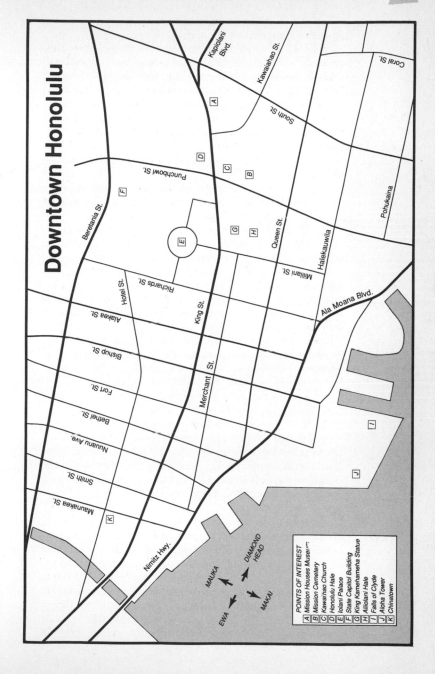

Downtown Honolulu

POINTS OF INTEREST

A Mission Houses Museum
B Mission Cemetery
C Kawaiahao Church
D Honolulu Hale
E Iolani Palace
F State Capitol Building
G King Kamehameha Statue
H Aliiolani Hale
I Falls of Clyde
J Aloha Tower
K Chinatown

MAUKA
DIAMOND HEAD
EWA
MAKAI

is the Kalakaua Boathouse (adjacent to the *Falls of Clyde*), an outstanding museum that traces the archipelago's maritime history from the era of Polynesian exploration to the days of the great ocean liners and beyond. Other displays focus on the old whaling trade, the invention of surfing and the natural history of the ocean. The audio tour is worth taking. Admission. ~ Pier 7; 536-6373.

It's also fun to wander the nearby wharves, catching glimpses of the shops and pleasure boats that still tie up around Honolulu's historic port. You can take in the city's fishing fleet, as well as several tour boats, at **Kewalo Boat Basin**, also known as Fisherman's Wharf, midway between Waikiki and Downtown Honolulu. ~ Ala Moana Boulevard and Ward Avenue.

From the Hawaii Maritime Center, follow the roadway along the water to **Aloha Tower** at Pier 9. You'll see it nearby, rising like a spire along the water's edge. Earlier in the century, when many visitors arrived in luxurious ocean liners, this slender structure was Hawaii's answer to the Statue of Liberty. It greeted guests when they arrived and bade them farewell upon departure. Now dwarfed by the skyscrapers of Downtown Honolulu, proud Aloha Tower still commands an unusual view of the harbor and ocean. Any day between 9 a.m. and 9 p.m. you can ride an elevator to the tenth floor observation deck for a crow's nest view. ~ For ship arrival and departure information, call 537-9260.

Today, **American Hawaii Cruises** carries on the oceanliner tradition in part. They operate the SS *Independence* and the SS *Constitution*, which ply the waters between the islands regularly, docking at Kauai, Maui and the Big Island, and in Honolulu near Aloha Tower. ~ For information on their week-long cruises around the Hawaiian islands, call 800-765-7000.

It's not far to **Fort Street Mall**, a seven-block stretch of Downtown Honolulu that has been refurbished and converted into an attractive pedestrian thoroughfare. There are restaurants galore here. The mall is also a good place to spend a little time shopping. Located miles from the Waikiki tourist beat, the stores here cater to local people, so you'll be able to discover objects unobtainable in kitschier quarters.

A one-block detour leads to Bethel Street, where you'll find the **Hawaii Theatre**. After years of painstaking restoration, it is again a study in neoclassical architecture. With gilded decor, Corinthian columns and striking mosaics, it has been elevated again to the grand status it enjoyed when the theater first opened in 1922. In 1929, it was the first movie theater in the islands to show movies with sound. Tours are available at this nationally registered historic place. Admission. ~ 1130 Bethel Street; 528-5535.

Fort Street Mall leads to **Merchant Street**, center of the old downtown section of Honolulu. The 19th- and early-20th-century buildings in this neighborhood re-create the days before Hawaii

became the 50th state, when the islands were almost totally controlled by "The Big Five," an interlocking group of powerful corporations. Today the brick rococo district remains much the same
on the outside. But the interiors of the buildings have changed
markedly. They now house boutiques and gourmet restaurants
downstairs and multinational corporations on the upper floors.

After proceeding away from the waterfront all the way to the
end of Merchant Street, take a right on Nuuanu Avenue, then a left
on Hotel Street. As you walk along this thoroughfare, which seems
to change its identity every block or two, you will pass from Honolulu's conservative financial district into one of its most intriguing
ethnic neighborhoods, **Chinatown**.   ◄ HIDDEN

The Chinese first arrived in Hawaii in 1852, imported as plantation workers. They quickly moved to urban areas, however, became merchants and proved very successful. Many settled right here
in this weather-beaten district, which has long been a center of con-
troversy and an integral part of Honolulu's history. When bubonic
plague savaged the Chinese community in 1900, the Caucasian-led
government tried to contain the pestilence by burning down af-
flicted homes. The bumbling white fathers managed to raze most of
Chinatown, destroying businesses as well as houses.

Today Hotel Street, the spine of Chinatown, is undergoing a
major renovation. Many buildings have already been restored and
newly refurbished shops now stand cheek-by-jowl with quaint, time-
worn stores. Even here, however, you can still encounter the other
side of Chinatown, the seedy, late-night face of the neighborhood.
Strung like a neon ganglion along the thoroughfare are porno movie
places, flophouses, barrooms and pool halls. This was once a booming red-light district, the haunt of sailors and ragged characters.

The ultimate emblem of Chinatown's revitalization is **Maunakea Marketplace**. This Amerasian shopping mall, with a statue of
Confucius overlooking a brick courtyard, houses an Oriental antique shop and a Chinese art store. The most interesting feature is
the produce market, a series of traditional hanging-ducks-and-live-
fish stalls inside an air-conditioned building. ~ Hotel and Maunakea streets.

THE MERRY MONARCH

The king who commissioned the Iolani Palace, David Kalakaua, was a
world traveler with a taste for the good life. Known as the Merry
Monarch, he planned for his coronation the greatest party Hawaii had
ever seen. He liked to spend money with abandon and managed to
amass in his lifetime a remarkable collection of material goods, not
the least of which was his palace.

HIDDEN ▶

The best way to visit this neighborhood is on one of the **China-town Walking Tours** sponsored by the Chinese Chamber of Commerce. Chinatown today is an eclectic community, containing not only Chinese, but Filipinos, Hawaiians, and recent arrivals from Vietnam and Laos. To fully understand Hawaii's melting-pot population, it's important to visit this vibrant district. The walking tour is given on Tuesday mornings, and will carry you past temples and other spots all around the neighborhood. Fee. ~ 42 North King Street; 533-3181.

Continuing north along Hotel Street across Nuuanu Stream, turn right on College Walk and follow it a short distance upstream. You'll pass the **Izumo Taishakyo Mission**, a Shinto Shrine.

Proceed farther and you will arrive at **Foster Botanical Garden**. This 14-acre plot is planted with orchids, palms, coffee trees, poisonous plants and numerous other exotic specimens. There are about 4000 species in all, dotted around a garden that was first planted over 125 years ago. You can meditate under a bo tree or wander through a "prehistoric glen," a riot of ancient ferns and unusual palms. Or you can stroll through and marvel at the universe of color crowded into this small urban garden. Admission. ~ 50 North Vineyard Boulevard; 522-7065.

On the way back to Chinatown, walk along the other side of Nuuanu Stream and stop at the **Cultural Plaza**. This Asian-style shopping mall is bounded by Kukui, Maunakea and Beretania streets, and by the stream. You'll find porcelain, Chinese jewelry, spices and perhaps even acupuncture supplies.

Another important cultural point in the downtown district is the **Honolulu Academy of Arts**. This outstanding museum often displays author James Michener's collection of woodblocks from Japan. There are also works by European, Asian and American masters, as well as important art by local painters and sculptors. Several elegantly landscaped courtyards add to the beauty here. Closed Monday. Admission. ~ 900 South Beretania Street; 532-8700.

Farther afield lies **Dole Cannery Square**, once the site of Hawaii's largest pineapple cannery. The 195-foot-high pineapple tower

◆◆

HEART OF A NEIGHBORHOOD

Some of Chinatown's woodframe buildings still suggest the old days and traditions. Wander down side streets like Maunakea Street and you will encounter import stores, Chinese groceries and noodle factories. You might also pop into one of the medicinal herb shops, which feature strange potions and healing powders. There are chop suey joints, acupuncturists and outdoor markets galore, all lending a priceless flavor of the Orient.

is currently down for repairs, but when it's standing, the factory is one of Honolulu's most recognizable landmarks. Visitors can watch a slideshow on the history of the pineapple industry and enjoy fresh pineapple juice. ~ 650 Iwilei Road; 528-2236.

LODGING

Centrally located between Waikiki and Downtown Honolulu is the **Nakamura Hotel**. It's a pleasant place, but the only reason I can conceive for staying here is the locale. The hotel itself is adequate; the rooms are neatly furnished, carpeted and equipped with private telephones for guests (though phone service is cut off at night). I'd ask for accommodations on the *mauka* side, since the other side fronts noisy King Street. ~ 1140 South King Street; 593-9951. BUDGET.

The **Pagoda Hotel** is sufficiently removed from the crowds but still only a ten-minute drive from the beach. Spacious studio and one-bedroom units put the accent on rattan furniture. The carpeted rooms feature views of the hotel garden or distant mountains. Two-bedroom units in the adjoining Pagoda Terrace offer kitchens. ~ 1525 Rycroft Street; 941-6611, 800-367-6060, fax 955-5067. MODERATE TO DELUXE.

On the outskirts of Chinatown is the **Town Inn**. This is an excellent spot to capture the local color of Honolulu's Chinese section, though the hotel itself is rather nondescript. The rooms are clean, carpeted and sparsely furnished—some even have air conditioning—and all are practically devoid of decoration. First-come, first-serve. ~ 250 North Beretania Street; 536-2377. BUDGET.

DINING

Rather than list the city's restaurants according to price, I'll group them by area. As you get away from Waikiki you'll be dining with a more local crowd and tasting foods more representative of island cuisine, so I would certainly advise checking out some of Honolulu's eating places.

Right next to Waikiki, in Ala Moana Center, there are numerous ethnic takeout restaurants that share a large dining pavilion called **Makai Market**. Best of all is **Patti's Chinese Kitchen** (946-5002), a crowded and noisy gathering place. At Patti's you can choose two or more main dishes plus a side order of fried rice, or *chow fun*. The courses include almond duck, lemon-sauce chicken, tofu, beef tomato, sweet-and-sour pork, barbecued ribs, pigs' feet and shrimp with vegetables. It's quite simply the best place near Waikiki for a low-cost meal. There's also the **Poi Bowl** (949-8444), a takeout stand serving Hawaiian dishes. ~ 1450 Ala Moana Boulevard. BUDGET.

◀ *HIDDEN*

Or you can ride the escalator to the upper level of Ala Moana Center. Here **Shirokiya**, a large Asian department store, features an informal Japanese restaurant and deli. ~ 973-9111. MODERATE.

A few blocks away at **Daiei**, a grocery and department store filled with an amazing variety of Asian and Hawaiian foods and

◀ *HIDDEN*

goods features the **Daiei Food Court**, an incredibly popular spot with local shoppers. Choose from places like **Sushi Robot**, which serves pre-made bento lunch boxes and made-to-order sushi, or **Yummy Korean Barbecue**, which specializes in barbecued beef, ribs and chicken. **Harpos** turns out pizza and spaghetti, and **Manapua** creates such Chinese favorites as roast duck and pork and noodles. ~ 801 Kaheka Street; 973-4800. BUDGET. Hawaiian regional cuisine accented by island fruits is featured at the **Prince Court**. The Hawaii Prince Hotel's harborside restaurant, this dining room is known for dishes like sea scallops, Kahuku shrimp, lobster and mahi salad niçoise. A big wine list is another plus at this Polynesian-style dining room appointed with floral bouquets. ~ 100 Holomoana Street; 956-1111. MODERATE TO DELUXE.

> You'll discover in Downtown Honolulu that in the course of a few short blocks you have passed from Hong Kong into Tokyo.

Ward Centre, midway between Waikiki and Downtown Honolulu, is a focus for gourmet dining. A warren of wood-paneled restaurants, it features several outstanding eateries. Particularly recommended for the price is **Scoozee's**, a "pasta, pizza, pizzazz" restaurant that has nothing on its menu above $10. ~ 1200 Ala Moana Boulevard; 597-1777. BUDGET.

Also consider **Compadres**, upstairs in the same complex. This attractive Mexican restaurant, with oak bar and patio dining area, prepares a host of dishes from south of the border as well as sandwiches, salads, steaks and seafood. It specializes in tropical ambience, good food and fishbowl-size margaritas. ~ 1200 Ala Moana Boulevard; 591-8307. MODERATE.

Ryan's Grill is one of Honolulu's hottest after-work hangouts for singles who want to become un-single, and the place is packed from 5 p.m. until after 10 p.m. Comfortable leather chairs and marble-topped tables create a cozy, modern atmosphere. Grilled and steamed fish and fowl, pizzas, salads and fettucine are among the many culinary options for those who go to eat instead of drink. ~ 1200 Ala Moana Boulevard; 591-9132. MODERATE TO DELUXE.

There are lots of other options at Ward Warehouse next door. Dinner at **The Old Spaghetti Factory**, which many locals rank as the city's best bargain, is like eating in a mansion where the Victorian designer got carried away. There are overstuffed chairs, a brass bed made into a table, stained-glass windows and elaborate chandeliers. And there's also spaghetti, of course, in a variety of styles, as well as other Italian treats. Each dinner comes with a salad and an individual loaf of homemade bread. This is a great place for kids. There's even a diaper-changing station in the restroom. ~ 1050 Ala Moana Boulevard; 591-2513. BUDGET.

Located in the ultracontemporary Restaurant Row shopping mall, **Sunset Grill** is a minimalist's delight. Track lights, exposed

Plate Lunches

There's nothing more Hawaiian than the plate lunch. It's soul food at its finest, but not for the faint at heart. Nor for those counting calories or concerned about the fat content of their food. A local culinary tradition, the plate lunch combines Japanese, Chinese, Korean, Hawaiian, American and Filipino fare into a meal that is not only delicious but more food for the price than you're likely to find anywhere.

The plate lunch tradition began in the sugar plantation days when women would deliver plates of food to family plantation workers. These plates would usually consist of two scoops of white rice, a scoop of potato or macaroni salad and a variety of meat and fish, including teriyaki pork, beef, chicken or fish; pork or chicken *lau lau*; or kalua pig. Some entrepreneurial villagers started up businesses selling lunches to field workers without families.

Little-changed today, the plate lunch still consists of two scoops of white rice and possibly a third scoop of macaroni or potato salad, as well as the main selections, which could be just about anything. A local favorite is *loco moco*, a hamburger steak topped with fried egg and gravy. There are also *kalbi* (Korean pork ribs), teriyaki beef, chicken and pork katsu, and stir-fried shrimp.

Plate lunches are served in simple restaurants, usually a drive-in or coffee shop. They also can be found at any of the lunch trucks parked at places around Honolulu, near the University of Hawaii or on the North Shore. Although there are probably as many opinions on the best plate lunches as there are people in Oahu, here are a few favorites.

Like Like Drive Inn is one of the oldest and most well-established plate lunch eateries in Honolulu and very popular with the locals. This comfy coffee shop has the feel of the '50s and serves up some good home-style comfort food. ~ 735 Keeaumoku Street; 941-2515.

Grace's Inn, with several locations around Oahu, is famed for its chicken *katsu* and homemade *kimchi*. It also serves beef stew, beef curry and a variety of other dishes. Their Beretania eatery is the best known of the "chain." ~ 1296 South Beretania Street; 593-2202.

You'll never be far from an **L & L Drive-Inn**. With more than 20 restaurants around Oahu, the chain has been voted by the readers of the *Honolulu Advertiser* as serving the best plate lunches. Stir-fried shrimp and hamburger steak are among the offerings, and the breakfasts come complete with Portuguese sausage and a Hawaiian favorite, spam. Check out the Kapiolani Boulevard diner. ~ 1471 Kapiolani Boulevard; 943-8808.

pipes, raw wood and poured concrete establish a kind of early-21st-century motif. The only area devoted to excess is the kitchen, which serves up a lavish array of *kiawe*-grilled dishes, such as smoke-infused marinated salmon. ~ 500 Ala Moana Boulevard; 521-4409. MODERATE TO DELUXE.

Fresh *ono*, mahimahi, *opakapaka* and ahi highlight the vast seafood menu at **John Dominus**. A sprawling establishment midway between Waikiki and downtown Honolulu, it features huge pools filled with hundreds of live lobsters. The wood-paneled dining room overlooks the water and the chefs know as much about preparing seafood as the original Polynesians. For landlubbers, steak and veal are also on the menu. ~ 43 Ahui Street; 523-0955. DELUXE TO ULTRA-DELUXE.

For sushi, sukiyaki, tempura and other Japanese specialties, try the **Pagoda Floating Restaurant**. This restaurant-in-the-round sits above a pond populated with gaily colored koi fish. Several cascades and a fountain feed the pond. The surrounding grounds have been carefully landscaped. This dining room, which offers a lunch and dinner buffet, also serves steaks, scampi and other Western dishes. ~ 1525 Rycroft Street; 941-6611. MODERATE.

Honolulu has numerous seafood restaurants. Some of them, fittingly enough, are located right on the water. But for an authentic seafront feel, it's nice to be where the fishing boats actually come in. **Fisherman's Wharf** provides just such an atmosphere. This sprawling facility is festooned with nautical gear. The "Seafood Grotto" topside has a shoalful of seafood selections ranging from live Maine lobster to Dungeness crab. ~ 1009 Ala Moana Boulevard; 538-3808. MODERATE TO DELUXE.

Up on the second level of the Aloha Tower Marketplace, toward the back overlooking the water, there's the **Kau Kau Corner Food Lanai**. This cluster of food stands ranges from Villa Pizza to Belinda's Aloha Kitchen to the Pacific Vegetarian Cafe and beyond. There's comfortable seating in an attractive setting, all at economical prices. ~ Aloha Tower Marketplace, Pier 8; 528-5700. BUDGET.

Saddles, hubcaps and cowboy boots hang from the ceiling of **Rodeo Cantina**, a crazy Tex-Mex joint overlooking the harbor. Crates of vegetables and boxes of beer cover corners of the room, and a collection of more than 100 hot-sauce bottles hangs on the wall. Mismatched silverware sits in wooden containers and cardboard six-packs on the tables. The food is nothing to write home to Aunt Bertha about, but the chips and salsa are great, the tequila selection is said to be the best in Hawaii, and there's a happy hour from 3:30 to 6 p.m. Monday through Friday, with a nacho and taco bar and cheap margaritas. The decor and country music make this place seem like a party. A true original. ~ Aloha Tower Marketplace, Pier 8; 545-1200. BUDGET TO MODERATE.

There are several other dining spots situated along interior streets away from the water that I particularly like. These are also located between Waikiki and Downtown Honolulu. For Italian-style seafood, **Philip Paolo's** is highly recommended by local residents. Set in a trim woodframe house, it features scampi, *frutti di mare* (seafood combination) and a host of pasta dishes. The interior is very fashionably done. ~ Two locations: 407 Uluniu Avenue and Keahole Street; 263-3287. MODERATE.

The decor at **Jimbo's Restaurant** is simple, but the noodles are ◀ *HIDDEN* superb. Jimbo's serves Japanese udon—thick, white and perfectly cooked—in a broth so delicious your taste buds will rejoice. This is Japanese soul food at its finest and no doubt the best udon this side of Tokyo. No wonder there's always a line outside. ~1936 South King Street; 947-2211. BUDGET.

Just down the street, **Wisteria Restaurant** has been pleasing local Japanese-Hawaiians for years. This is where they come to celebrate birthdays, anniversaries and other milestones. The setting is padded booths–coffeeshop style. The food is Japanese home-style cooking, just like *obachan* (grandma) used to make. The sukiyaki and teriyaki are particularly tasty. ~ 1206 South King Street; 591-9276. MODERATE.

In the same part of town sits one of Honolulu's best budget-priced Chinese restaurants. The decor at **King Tsin Restaurant** is rather bland, but the Mandarin cuisine adds plenty of spice. You can order Szechuan dishes like shredded pork or a Mongolian beef dish. These are plenty hot; you might also want to try the milder seafood, pork, vegetable, fowl and beef dishes. ~ 1110 McCully Street; 946-3273. BUDGET.

Auntie Pasto's is a popular Italian restaurant with oilcloth on the tables and a map of the mother country tacked to the wall. Pasta is served with any of a dozen different sauces—meat sauce,

---

✔ **CHECK THESE OUT**

- Tour **Iolani Palace**, the only royal manor in the entire United States, and discover what life was like for Hawaii's monarchs. *page 95*
- Escape the bustle of Waikiki at the **Pagoda Hotel** while you relax in a rattan chair and gaze at the tropical garden below. *page 101*
- Tuck yourself into a wicker chair, listen for the ornamental gong and order the seven-spice duck confit at **Indigo**. *page 107*
- Go on a treasure hunt as you browse through the hodgepodge at **Aloha Antique & Collectibles** in search of that special gem. *page 109*
- Ride the elevator to the top of **Aloha Tower** for an open-air bird's-eye view of the city and the sea. *page 98*

clams and broccoli, creamy pesto, carbonara and seafood. There are salads aplenty plus an assortment of entrées that includes veal marsala, chicken cacciatore and calamari steak. ~ 1066 South Beretania Street; 523-8855. BUDGET TO MODERATE.

For Southeast Asian cuisine, try the **Thai Taste**. At this modest café you can savor *kang som* (hot-and-sour fish soup), fried pork with garlic and pepper, or a tasty garlic prawn dish. ~ 1246 South King Street; 596-8106. BUDGET.

HIDDEN ► In Downtown Honolulu, near the city's financial center, there's a modest restaurant that I particularly like. **People's Café** has been serving Hawaiian food for over 60 years. The place is owned by a Japanese family, which helps explain the teriyaki dishes on the menu. But primarily the food is Polynesian: This is a splendid spot to order poi, *lomi* salmon, *kalua* pig and other island favorites. *Ono, ono!* ~ 1310 Pali Highway; 536-5789. BUDGET TO MODERATE.

HIDDEN ► **Itochan Sushi** serves sushi-bar quality sushi at economical prices in a tiny four-table-and-counter hole in the wall in The Arcade, a minimall of shops and restaurants on Merchant Street in the heart of downtown. ~ 212 Merchant Street; 545-7848. BUDGET.

For Chinese food, try **Yong Sing Restaurant**. This high-ceilinged establishment, catering to local businesspeople, has some delicious dishes. I thought the oyster sauce chicken particularly tasty. With its daily lunch specials, Yong Sing is a perfect stop off when you're shopping or sightseeing downtown. ~ 1055 Alakea Street; 531-1367. BUDGET TO MODERATE.

HIDDEN ► But for the true flavor of China, head over to Chinatown, just a few blocks from the financial district. Amid the tumbledown buildings and jumble of shops, you'll happen upon **Double Eight Restaurant**. Although the service is forgettable and the decor non-existent, they do know how to cook up Hong Kong–style delicacies. One fortuitous sign of quality is that few of the employees speak any English. Good luck and bon appetit! ~ 1113 Maunakea Street; 526-3887. BUDGET.

HIDDEN ► There's **A Little Bit of Saigon** right in the heart of Chinatown. Small it may be, but this café represents a triple threat to the competition—attractive decor, good prices and excellent food. Little wonder it has gained such a strong reputation among the local gentry. The menu covers the spectrum of Vietnamese dishes, and the interior, lined with tropical paintings, is easy on the eyes. ~ 1160 Maunakea Street; 528-3663. BUDGET TO MODERATE.

And there's a little bit of every other ethnic cuisine at the food stalls in **Maunakea Marketplace**. Here you'll find vendors dispensing steaming plates of Thai, Chinese, Japanese, Hawaiian, Filipino, Korean, Vietnamese and Italian food. Italian? Small tables are provided. ~ Hotel and Maunakea streets. BUDGET.

By way of Filipino food, **Mabuhay Cafe** comes recommended by several readers. It's a plainly adorned place on the edge of Chinatown that serves a largely local clientele. The menu is extensive, covering the full spectrum of Filipino dishes. ~ 1049 River Street; 545-1956. BUDGET.

For upscale dining in Chinatown, the address is **Indigo**. This Eurasian dining room casts an aura of the Orient with its dark wicker chairs, ornamental gong and intaglio-carved furnishings. Expect more than a dozen dim sum dishes plus "Peking pizzettas." The soups and salads include tea-smoked chicken jook and grilled goat cheese in lotus leaf. Among the entrées, they offer peppered Mongolian beef, a "Buddhist vegetable" medley and seven-spice duck confit. What an adventure! No lunch on Sunday. ~ 1121 Nuuanu Avenue; 521-2900. MODERATE.

Eating at **Duc's Bistro** is like entering a French salon. This quiet oasis may be on the edge of Chinatown, but it seems a world away. White tablecloths and vases full of flowers adorn the tables and gallery-quality paintings decorate the walls. Quiet classical music provides a soothing atmosphere to enjoy the French-Vietnamese cuisine that has gained this restaurant a loyal following among locals. Fish, prawns, duck and chicken are prepared French fashion with a touch of Vietnam. ~ 1188 Maunakea Street; 531-6325. DELUXE.

GROCERIES

Midway between Waikiki and Downtown Honolulu there's a **Times Supermarket**. ~ 1290 South Beretania Street; 524-5711. Nearby is a **Safeway** store. ~ 1121 South Beretania Street; 591-8315. There's another **Safeway** in Downtown Honolulu. ~ 1360 Pali Highway; 538-3953.

Also look for **The Carrot Patch** with its health and diet products. ~ 700 Bishop Street; 531-4037.

You might want to browse around the mom-and-pop grocery stores spotted throughout Chinatown. They're marvelous places to pick up Chinese foodstuffs and to capture the local color.

◄ HIDDEN

Don't miss the **Open Market** in Chinatown. It's a great place to shop for fresh foods. There are numerous stands selling fish, produce, poultry, meat, baked goods and island fruits, all at low-overhead prices. ~ Along North King Street between River and Kekaulike streets.

SHOPPING

Ala Moana Center, on the outskirts of Waikiki, is the state's largest shopping center. This multitiered complex has practically everything. Where most self-respecting malls have two department stores, Ala Moana has four: **Sears** (947-0211), **JC Penney** (946-8068), Hawaii's own **Liberty House** (941-2345) and a Japanese emporium called **Shirokiya** (973-9111). There's also a **Longs Drug Store** (941-4433), a good place to buy inexpensive Hawaiian curios. For contemporary fashion there is **United Colors of Benetton** (973-2670), among numerous other shops. You'll also find an assortment of stores selling liquor, antiques, tennis and golf supplies, stationery, leather goods, cameras, shoes, art, tobacco. You name it, they have it. ~ 1450 Ala Moana Boulevard.

And, in a paragraph by itself, there's the **Honolulu Book Shop**. Together with its sister store downtown at 1001 Bishop Street, this is Hawaii's finest bookstore. Both branches contain excellent selections of Hawaiiana books, bestsellers, paperbacks, calendars, magazines and out-of-town newspapers. ~ Ala Moana Center; 941-2274.

For an excellent selection of women's clothing and accessories, head to **Pomegranates In The Sun**. ~ 1050 Ala Moana Boulevard; 591-2208.

One of Honolulu's sleeker shopping malls is the ultramodern **Ward Centre**. Streamlined and stylized, it's an elite enclave filled with designer shops and spiffy restaurants. In addition to boutiques and children's shops, there's a bookstore and a gourmet grocery, **R. Field Wine Co.** (596-9463). Adorned with blond-wood facades, brick walkways and brass-rail restaurants, the complex provides a touch of Beverly Hills. ~ 1200 Ala Moana Boulevard.

Anchoring Ward Centre at the far end is **Borders Books & Music**, a superstore that is chockablock with everything for your reading and listening pleasure. They have two floors of paperbacks, hardbacks, audiotapes and CDs. ~ 591-8995.

Just down the walkway, you can home in on **Sedona**, the self-proclaimed "unique place to find yourself." If you're looking for aromatherapy oils, visionary music, inspirational gifts or a personal psychic reading, you have discovered the place. ~ 591-8115.

At **Art a la Carte** you'll find some of the most avant garde jewelry, paintings and prints this side of San Francisco. ~ 897-8034.

Tropical Clay sells island-inspired pottery in vivid colors and some pretty wild designs. ~ 597-1811.

Ala Moana may be the biggest, but **Ward Warehouse**, located on Ala Moana Boulevard between Waikiki and Downtown Honolulu, is another very interesting shopping center. It features stores such as **Mamo Howell** (592-0616), which stocks original Hawaiian wear—aloha shirts and dressy muumuus. **Out of Africa** (591-6260) is a gallery with art, masks and jewelry from all over the

ASIAN IMPORTS

If you're seeking Oriental items, then Chinatown is the place. Spotted throughout this refurbished neighborhood are small shops selling statuettes, pottery, woodcrafts and other curios. It's also worthwhile wandering through the **Cultural Plaza**. This mall is filled with Asian jewelers, bookstores and knickknack shops. ~ Corner of Beretania and Maunakea streets; 521-4934.

world. **East of Sun–West of Moon** (596-8046) sells all kinds of crystals, candles, CDs and assorted new age paraphernalia. At **Kris Kringle's Den** (591-8844), it's Christmas all year long. **My Favorite Things** (596-8048) has enough miniatures to furnish the most elaborate dollhouse—or an entire wee neighborhood. **Nohea Gallery** (596-0074) displays quilts, jewelry, pottery, glassware, laps and wooden bureaus—all made in Hawaii by local artists.

Honolulu's newest shopping complex is a California-style affair complete with white stucco walls and curved tile roof. **Aloha Tower Marketplace** is on the waterfront overlooking Honolulu Harbor. With its flagstone walkways and open-air courtyards, it's worth visiting even if buying something is the last thing on your mind. Among the over 100 shops and restaurants are about 25 devoted to apparel, a handful of galleries and perhaps three dozen specialty shops. Among them are **Hula Prints** (528-0395), which sells Hawaiian tourist poster prints of the 1920s and other art. **Automobilia Hawaii** (524-7300) specializes in all kinds of car stuff, from T-shirts, hats and key chains with automobile logos to model cars. At **Flags Flying** (537-1300) the flags of more than 150 countries decorate T-shirts, shorts, stickers and even soccer balls. **Hush-a-bye Baby** (537-2427) sells adorable safari suits and sun dresses that make great souvenirs for the knee-highs. Betty Boop meets Mickey Mouse and the Simpsons at **Animation Magic** (545-8666) a shop where customers of all ages can celebrate cartoons. There are also inexpensive food stands and several full-service restaurants. Tucked between the Hawaii Maritime Museum and Aloha Tower, it's set near one of the busiest parts of the harbor. ~ Pier 8; 528-5700.

If you love those claustrophobic antique stores that have keepsakes stacked to the rafters and spilling into the aisles, then the 900 block of Maunakea Street is calling. Here **Aloha Antique & Collectibles** extends for three storefronts with everything imaginable in the priceless-to-worthless range. ~ 930 Maunakea Street; 536-6187.

At the edge of Chinatown along Nuuanu Avenue are several galleries and shops worthy of a visit. The **Pegge Hopper Gallery** is here, displaying line drawings and the female portraits for which she is renowned. ~ 1164 Nuuanu Avenue; 524-1160.

NIGHTLIFE

The first thing you'll see upon entering the Prince Kuhio Hotel is **Cupid's Lobby Bar**. The lounge area features tropical palms, tapestries, rock walls and a small mirrored bar. Order drinks and *pupus* while enjoying light piano music and vocalists. An outdoor garden is adjacent. ~ 2500 Kuhio Avenue; 922-0811.

At **Rumours**, theme nights are the spice of life. Ballroom dancing, college night and karaoke are all featured, along with dancing to Top-40 music provided by deejays. Located in the Ala Moana Hotel, this club is decorated with artwork and neon fixtures. Weekend cover. ~ 410 Atkinson Drive; 955-4811.

A harbor view and Hawaiian/contemporary music played on weekends by an acoustic guitarist make **Kincaid's** a good choice for a relaxing evening. This lounge is part of a popular Honolulu restaurant. ~ 1050 Ala Moana Boulevard; 591-2005.

Located east of Waikiki, the **Hard Rock Cafe** is always a kick. Decorated with tons of rock-and-roll memorabilia, this restaurant/ bar is a popular nightspot for those who like loud music and a big crowd. Live bands play on Friday and Saturday night. ~ 1837 Kapiolani Boulevard; 955-7383.

Near Downtown Honolulu, the ultracontemporary Restaurant Row, offers several nightspots including a restaurant called **The Ocean Club**. This upscale club with a dress code features nightly deejay dance music and live music on Thursday night. Cover. ~ 500 Ala Moana Boulevard; 526-9888.

Also on Restaurant Row, there's dancing and billiards at the **World Cafe**. ~ 500 Ala Moana Boulevard; 599-4450.

For something more refined and classical, consider **Chamber Music Hawaii**, which presents 20 to 25 concerts annually at several different locations around the city. They also perform on the windward side of the island. ~ 947-1975.

The **Hawaii Theatre** offers the best in Broadway performances, dance troupes, classical music and much more. The Hawaii International Film Festival is held here every November. ~ 1130 Bethel Street; 528-0506.

The **Honolulu Symphony**, with a season that runs from September to May, provides a delightful schedule of programs. ~ 524-0815.

At the **Hawaii Opera Theater**, you can see works like Saint-Saens' *Samson and Delilah*, Puccini's *Madame Butterfly* and *Die Fledermaus* by Strauss. This regional company features stars from the international opera scene. ~ 987 Waimanu Street; 596-7372, box office 596-7858.

A variety of youth- and family-oriented productions are performed by the **Honolulu Theater for Youth**, at a number of venues throughout Oahu. The company also tours the neighbor islands twice a year. ~ 2846 Ualena Street; 839-9885.

At the other end of the cultural spectrum (and at the other end of town), the Honolulu red-light scene centers around Hotel Street in Chinatown. This partially refurbished, partially rundown strip is lined with hostess bars and adult bookstores. Prostitutes, straight and gay, are on the street regularly.

BEACHES & PARKS

ALA MOANA REGIONAL PARK 🚲 🏊 🎣 ⛵ This 119-acre park is a favorite with Hawaii residents. On weekends every type of outdoor enthusiast imaginable turns out to swim, surf, fish (common catches are *papio*, bonefish, goatfish and *moano*), jog, fly model airplanes, sail model boats and so on. It's also a good

HIDDEN ►

place to bodysurf. The three separate breaks here, "Concessions," "Tennis Courts" and "Baby Haleiwa," all have summer waves. There's a curving length of beach, a grassy park area, a helluva lot of local color and facilities that include a picnic area, restrooms, showers, concession stands, tennis courts, a recreation building, a bowling green and lifeguards. ~ On Ala Moana Boulevard at the west end of Waikiki, across from Ala Moana Center.

SAND ISLAND STATE RECREATION AREA 🛶 This 140-acre   ◀ *HIDDEN*
park wraps around the south and east shores of Sand Island, with sections fronting both Honolulu Harbor and the open sea. Despite the name, there's only a small sandy beach here, and jet traffic from nearby Honolulu International might disturb your snoozing. But there is a great view of Honolulu. While the swimming and snorkeling are poor here, there are good surf breaks in summer and fishing is usually rewarding. Bonefish, goatfish, *papio* and *moano* are the prime catches. Facilities include restrooms and a picnic area. ~ From Waikiki, take Ala Moana Boulevard and Nimitz Highway several miles west to Sand Island Access Road.

▲ State permit required for tent camping in the grassy area facing the ocean.

SIX

Greater Honolulu

Framed by the Waianae Range in the west and the Koolau Range to the east, Honolulu is a nonstop drama presented within a natural amphitheater. Honolulu Harbor sets the stage to the south; at the center lie Waikiki and Downtown Honolulu. Wrapped around these tourist and business centers is a rainbow-shaped congeries of sights and places that for lack of a better name constitutes "Greater Honolulu."

Greater Honolulu is where most of the people of Honolulu live. It extends from navy-gray Pearl Harbor to the turquoise waters of the prestigious Kahala district and holds in its ambit some of the city's prettiest territory. Here are the neighborhoods, which, as the city grew, stretched farther east, west and north. Here are working-class enclaves with neat, even rows of houses and wonderful ethnic restaurants. Here, too, is the realm of the well-to-do with their neighborhoods by the waterfront and homes perched on the hillsides overlooking the city.

Each part of greater Honolulu is defined not only by its geographic characteristics but also by the type of people who settled there. Manoa Valley, for example, became home to the descendants of the early missionaries, who built New England saltbox–style homes quite different than those in other areas. Portuguese immigrants, many of whose families had come to work on the sugar plantations, put down roots on the slopes of Punchbowl and named their streets after Lisbon, the Azores, Madeira and other places that reminded them of home.

The sights of Greater Honolulu are dotted all across the city and require a bit of planning to see. You'll need to ride buses or taxis or rent a car, but it is well worth the extra effort. You'll be away from the crowds of tourists and get a chance to meet the locals and get a singular perspective on island life and culture.

Many of the points of interest below are frequented more by local residents than tourists. Others contain an interesting mix of local folk and out-of-towners. In any case, be sure to take the time to explore some of these outlying spots.

NUUANU AVENUE The first district is actually within walking distance of Downtown Honolulu, but it's a relatively long walk, so transportation is generally advised.

Nuuanu Avenue begins downtown and travels uphill in a north-easterly direction past several points of interest. First stop is Soto Mission of Hawaii, home of a meditative Zen sect. Modeled after a temple in India where the Buddha gave his first sermon, this building is marked by dramatic towers, and beautiful Japanese bon-sai plants decorate the landscape. ~ 1708 Nuuanu Avenue. Here and at nearby Honolulu Myohoji Temple the city seems like a dis-tant memory. The latter building, placidly situated along a small stream, is capped by a peace tower. ~ 2003 Nuuanu Avenue.

Uphill from this Buddhist shrine lies **Honolulu Memorial Park**. There is an ancestral monument here, bordered on three sides by a pond of flashing carp and a striking three-tiered pagoda. ~ 22 Craig-side Place. This entire area is a center of simple yet beautiful Asian places of worship. For instance, **Tenrikyo Mission** is a woodframe temple that was moved here all the way from Japan. One intrigu-ing fact about this fragile structure is that large sections were built without nails. ~ 2236 Nuuanu Avenue.

The Hawaiian people also have an important center here. The **Royal Mausoleum** is situated across the street from the Tenrikyo Mission. This was the final resting place for two of Hawaii's royal families, the Kamehameha and Kalakaua clans. Together they ruled 19th-century Hawaii. Today the area is landscaped with palms, ginger, plumeria and other beautiful plants and flowers. ~ 2261 Nuuanu Avenue.

◄ HIDDEN

PUNCHBOWL AND TANTALUS   It is a few miles from Downtown Honolulu to **Punchbowl**, the circular center of an extinct volcano. You'll find it northeast of town, at the end of Ward Avenue and just off Prospect Drive, which circles the crater. A youngster in ge-ologic terms, the volcano is a mere 150,000 years old. From the lip of the crater, there is a marvelous vista sweeping down to Diamond Head, across Honolulu and all the way out to the Waianae Range.

The most important feature here, however, is the **National Me-morial Cemetery**, where more than 25,000 war dead have been in-terred. Victims of both World Wars, as well as the Korean, Spanish-American and Vietnam wars, are buried here. There is also an impressive monument to the "Courts of the Missing," which lists the names of soldiers missing in action. Ironically, of all the people buried here, the most famous was not a soldier but a journalist— Ernie Pyle, whose World War II stories about the average GI were eagerly followed by an entire nation. Near his grave you will also find the burial site of Hawaii's first astronaut, Ellison Onizuka, who died in the *Challenger* space shuttle disaster. Guided walking tours are offered by the American Legion. Fee. ~ 946-6383.

You can explore the heights by following Tantalus Drive as it winds up the side of **Tantalus**, a 2013-foot mountain. Together with Round Top Drive, Tantalus Drive forms a loop that circles through

◄ HIDDEN

the residential areas hidden within this rainforest. There are spectacular views all along the route, as well as hiking trails that lead from the road into verdant hilltop regions. Here you'll encounter guava, banana, eucalyptus and ginger trees as well as wildflowers and an occasional wild pig. One of the best views of all is found at **Puu Ualakaa Park**, a lovely retreat located along the drive. The vista here extends from Diamond Head west to Pearl Harbor, encompassing in its course a giant swath of Honolulu and the Pacific.

Of all the exhibits at the Bishop Museum, the most spectacular are cloaks worn by Hawaiian kings and fashioned from tens of thousands of tiny feathers.

En route stop by the **Contemporary Museum**. In addition to changing exhibitions of contemporary art, the museum features the works of several well-known artists in its sculpture garden including David Hockney, Robert Arneson, Charles Arnoldi and Tom Wasselman. Boasting five galleries, an inspired gift shop and a gourmet café, the museum is nevertheless upstaged by its magnificently landscaped grounds. Closed Monday. Admission. ~ 2411 Makiki Heights Drive; 526-1322.

CROSS-ISLAND EXPRESS   Along the outskirts of Honolulu, there are several more points of interest. The best way to tour them is while traveling along the two highways that cut across the Koolaus, connecting Honolulu directly with the island's Windward Coast.

The Likelike Highway, Route 63, can be reached from Route H-1, the superhighway that serves Honolulu. Before heading up into the mountains, you will encounter the **Bishop Museum** near the intersection of Routes 63 and H-1. Built around the turn of the century, it houses an excellent collection of Hawaiian and Pacific artifacts.

Here you'll find outrigger canoes, thrones, primitive artworks, royal feather capes and fascinating natural-history exhibits. There are plaited mats woven from pandanus, drums made with shark skin, 19th-century surfboards, and helmets decorated with dog teeth and pearl shells. The 19th-century whaling trade is represented with menacing harpoons and yellowing photographs of the oil-laden ships. There are displays capturing the Japanese, Chinese and Filipino heritage in Hawaii and a hall devoted to other cultures of the Pacific.

The museum also offers a planetarium, a Hall of Discovery with children's activities, and classes in quilting, hula dancing, lei-making and weaving. The Bishop is truly one of the finest museums of its kind in the world. Admission. ~ 1525 Bernice Street; 847-3511.

The other, more scenic road across the mountains is the Pali Highway, Route 61. As it ascends, it passes **Queen Emma's Summer Palace**. Constructed in 1848, the palace was originally used by King Kamehameha IV and his wife, Queen Emma. Today the gra-

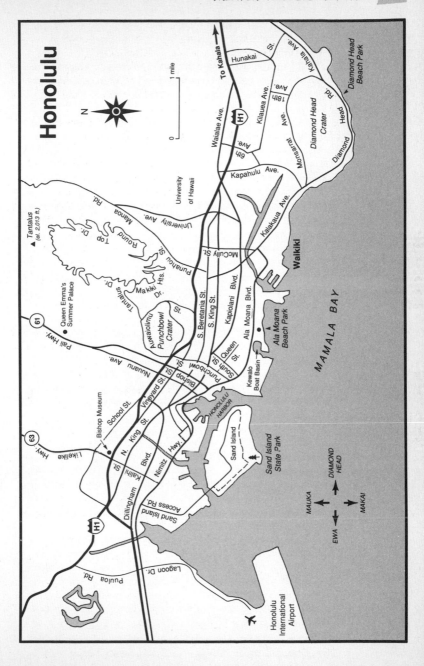

Honolulu

N

0   1 mile

▲ Tantalus
(el. 2,013 ft.)

To Kahala

Hunakai
St.

Kilauea Ave.

18th Ave.

Kahala Ave.

Diamond Head
Beach Park

H1

6th Ave.

Monsarrat Ave.

Diamond Head
Crater

Diamond Head

Diamond Head
Rd.

Waialae Ave.

Kapahulu Ave.

University
of Hawaii

University Ave.

Manoa Rd.

Round Top Dr.

Punahou St.

McCully St.

Kalakaua Ave.

Waikiki

Queen Emma's
Summer Palace

Tantalus Dr.

Makiki
Hts. Dr.

S. Beretania St.

S. King St.

Kapiolani Blvd.

Queen St.

Ala Moana Blvd.

Ala Moana
Beach Park

MAMALA BAY

61

Pali Hwy.

Nuuanu Ave.

Awaiolimu St.

Punchbowl
Crater

Punchbowl St.

Bishop St.

South St.

Kewalo
Boat Basin

Bishop Museum

School St.

Vineyard St.

N. King St.

HONOLULU
HARBOR

Sand Island

Sand Island
State Park

63

Likelike Hwy.

Kalihi St.

Nimiz Blvd.

Hwy.

Sand Island

MAUKA

DIAMOND
HEAD

EWA

MAKAI

H1

Dillingham Blvd.

Sand Island
Access Rd.

Lagoon Dr.

Puuloa Rd.

Honolulu
International
Airport

cious white-pillared house is a museum. Here you can view the
Queen's personal artifacts, as well as various other period pieces.
Admission. ~ 595-3167.

HIDDEN ▶

You can also walk the tree-shaded grounds of **Nuuanu Pali
Drive** and follow until it rejoins the highway. This residential boul-
evard, with its natural canopy and park-like atmosphere, is one of
Honolulu's many idyllic hideaways.

Farther along Pali Highway, there is a turnoff to **Nuuanu Pali
Lookout**. It is a point that must not be missed, and is without doubt
Oahu's finest view. Gaze down the sheer, rugged face of the Koolau
cliffs as they drop 3000 feet to a softly rolling coastal shelf. Your
view will extend from Makapuu Point to the distant reaches of
Kaneohe Bay, and from the lip of the cliff far out to sea. It was from
these heights, according to legend, that a vanquished army was
forced to plunge when Kamehameha I captured Oahu in 1795.

PEARL HARBOR   Many people consider a trip to Pearl Harbor a
pilgrimage. It was here on a sleepy Sunday morning, December 7,
1941, that the Japanese launched a sneak attack on the United
States naval fleet anchored in the port, immediately plunging the
nation into World War II. As Japanese planes bombed the harbor,
over 2400 Americans lost their lives. Eighteen ships sank that day
in the country's greatest military disaster.

The battleship USS *Arizona* was hit so savagely by aerial bombs
and torpedoes that it plunged to the bottom, entombing over 1100
sailors within its hulk; today they remain in that watery grave. A
special **USS Arizona Memorial** was built to honor them; it's a museum constructed directly above the ship, right in the middle of
Pearl Harbor. In addition to the museum displays, the memorial
includes a shrine with the name of each sailor who died aboard the
ship carved in marble. Gazing at this too, too long list of names,
and peering over the side at the shadowy hull of the ship, it's hard
not to be overcome by the tragic history of the place. Daily from 8
a.m. to 3 p.m., the United States Navy sponsors free boat tours out
to this fascinating memorial. Before boarding, be sure to remember, no bathing suits, bare feet or children under 45 inches are permitted. Pearl Harbor, several miles northwest of Downtown Honolulu, can be reached by car or bus. ~ 422-0561.

Anchored nearby the *Arizona* visitors center is the **USS Bow-
fin/Pacific Submarine Museum**. This World War II–era submarine
is a window into life beneath the waves. It provides an excellent
opportunity to tour the claustrophobic quarters in which 80 men
spent months at a time. The accompanying museum, filled with
submarine-related artifacts, will help provide an even fuller perspective. Admission. ~ 423-1341.

MANOA VALLEY   Residents of a different sort are found in the
city's beautiful Manoa Valley, a couple of miles northeast of Wai-

The Neighborhoods

The neighborhoods of Honolulu stretch along the flat-
lands that spread out from downtown and snake their way up
the valleys and over the hills that surround the city. They provide
a social history of this Polynesian metropolis, as its population
grew and its economy expanded.

One of the oldest neighborhoods, **Kalihi**, still thrives as a working-
class enclave west of downtown. As Honolulu grew, wealthy and middle-
class people moved farther eastward and northward to the outer reaches
of the city. The poor Hawaiian residents of Kalihi were joined by immigrants
and people leaving the plantations for an urban lifestyle. In Kalihi, they were
close to factory jobs and small farms still scattered through the area. They
opened clubs and restaurants and established schools and churches, many of
which still exist today.

Manoa, the valley neighborhood that serves as home to the University
of Hawaii, served as a popular retreat of Hawaiian royalty in the early 19th
century. It was later settled by descendants of missionaries, who built
homes reminiscent of their New England origins. The estate of the Cooke
family, who founded Castle & Cooke, one of the Big Five companies that
controlled the state, can be found here.

The neighborhood was also settled by Chinese, who favored Manoa for
its excellent *feng shui*. Because the mountains on both sides act as protection and funnel energy through the valley, the Chinese people believed living
there would bring good luck. Manoa owes its natural heritage partly to the
founder of the Lyons Arboretum, who at the turn of the century planted
trees from around the world in what was to become a verdant valley.

The **Kahala District**, which stretches out along the coast east of
Diamond Head became one of the realms of the rich, with their beautiful
homes lined along the beach. This neighborhood remains quiet and peaceful,
blessed by the breezes that blow in from its shores and unsullied by the
kind of development that has commercialized other urban beach areas.
Although the beach is shaded by coconut palms, local residents don't have
to worry about falling coconuts. They're all picked by local Tongan tree
climbers, hired to prevent the dropping fruit from bonking heads.

kiki. Among the elegant homes decorating the region are some owned by the New England families that settled in Hawaii in the 19th century.

The **University of Hawaii** has its main campus here; almost 20,000 students and 2000 faculty members attend classes and teach on these grounds, which are set amid rolling lawns and backdropped by the Koolau Mountains. ~ 2444 Dole Street; 956-8111.

HIDDEN ►   On campus is the **East-West Center**, a private research facility. Designed by noted architect I. M. Pei, the center is devoted to the study of Asian and American cultures. The center also contains a number of priceless Asian artworks, well worth viewing. ~ John Burns Hall, 1601 East-West Road; 944-7111.

From here you can head deeper into Manoa Valley along Oahu Avenue and Manoa Road. At the end of Manoa Road is **Lyon Arboretum**, a magnificent 194-acre garden with more than 8000 plant species, research greenhouses, hiking trails and perhaps the world's largest collection of palm trees. The arboretum also offers a variety of one-day classes on topics such as horticulture and lei-making. Closed Sunday. ~ 3860 Manoa Road; 988-3177.

KAHALA   On the far side of Diamond Head, along a string of narrow beaches, lie many of Honolulu's most admired addresses. To reach this residential promised land follow Diamond Head Road.

Diamond Head Beach Park, a twisting ribbon of white sand, nestles directly below the famous crater. Whenever the wind and waves are good, you'll see windsurfers and surfers galore sweeping in toward the shoreline. The coral reef here makes for good skin-diving, too. It's a pretty beach, backdropped by the Kuilei cliffs and watched over by the **Diamond Head Lighthouse**.

From Diamond Head, continue east along Diamond Head Road and Kahala Avenue. These will lead through the Kahala District, home to the island's elite. Bordered by the ocean and the exclusive Waialae Country Club is a golden string of spectacular oceanfront homes with carefully manicured lawns.

LODGING   The **Nuuanu YMCA** has inexpensive accommodations for men. Complete athletic facilities are available. ~ 1441 Pali Highway; 536-3556. BUDGET.

Hawaii's foremost bed-and-breakfast inn rests in a magnificent old mansion near the University of Hawaii campus. Set in the lush

HIDDEN ►   Manoa Valley, the **Manoa Valley Inn** is a 1915 cream-colored Victorian featuring seven guest rooms and an adjacent cottage. Decorated with patterned wallpaper and old-style artworks, the rooms are furnished in plump antique armchairs. Guests enjoy a sunroom and parlor, as well as a spacious veranda and lawn. For luxury and privacy, this historic jewel is one of the island's finest spots. Continental breakfast and evening wine and cheese are included. ~ 2001

Vancouver Drive; 947-6019, 800-634-5115, fax 946-6168. DELUXE
TO ULTRA-DELUXE.

Also in Manoa Valley, the **Fernhurst YWCA** is an appealing three-
story lowrise that provides a residence for women. Rooms are single or double occupancy with connecting baths. Among the facilities
are microwaves, refrigerators, laundry, dining room, swimming pool
and lounge. Rates include breakfast and dinner Monday through
Friday. ~ 1566 Wilder Avenue; 941-2231, fax 949-0266. BUDGET.

The **Atherton YWCA** is a coed facility with accommodations for
both men and women. Across the street from the University of Hawaii campus, it's open year-round to full-time students (of any institution, but you have to show registration and student ID) and
during the summer to the general public. There's a nonrefundable
application fee and a refundable deposit. Facilities include laundry,
lounge and a microwave. Reservations must be booked at least two
weeks in advance and the facility is closed weekends and holidays,
so plan accordingly. ~ 1810 University Avenue; 946-0253, fax 941-
7802. BUDGET.

The **Honolulu International Youth Hostel** is a dormitory-style
crash pad with separate living quarters for men and women. Shared
kitchen facilities, television lounge, garden patio and laundry are
available. ~ 2323-A Sea View Avenue; 946-0591, fax 946-5904.
BUDGET.

With two rooms and a cottage, **Bed & Breakfast Manoa** offers   ◀ HIDDEN
cozy surroundings as well as spectacular views of Diamond Head.
Light pastels and a Southern-style decor add to the homey aura,
and those mild Hawaiian nights make it possible to sleep outdoors.
~ 2651 Terrace Drive; 988-6333, fax 988-5240. MODERATE TO
DELUXE.

✔ **CHECK THESE OUT**

- Learn the hula, look into 19th-century Hawaiian history and gaze at the
  outrigger canoes and royal feather capes at the **Bishop Museum**. *page 114*
- Step back to the Victorian era and relax out on the veranda of the
  Manoa Valley Inn, one of the island's finest lodging spots. *page 118*
- Head for **Helena's Hawaiian Foods** to check out the luau chicken with
  taro leaves and coconut milk, a true local culinary treat. *page 121*
- Browse through the finely made goods at **Lanakila Crafts**, where
  woven handbags and monkeypod bowls are some of the bargains
  you'll find, all made by the disabled. *page 122*
- Explore the remains of a *heiau*, an arboretum of medicinal plants
  and a rainforest extending to the far reaches of the Koolaus at
  Keaiwa Heiau State Recreation Area. *page 122*

With its breezy corner rooms and strict nonsmoking policy, **The Mango House** caters solely to women. There are two guest rooms and a cottage, each comfortably furnished and decorated with local artwork. One of the rooms includes a hot tub, which is almost as appealing as the homemade mango jam that is served for breakfast. Set in a residential neighborhood, The Mango House enjoys panoramic views of Honolulu. Three-night minimum stay. ~ 2087 Iholina Street; phone/fax 595-6682, 800-776-2646, e-mail mango@pixi.com. MODERATE TO DELUXE.

DINING

HIDDEN ►

Liliha Seafood Restaurant, a neighborhood café out past Downtown Honolulu, comes highly recommended by local folks. This could very well be the only Hawaiian dining spot that offers sweet-and-sour sea bass, squid with sour mustard cabbage and fried squid with *ong choy*. In addition to two dozen seafood dishes, they have a host of chicken, pork, vegetable and noodle selections. ~ 1408 Liliha Street; 536-2663. BUDGET.

One of the ethnic restaurants most popular with local folks is **Keo's Thai Cuisine**. Fulfilling to all the senses, this intimate place is decorated with fresh flowers and tropical plants. The cuisine includes such Southeast Asian dishes as the "evil jungle prince," a sliced beef, shrimp or chicken entrée in hot sauce. You can choose from dozens of fish, shellfish, fowl and meat dishes. The food is very, very spicy, and highly recommended. Dinner only. ~ 625 Kapahulu Avenue; 737-8240. MODERATE TO DELUXE.

HIDDEN ►

For Japanese dining, one of my favorites is **Irifune**, a warm and friendly place frequented by a local crowd. There are tasty curry, teriyaki and tempura dishes, plus several other Asian delectables. Closed Monday. ~ 563 Kapahulu Avenue; 737-1141. MODERATE.

If the thought of not checking your e-mail for days leaves you feeling faint, knock back an espresso, wolf down a sandwich and log on at the **Internet Café**. Travelers can access their own e-mail accounts at this 24-hour communication waystation, or use the guest account to send mail—and food and drink *are* allowed at the dozen or more workstations! ~ 559 Kapahulu Avenue; 735-5282; www.aloha-cafe.com. BUDGET.

Quantity and quality don't usually come together, particularly where gourmet restaurants are concerned. But at **Sam Choy** you can count on platter-size portions of macadamia-crushed *ono*, Oriental lamb chops, oven-roasted duck or tofu lasagna. Considered one of the top Hawaiian cuisine restaurants on the island, it sits with unassuming grace on the second floor of a strip mall. Eat heartily (and well)! Dinner and Sunday brunch. ~ 449 Kapahulu Avenue, Suite 201; 732-8645. DELUXE TO ULTRA-DELUXE.

For local-style plate lunches, cruise in to **Rainbow Drive-In**. Popular with *kamaainas* and tourists alike, the menu includes hamburger steak, beef curry, chili and fried chicken served with two scoops of rice and macaroni salad. ~ 3308 Kanaina Avenue; 737-0177. BUDGET.

Ono Hawaiian Foods is a must for all true Hawaii lovers. It's a hole-in-da-wall eatery on a busy street. But if you're lucky enough to get one of the few tables, you can feast on *laulau*, kalua pig, *pipikaula*, poi and *haupia*. The walls are papered with signed photographs of local notables and the place is packed with locals, notable and otherwise. Closed Sunday. ~ 726 Kapahulu Avenue; 737- 2275. BUDGET.

Near the University of Hawaii campus, there are pizzas, hero sandwiches, spaghetti and a salad bar at **Mama Mia**. Open for lunch on weekends and dinner every day, it's a great place to snack or stop for a cold beer. ~ Puck's Alley, 1015 University Avenue; 947-5233. MODERATE.

Or you can check out **Anna Banana's**, a combination bar and Mexican restaurant that draws a swinging crowd. Located a half-mile from campus, this dim eatery serves burritos, enchiladas and other south-of-the-border favorites. Decorated in slapdash fashion with propellers, antlers, surfboards, boxing gloves and trophies, Anna's is the local center for slumming. ~ 2440 South Beretania Street; 946-5190. BUDGET.

Waialae Avenue, a neighborhood strip several miles outside Waikiki, has developed into a gourmet ghetto. **Azteca Mexican Restaurant** is a vinyl-booth-and-plastic-panel eatery that serves a delicious array of Mexican food. ~ 3617 Waialae Avenue; 735-2492. BUDGET TO MODERATE.

For spicy and delicious Asian dishes, it is hard to find a more appealing place than **Hale Vietnam**. A family restaurant that draws a local crowd, it features traditional Vietnamese soup and a host of excellent entrées. ~ 1140 12th Avenue; 734-7581. MODERATE.   ◄ HIDDEN

Quietly hidden away in a tiny storefront in the Kalihi district, **Helena's Hawaiian Foods** has been dishing up kalua pig, *lomi* salmon and *pipikaula* from its tiny kitchen for more than 50 years. The food is served in tiny dishes, so you can sample a selection. The luau chicken cooked with taro leaves and coconut milk is a knock-out. The place only has ten tables, which means there's often a wait. But it's worth it. Lunch only. ~ 1364 North King Street; 845-8044. BUDGET.   ◄ HIDDEN

A few blocks down the street is **Elena's,** another Kalihi culinary treasure. This '50s-style coffee shop with a counter, booths and paneled and mirrored walls specializes in such Filipino favorites as pork adobo, *pansit*, *bangus sinigang*, beef *asada* and *lumpia*. It claims to be the "home of the finest Filipino food in Kalihi." Some say it's the finest in all of Honolulu. ~ 2153 North King Street; 845-0340. BUDGET.

Kelly's Restaurant & Bakery has been serving fish, steak and shrimp plate lunches for more than 44 years. This bright and cheerful 24-hour coffee shop near the airport has a long counter and bright green booths. The miso-grilled fish is a meal to be remembered. ~ 2908 Kamehameha Highway; 836-3444. BUDGET.

GROCERIES   A good place to shop near the University of Hawaii's Manoa campus is at **Star Market**. ~ 2470 South King Street; 973-1666.

The best place in Honolulu to buy health foods is at **Down To Earth Natural Foods**. ~ 2525 South King Street; 947-7678. **Kokua Market** is another excellent choice. ~ 2643 South King Street; 941-1922.

SHOPPING   Scattered around town are several shops that I recommend you check out. At **Lanakila Crafts** most of the goods are made by the

HIDDEN ▶   disabled, and the craftsmanship is superb. There are shell necklaces, woven handbags, monkeypod bowls and homemade dolls. You'll probably see these items in other stores around the islands, with much higher price tags than here at the "factory." ~ 1809 Bachelot Street; 531-0555.

Out at the Bishop Museum be sure to stop by **Shop Pacifica**, which offers a fine selection of Hawaiiana. There are books on island history and geography, an assortment of instruments that include nose flutes and gourds, plus cards, souvenirs and wooden bowls. ~ 1525 Bernice Street, near the intersection of Routes 63 and H-1; 848-4158.

One of Honolulu's most upscale shopping centers is **Kahala Mall**, where you'll find designer shops galore. This attractive complex also hosts an array of moderately priced stores. ~ 4211 Waialae Avenue; 732-7736.

Barnes & Noble has a superstore here. In addition to a comprehensive line of books, they sell tapes and CDs and feature a café on the premises. ~ Kahala Mall, 4211 Waialae Avenue; 737-3323.

NIGHTLIFE   Outside Honolulu there are usually a couple of spots to hear Hawaiian music. Pick up a copy of *Spotlight* or *This Week* magazine to see what's going on.

Over by the University of Hawaii's Manoa campus, there's **Anna Banana's**. A popular hangout for years, this wildly decorated spot has live entertainment several nights a week. There's likely to be a local band cranking it up and a local crowd headed for the dancefloor. Cover. ~ 2440 South Beretania Street; 946-5190.

BEACHES & PARKS   **KEAIWA HEIAU STATE RECREATION AREA** 🏃 As amazing as it sounds, this is a wooded retreat within easy driving distance of Honolulu. Situated in the Koolau foothills overlooking Pearl Har-

HIDDEN ▶   bor, it contains the remains of a *heiau*, a temple once used by Hawaiian healers. There's an arboretum of medicinal plants, a forest extending to the far reaches of the mountains and a network of hiking trails. Facilities include picnic area, showers and restrooms. ~ Located in Aiea Heights. To get there from Honolulu, take Route 90 west to Aiea, then follow Aiea Heights Drive to the park.

▲ Tents only. State permit required.

DIAMOND HEAD BEACH PARK A heaven to windsurfers, this twisting ribbon of white sand sits directly below the crater. It's close enough to Waikiki for convenient access but far enough to shake most of the crowds. The Kuilei cliffs, covered with scrub growth, loom behind the beach. Snorkeling is good here as a coral reef extends offshore through this area. There's also a good year-round surf break called "Lighthouse." And for the anglers, your chances are good to reel in *ulua*, *papio* or *mamao*. A shower and picnic area are the only facilities. ~ Located just beyond Waikiki along Diamond Head Road at the foot of Diamond Head; watch for parked cars.

◄ HIDDEN

KUILEI CLIFFS BEACH PARK AND KAALAWAI BEACH Extending east from Diamond Head Beach Park, these sandy corridors are also flanked by sharp sea cliffs. Together they extend from Diamond Head Lighthouse to Black Point. The aquatic attractions are the same as at Diamond Head Beach Park and both beaches can be reached from it (or from cliff trails leading down from Diamond Head Road). A protecting reef makes for good swimming at Kaalawai Beach (which can also be reached via a public accessway off Kulumanu Place).

WAIALAE BEACH PARK Smack in the middle of Honolulu's prestigious Kahala district, where a million dollars buys a modest house, sits this tidy beach. Its white sand neatly groomed, its spacious lawn shaded by palms, Waialae is a true find. It has good swimming and fishing. There are bathhouse facilities, beachside picnic tables and a footbridge arching across the stream that divides the property. To the west of the park lies **Kahala Beach**, a long, thin swath of sand that extends all the way to Black Point. There's good snorkeling near the Kahala Hilton. ~ Located on the 4900 block of Kahala Avenue in Kahala.

SEVEN

Southeast Oahu

Out past Honolulu, beyond the glitter of Waikiki and the gilded neighborhoods of Kahala, the pace slows down, the vistas open up and Oahu begins to look more like a tropical island. The road—Route 72, the Kalanianaole Highway—leads out of Honolulu and hugs the rugged coastline as it climbs up and down and back and forth along the edge of a series of volcanic ridges. The jagged, jade-colored peaks of the Koolau Mountains on one side and the sparkling blue sea on the other provide some of the most striking scenery the state has to offer.

Fortunately, there are lots of places to stop and admire it along the way. Some of Hawaii's best snorkeling is at Hanauma Bay, a marine nature preserve. Koko Head and Koko Crater have hiking trails, and a swim is an option at any of a number of pocket beaches that dot the shore. For those who long for more "traditional" amusements, there is also Sea Life Park, a marine theme park, about midway along the Southeast Coast.

Eventually the road drops down and continues alongside fields to Waimanalo, the center of a farming region that once long ago was a sugar plantation but now supplies much of the fruit and flowers that appear in Honolulu's markets. The town preserves a bit of the Hawaiian Wild West, with people parading through town in pickups and a yearly spring rodeo that attracts *paniolos* (cowboys) from around Oahu and the Neighbor Islands. Waimanalo, and the surrounding rural lands, are another side of the multifaceted island of Oahu, and one that warrants a closer look.

The highway also streams through Hawaii Kai and other residential areas, and approaches the slopes of an extinct volcano, 642-foot **Koko Head**. Here Madame Pele is reputed to have dug a hole for the last time in search of fiery volcanic matter. **Koko Crater**, the second hump on the horizon, rises to over 1200 feet. This fire-pit, according to Hawaiian legend, is the vagina of Pele's sister. It seems that Pele, goddess of volcanoes, was being pursued by a handsome demigod. Her sister, trying to distract the hot suitor from Pele, spread her legs across the landscape.

From the top of Koko Head, a well-marked sideroad and trail lead down to **Hanauma Bay**, one of the prettiest beaches in all Hawaii. This breathtaking place is a marine preserve filled with multicolored coral and teeming with underwater life. The word *hanauma* means "the curved bay," and you will clearly see that this inlet was once a circular volcano, one wall of which was breached by the sea. Little wonder that Hollywood chose this spot as the prime location for Elvis Presley's movie, *Blue Hawaii*. Elvis' grass shack was right here, and the strand was also a setting in the classic film *From Here to Eternity*.

The swimming and snorkeling are unmatched anywhere and the mazework of coral formations along the bottom adds to the snorkeling adventure. Or you can stroll along the rock ledges that fringe the bay and explore **Toilet Bowl**, a tidepool that "flushes" as the waves wash through it. The best time to come is early morning before other swimmers stir up the waters. Hanauma Bay is an extremely popular picnic spot among local folks, so it is also advisable to visit on a weekday rather than face bucking the crowds on Saturday and Sunday. Because of its popularity, there has been discussion of limiting access to a given number of people each day. Call to check the status before you go. ~ Hanauma Bay is located about 12 miles east of Waikiki; 924-0266.

From here the highway corkscrews along the coast. Among the remarkable scenes you'll enjoy en route are views of Lanai and Molokai, two of Oahu's sister islands. On a clear, clear day you can also see Maui, an island that requires no introduction.

At an overlook you will encounter **Halona Blowhole**, a lava tube through which geysers of seawater blast. During high tide and when the sea is turbulent, these gushers reach dramatic heights. *Halona* means "peering place," and that is exactly what everyone seems to do here. You can't miss the spot, since the roadside parking lot is inevitably crowded with tourists. Between December and April this vista is also a prime whale-watching spot.

Just beyond spreads **Sandy Beach**, one of Hawaii's most renowned bodysurfing spots. It's a long, wide beach piled with fluffy sand and complete with picnic areas and showers. Inexperienced bodysurfers are better off enjoying the excellent sunbathing here, since the dramatic shorebreak that makes the beach so popular among bodysurfers can overwhelm beginners.

Across from the beach a side road leads up to **Koko Crater Botanical Gardens**, a 200-acre collection of cacti, plumeria and other flowering plants. ~ 50 North Vineyard Boulevard; 522-7060.

◄ *HIDDEN*

Past this pretty spot, Route 72 rounds Oahu's southeastern corner and sets a course along the eastern shoreline. It also climbs to a scenic point from which you can take your first view of the Windward Coast. You will be standing on **Makapuu Point**. Above you rise sharp lava cliffs, while below are rolling sand dunes and open ocean. The slope-faced islet just offshore is Rabbit Island. The distant headland is Makapuu Peninsula, toward which you are bound.

From this perfect perch you can also spy a complex of buildings. That's **Sea Life Park**, a marine-world attraction comparable to those in California and Florida. Among the many features at this park is the "Hawaiian Reef," a 300,000-gallon oceanarium inhabited by about 4000 sea creatures. To see it you wind through a spiral viewing area that descends three fathoms along the tank's glass perimeter. At times a scuba diver will be hand-feeding the fish. Swimming about this underwater world are sharks, stingrays and a variety of lesser-known species. The park also features a touch pool, turtle lagoon, penguin habitat and the only known *wholphin* (half whale, half dolphin) living in captivity. ~ 41-202 Kalanianaole Highway, Makapuu Point; 259-7933.

Across the road from Sea Life Park spreads **Makapuu Beach Park**, another fabled but daunting bodysurfing spot that is set in a particularly pretty location. Nearby black lava cliffs are topped by a white lighthouse and **Rabbit Island** is anchored just offshore. Rabbit Island, located off Makapuu Point, resembles a bunny's head, but was actually named for a former rabbit-raising farm there. The beach itself is a short, wide rectangle of white sand. It's an ideal place to picnic, but when the surf is up, beware of the waves.

The road continues along the shoreline between soft sand beaches and rugged mountain peaks. For the next 30 miles your attention will be drawn back continually to those rocky crags. They are part of the **Koolau Range**, a wall of precipitous mountains that vault up from Oahu's placid interior. Their spires, minarets and fluted towers are softened here and there by lush, green valleys, but never enough to detract from the sheer beauty and magnitude of the heights. Light and shade play games along their moss-covered surfaces, while rainbows hang suspended between the peaks. If wind and weather permit, you will see hang gliders dusting the cliffs as they sail from the mountains down to the distant beach.

The road continues through **Waimanalo**, an old ranching area that today has been turned to fruit and flower cultivation. Outside town you will see **Olomana Peak**. Favored by rock climbers, it is a double-barreled peak that seems to belong in the Swiss Alps.

DINING   Spotted along Oahu's southeastern shore are a number of moderately priced restaurants (and a couple of expensive but worthy ones) that may prove handy if you're beachcombing or camping. Most are located on or near Route 72 (Kalanianaole Highway). For the sake of convenience, I'll list the restaurants as they will appear when you travel east and north.

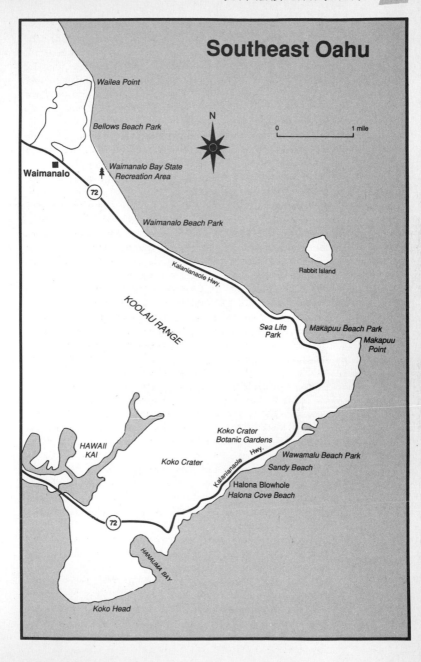

Southeast Oahu

Wailea Point

Bellows Beach Park

■
Waimanalo

Waimanalo Bay State
Recreation Area

(72)

N

0   1 mile

Waimanalo Beach Park

Kalanianaole Hwy.

Rabbit Island

KOOLAU RANGE

Sea Life
Park

Makapuu Beach Park

Makapuu
Point

*HAWAII
KAI*

Koko Crater
Botanic Gardens

Koko Crater

Wawamalu Beach Park

Sandy Beach

Kalanianaole Hwy.

Halona Blowhole
Halona Cove Beach

(72)

HANAUMA BAY

Koko Head

You're bound to feel Eurocentric at the **Swiss Inn**, where the menu includes wienerschnitztel, veal with a cream mushroom sauce and cheese fondue. There's also a beef fondue with 24-hour advance notice. On the dessert menu you'll find Swiss chocolate mousse, peach melba and fresh fruit tarts. The wood-paneled Old World look features pictures of villages that make you yearn for the Matterhorn. ~ Niu Valley Shopping Center, 5730 Kalanianaole Highway; 377-5447. DELUXE.

Tucked away in unassuming fashion in a business park is one of the area's top dining spots. You'll have to travel all the way to Hawaii Kai, several miles east of Waikiki, to find **Roy's Restaurant**. It is, to say the least, ultracontemporary, from the magazine clips framed on the walls to the cylindrical fish tank near the door. One of the most innovative of Hawaii's "Nouvelle Pacific" cuisine dining rooms, it specializes in fresh local ingredients. The main complaints you hear about this wildly popular restaurant are that it's too crowded and too noisy. ~ 6600 Kalanianaole Highway; 396-7697. DELUXE TO ULTRA-DELUXE.

HIDDEN ▶   **Thai Valley Cuisine** is tucked away in a tiny shopping center in Kalama Village, a suburban residential neighborhood built in the center of Koko Head Crater. The restaurant serves a variety of Thai appetizers, curries, noodles and such entrées as basil eggplant, fresh mushrooms in garlic sauté, stuffed chicken wings and deep-fried snapper. ~ 501 Kealahou Street, Kalama Village; 395-9746. BUDGET TO MODERATE.

The **Waimanalo Fish Market & Restaurant** at the Waimanalo Shopping Center looks like a market, with green-and-white checkered tablecloths on the tables, white plastic chairs and linoleum floors. It's also a plate-lunch place that specializes in Hawaiian food like Kalua pig, *lomi* salmon and *lau lau*. They make fresh poi daily. ~ 41-1537 Kalanianaole Highway, Waimanalo; 259-8008. BUDGET.

Dave's Ice Cream in the same complex scoops up gourmet ice cream in flavors like azuki bean, cotton candy and *poha*, made from gooseberries grown on the Big Island. It also serves guava and passion fruit sherbet, among a wide array of other selections. ~ 41-1537 Kalanianaole Highway. BUDGET.

Keneke's Bar-B-Q has breakfasts, plate lunches and sandwiches at greasy-spoon prices, as well as shaved ice and ice cream. No gourmet's delight, this tiny eatery is well placed for people enjoying Waimanalo's beaches. ~ 41-857 Kalanianaole Highway, Waimanalo; no phone. BUDGET.

HIDDEN ▶   A few doors down is one of Hawaii's great Mexican restaurants. **Bueno Nalo** may be short on looks, but it's definitely long on taste. ~ 41-865 Kalanianaole Highway, Waimanalo; 259-7186. BUDGET.

A convenient place to shop in Oahu's southeast corner is at the Koko Marina Shopping Center's **Foodland**. ~ 7192 Kalanianaole Highway, Hawaii Kai; 395-3131. **Mel's Market** is where all the locals come to shop. Its crowded aisles contain a cornucopia of Hawaii's culinary ingredients, from kimchee and cream cheese to ahi tuna and tempura mix. ~ 41-1029 Kalanianaole Highway, Waimanalo; 259-7550.

GROCERIES

HANAUMA BAY NATURE PRESERVE One of Oahu's prettiest and most popular beaches, this curving swath of white sand extends for almost a half-mile. The bottom of the bay is a maze of coral reef, and the entire area has been designated a marine preserve; fishing is strictly prohibited. As a result, the skindiving is unmatched and the fish are tame enough to eat from your hand. (Just beware of "Witches Brew," a turbulent area on the bay's right side, and the "Molokai Express," a wicked current sweeping across the mouth of the bay.) You can also hike along rock ledges fringing the bay and explore some mind-boggling tidepools. Crowded though it is, this is one strand that should not be bypassed. Get here early—the beach closes at 7 p.m. every day. Facilities include a picnic area, restrooms, showers, a snack bar, snorkeling equipment rentals and lifeguards. Call ahead to check whether or not access is limited. ~ Located about nine miles east of Waikiki. Take Kalanianaole Highway (Route 72) to Koko Head, then turn onto the side road near the top of the promontory. This leads to a parking lot; leave your vehicle and walk the several hundred yards down the path to the beach; 924-0266.

BEACHES & PARKS

HALONA COVE BEACH This is the closest you'll find to a hidden beach near Honolulu. It's a patch of white sand wedged between Halona Point and the Halona Blowhole lookout. Located

◄ *HIDDEN*

✔ CHECK THESE OUT

- Catch a glimpse of the world's only known wholphin (half whale, half dolphin) living in captivity in the tanks of **Sea Life Park**. *page 126*
- Join the savvy diners enjoying Hawaii regional cuisine in ultrachic surroundings at **Roy's Restaurant**, an award-winning restaurant. *page 128*
- Pick up a bag of rice crackers and a drink and check out the local scene in **Mel's Market**, where the Waimanaloans come to shop. *page 129*
- Don fins and mask for an exploration of **Hanauma Bay**, where you can spy moray eels, needlenose fish and schools of colorful reef fish at one of the state's best snorkeling spots. *page 129*

directly below Kalanianaole Highway (Route 72), this is not exactly a wilderness area. But you can still escape the crowds massed on the nearby beaches. Swimming and snorkeling are good when the sea is gentle but extremely dangerous if it's rough. Prime catches are *ulua*, *papio* and *mamao*. There are no facilities. ~ Stop at the Halona Blowhole parking lot on Kalanianaole Highway (Route 72), about ten miles east of Waikiki. Follow the path from the right side of the lot down to the beach.

People come from all over the world to body surf Sandy Beach and Makapuu Beach Park.

SANDY BEACH This long, wide beach is a favorite among Oahu's youth. The shorebreak makes it one of the finest, and most dangerous, bodysurfing beaches in the islands. Surfing is good and very popular but beware of rip currents. Lifeguards are on duty. It's a pleasant place to sunbathe, but if you go swimming, plan to negotiate a pounding shoreline. Anglers try for *ulua*, *papio* and *mamao*. There are picnic areas, restrooms and showers. Should you want to avoid the crowds, head over to **Wawamalu Beach Park** next door to the east. ~ Head out on Kalanianaole Highway (Route 72) about 12 miles east of Waikiki.

MAKAPUU BEACH PARK Makapuu is set in a very pretty spot with lava cliffs in the background and Rabbit Island just offshore. This short, wide rectangle of white sand is Hawaii's most famous bodysurfing beach. With no protecting reef and a precipitous shoreline, Makapuu is inundated by awesome swells that send wave riders crashing onto shore. Necks and backs are broken with frightening regularity here, so if the waves are large and you're inexperienced—play the spectator. If you take the plunge, prepare for a battering! Snorkeling is usually poor and surfing is not permitted here. Common catches are *ulua*, *papio* and *mamao*. The only facilities are restrooms and a lifeguard. There's a restaurant across the road in Sea Life Park. ~ Located on Kalanianaole Highway (Route 72) about 13 miles east of Waikiki.

▲ Currently not permitted, but it will probably reopen to the public so it's worth checking out.

WAIMANALO BEACH PARK AND WAIMANALO BAY STATE RECREATION AREA Located at the southeast end of Waimanalo's three-and-a-half-mile-long beach, this is a spacious 38-acre park. It's studded with ironwood trees and equipped with numerous recreation facilities including a playground, a basketball court and a baseball field. Waimanalo Beach Park and Waimanalo Bay State Recreation Area, a mile farther north, are both excellent spots for picnicking, swimming, surfing and sunbathing. The latter is farther removed from the highway in a grove of ironwood trees known to local residents as "Sherwood Forest." Waimanalo is a good place to fish for *papio*, bonefish, milkfish and goatfish. There

TheBus

There is perhaps no greater Hawaiian bargain than TheBus. Although you can rent a car to explore Oahu, you can also do it by the island's remarkable public transportation system, known quite simply as TheBus.

TheBus is a great way to sightsee at a leisurely pace—and peoplewatch at the same time. Hop aboard the #19 (or another downtown-bound bus) from Waikiki and you'll pass Ala Moana Center, the fishing boats of Kewalo Boat Basin and the historic Mission Houses before entering Chinatown. There tiny wizened *obachans* (grandmas) speaking a patois of Japanese-English climb patiently aboard, while mothers with a child in one arm and a shopping bag in the other negotiate the steep steps.

Or take the #52 Circle Island route and get the grand tour of the island. You'll pass through sleepy villages and alongside strands of sandy beaches while getting an upclose view of local life. Twice hourly buses give ample opportunity to stop and check out the sights along the way.

TheBus covers 90 percent of the 60-square-mile island. The fleet of 440 buses that are on the road travel a combined total of 60,000 miles every day, carrying 210,000 passengers daily—between 30,000 and 35,000 of them are visitors.

Buses operate 22 hours each day, shutting down between 2:30 and 4:30 a.m. Unless you have to be somewhere during rush hour, the best times to travel are between 9 a.m. and 3 p.m. or after 6 p.m. Some 60 percent of all buses operate with wheelchair lifts, making them accessible to physically disabled riders.

Because so many local residents rely on public transportation, service is reliable and buses run frequently, even outside of Honolulu. With each ticket, riders can request a transfer that must be used to transfer to a different route within one and a half hours. The transfer can't be used for another ride on the same bus route. There's also a four-day Oahu Discover Passport with unlimited rides that is sold at all ABC stores.

TheBus operates a 24-hour recorded information line (296-1818) that lists which buses to take to various attractions and destinations from Waikiki. There's also a customer bus information service (848-5555), with operators giving directions between the hours of 5:30 a.m. and 10 p.m. Those with Internet access can print out directions and time tables by contacting www.thebus.org.

are picnic areas, restrooms and showers at both. ~ Waimanalo Beach Park is located at 41-471 Kalanianaole Highway (Route 72) about 15 miles east of Waikiki. Waimanalo Bay State Recreation Area is on Oloiloi Street a mile farther north.

▲ A county permit required at both of the parks for tent and trailer camping.

HIDDEN ▶ **BELLOWS BEACH PARK** ▵ ⚓ ♨ ⛵ This is one of Oahu's prettiest parks. There's a broad white-sand beach bordered by ironwood trees, with a marvelous view of the Koolau mountains. It's a great place for swimming and snorkeling. It's also a good surf spot for beginners and fishing usually rewards with *papio*, bonefish, milkfish and goatfish. Sounds great, huh? The catch is that Bellows Park is situated on a military base and is open to visitors only from Friday noon until 8 a.m. Monday. Facilities include a picnic area, showers, a restroom and a lifeguard; restaurants and markets are about a mile away in Waimanalo. ~ Turn off Kalanianaole Highway (Route 72) toward Bellows Air Force Station. The park is located near Waimanalo, about 17 miles east of Waikiki.

▲ County permit required.

EIGHT

Windward Coast

Named for the trade winds that blow with soothing predictability from the northeast, this sand-rimmed shoreline lies on the far side of the *pali* from Honolulu. Between fluted emerald cliffs and the turquoise ocean are the bedroom communities of Kailua and Kaneohe, and the agricultural regions of the Waiahole and Waikane valleys.

Kailua, which was previously a quiet suburb, has become a windsurfing mecca, attracting beginning and intermediate sailors from around the world to its shores. A protective reef, a lack of breakers and on-shore trade winds create near perfect conditions for the sport, and the residents of Kailua haven't overlooked the opportunities. Scores of families operate bed-and-breakfasts in residential neighborhoods, and windsurfers have become a part of the community. It's the kind of low-key place where even the likes of Robin Williams, who reportedly vacations there, can find an escape.

Moving north, the highway hugs the coast, revealing a steady succession of beaches, and passes through sleepy rural communities, where life seems little changed by the procession of tourists in rental cars and buses that pass by daily. In Laie, the Mormons set about creating a religious community that draws students from throughout the South Pacific to a branch of Brigham Young University and tourists to the Polynesian Cultural Center, which the students operate as the most popular tourist attraction on Oahu.

Leaving Laie, one returns to the sleepy ways of rural Oahu, arriving in Kahuku, where the former sugar mill has been turned into a tiny shopping mall. Tourism has replaced sugar as an economic endeavor, just as it has in most other places on Oahu.

From the southeastern corner of the island, the Kalanianaole Highway flows into Kailua, where it intersects with Route 61, or Kailua Road. If you go right for a quar-

HIDDEN ► ter of a mile along this road you will encounter **Ulupo Heiau** (it's behind the YMCA). According to Hawaiian legend, this temple (which stands 30 feet high and measures 150 feet in length) was built by *Menehunes*, who passed the building stones across a six-mile-long bucket brigade in a one-night construction project. The *Menehunes*, in case you haven't been introduced, were tiny Hobbit-like creatures who inhabited Hawaii even before the Polynesians arrived. They were reputed to be superhumanly strong and would work all night to build dams, temples and other structures. Several mysterious manmade objects in the islands that archaeologists have trouble placing chronologically are claimed by mythmakers to be *Menehune* creations.

Heading back to the main highway, you will find that Route 72 immediately merges into Route 61, which then continues for two miles to Route 83, the Kahekili Highway. Above this thoroughfare, HIDDEN ► spreading across 400 acres at the foot of the *pali* is **Hoomaluhia Botanical Garden**, a relaxing nature conservancy. With sheer cliffs rising on one side and a panoramic ocean view opening in the distance, it is a special place indeed. There is a 32-acre lake as well as a visitors center and hiking trails. The fruits, flowers and trees include hundreds of species native to Hawaii. ~ Off Route 83 at the end of Luluku Road, Kaneohe; 233-7323.

The Kahekili Highway will also carry you to the graceful **Haiku Gardens**, located just outside Kailua. Formerly a private estate, the gardens rest in a lovely spot with a lofty rockface backdrop. Within this preserve are acres of exotic plant life, including an enchanting lily pond as well as numerous species of flowers. Hawaii specializes in beautiful gardens; the frequent rains and lush terrain make for luxuriant growing conditions. This happens to be one of the prettiest gardens of all. ~ 46-336 Haiku Road, Kaneohe; 247-6671.

Farther along you'll encounter the "Valley of the Temples," a verdant chasm folded between the mountains and the sea. Part of the valley has been consecrated as a cemetery honoring the Japanese. Highlighting the region is the **Byodo-In Temple**. Rimmed by 2000-foot cliffs, this Buddhist shrine is a replica of a 900-year-old temple in Uji, Japan. It was constructed in 1968 in memory of the first Japanese immigrants to settle in Hawaii. The simple architecture is enhanced by a bronze bell weighing seven tons that visitors are permitted to ring. A statue of Buddha dominates the site. Walk along the placid reflecting pool with its swans, ducks and multihued carp and you will be drawn a million miles away from the bustle of Honolulu. Admission. ~ 47-200 Kahekili Highway, Kaneohe; 239-8811.

An alternate route through Kailua and Kaneohe will carry you near the water, though the only really pretty views of Kaneohe Bay come near the end. Simply follow North Kalaheo Avenue through

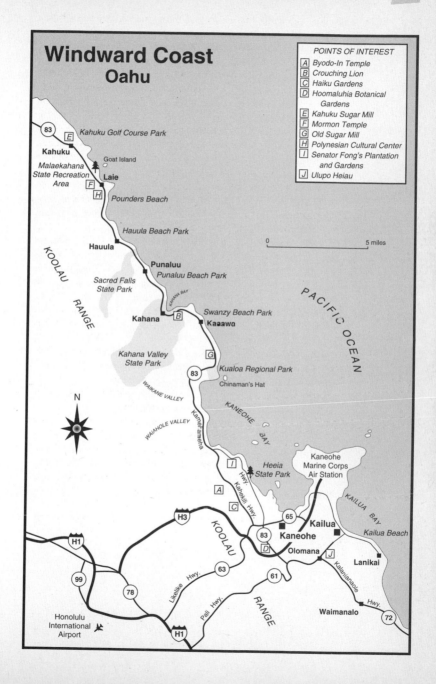

Windward Coast
Oahu

POINTS OF INTEREST

- A Byodo-In Temple
- B Crouching Lion
- C Haiku Gardens
- D Hoomaluhia Botanical
     Gardens
- E Kahuku Sugar Mill
- F Mormon Temple
- G Old Sugar Mill
- H Polynesian Cultural Center
- I Senator Fong's Plantation
     and Gardens
- J Ulupo Heiau

83

E Kahuku Golf Course Park

Kahuku

Goat Island

Malaekahana
State Recreation
Area

F Laie
H

Pounders Beach

Hauula Beach Park

Hauula

Punaluu

Punaluu Beach Park

Sacred Falls
State Park

KAHANA BAY

B **Kahana**

Swanzy Beach Park

Kaaawa

G

Kahana Valley
State Park

PACIFIC OCEAN

0   5 miles

83

Kualoa Regional Park

Chinaman's Hat

WAIKANE VALLEY

WAIAHOLE VALLEY

Kamehameha Hwy.

KANEOHE BAY

N

I

Heeia
State Park

Kaneohe
Marine Corps
Air Station

A

Kahekili Hwy.

C

KOOLAU

RANGE

H3

65

Kailua

KAILUA BAY

Kaneohe

83

Kailua Beach

D

Olomana

J

H1

KOOLAU

Lanikai

99

63

61

Kalanianaole

78

Likelike Hwy.

RANGE

Honolulu
International
Airport

Pali Hwy.

H1

Waimanalo

Hwy.

72

Kailua, then pick up Kaneohe Bay Drive, and turn right on Route 836, which curves for miles before linking with Route 83. At Heeia Kea Boat Harbor you can take an hour-long glass-bottom boat ride aboard the **Coral Queen.** ~ 235-2888.

Kaneohe Bay is renowned for its coral formations and schools of tropical fish that are as brilliantly colored as the coral. This expansive body of water possesses the only barrier reef in Hawaii. Along its shores are ancient Hawaiian fish ponds, rock-bound enclosures constructed by the early Polynesians to raise fresh seafood. Though they once lined the shores of Oahu, today only five remain; four rest along this Windward Coast. As a matter of fact, the largest of all is located at **Heeia State Park.** It's an impressive engineering feat that measures 500 feet in length and once contained an 88-acre fish farm. The stone walls in places are 12 feet thick. ~ Located along Route 836 a few hundred yards before it merges with Route 83.

High above Kaneohe, gazing down upon the bay, is **Senator Fong's Plantation and Gardens.** Here you can take a narrated tram tour of 725 acres of gardens and orchards. This luxurious preserve was donated by one of Hawaii's most famous U.S. senators, so be prepared to venture from Eisenhower Valley to Kennedy Valley (sugar cane) to the Johnson Plateau (fruit orchards) to Nixon Valley (gardens) to the Ford Plateau (pine trees)! Admission. ~ 47-285 Pulama Road, Kaneohe; 239-6775.

Route 83 soon becomes known as the Kamehameha Highway as it courses past taro patches and lazy fishing boats, then enters **Waiahole Valley** and **Waikane Valley,** some of the last places on the island where Hawaiian farmers grow crops in the traditional way.

Just down the road, the **Old Sugar Mill,** Oahu's first, lies in ruin along the side of the road. Built during the 1860s, it fell into disuse soon after completion and has since served only as a local curiosity.

Three miles later you will arrive at a rock profile that resembles a **Crouching Lion.** To the ancient Hawaiians, who had never experienced the king of the jungle, the stone face was, in fact, that of Kauhi, a demigod from the island of Tahiti.

RORSCHACH TEST, HAWAIIAN STYLE

That cone-shaped island offshore is **Chinaman's Hat.** It was named for its resemblance to a coolie cap, though the Hawaiians had another name for it long before the Chinese arrived in the islands. They called it Mokolii Island, or "little dragon," and claimed it represented the tail of a beast that resided under the water. Watch for frigate birds and delicate Hawaiian stilts flying overhead.

Next is coral-studded **Kahana Bay**. Then the road, still crowding the coastline, traverses the tiny towns of Punaluu and Hauula. The old **Hauula Door of Faith Church**, a small chapel of clapboard design, is surrounded by palms. Not far from here is another aging woodframe sanctuary, **Hauula Congregational Christian Church**, built of wood and coral back in 1862.

The nearby town of Laie is populated by Mormons. The Hawaii campus of **Brigham Young University** is located here, as well as the **Mormon Temple**. The Mormons settled here back in 1864; today there are about 25,000 in Hawaii. The courtyards and grounds of the temple are open to the public, but only Mormons are permitted to enter the temple sanctuary.

The Mormons also own Oahu's most popular tourist attraction, the **Polynesian Cultural Center**. Set right on Kamehameha Highway in Laie, it represents one of the foremost theme parks in the entire Pacific, a 42-acre attempt to re-create ancient Polynesia. As you wander about the grounds you'll encounter ersatz villages portraying life in the Marquesas, Tahiti, Fiji, Tonga, New Zealand and old Hawaii. Step over to the Tahitian hamlet and you will experience the rocking *tamure* dance. Or wander onto the islands of Samoa where the local inhabitants demonstrate how to climb coconut trees. In Tonga a native will be beating tapa cloth from mulberry bark, while the Fijians are pounding rhythms with poles of bamboo. These mock villages are linked by waterways and can be visited in canoes. The boats will carry you past craftsmen preparing poi by mashing taro roots and others husking coconuts.

The most popular shows are the "Pageant of the Long Canoes," in which the boats head up a lagoon amid a flurry of singing and dancing, and "Horizons." The latter is an evening show similar to Waikiki's Polynesian revues, though generally considered more elaborate. Most of the entertainers and other employees at this Hawaiian-style Disneyland are Mormon students attending the local university. Closed Sunday. Admission. ~ Kamehameha Highway, Laie; 293-3000.

Be sure to take in the town's natural wonder, **Laie Point**. This headland provides extraordinary ocean views sweeping for miles along the shoreline. Since the breezes and surf are wilder here than elsewhere on the Windward Coast, you'll often encounter waves lashing at the two offshore islets with amazing force. ~ Anemoku Street, off Kamehameha Highway.

Then the main road goes to Kahuku, past the **Kahuku Sugar Mill**, a turn-of-the-century plant. In an effort to refurbish the old mill several years ago, gears and crushers were painted tropical hues and the entire complex was turned into an entertaining museum-cum-shopping mall. You'll find a few restaurants and gift shops, and the machinery of the old mill.

LODGING Out in the suburban town of Kailua, where trim houses front a beautiful white-sand beach, you'll discover **Kailua Beachside Cottages**. Overlooking Kailua Beach Park and about 100 yards from the beach sits a cluster of woodframe cottages. Each is equipped with a full kitchen, cable television and a telephone. Some of the furniture is nicked, but these duplex units are clean and cozy. They sit in a yard shaded with *hala*, coconut and breadfruit trees and provide an excellent value. ~ 204 South Kalaheo Avenue, Kailua; 262-4128, 261-1653, fax 261-0893. MODERATE TO DELUXE.

Carol Naish of **Naish Hawaii**, the oldest windsurfing business in Hawaii, operates a bed-and-breakfast referral service for windsurfers and others who would prefer to stay in a quiet community rather than busy Waikiki. She represents 40 homes and attempts to carefully match guests with hosts so that all will have a good time. ~ 155 Hamakua Drive, Kailua; 261-3539, fax 263-9723. BUDGET TO DELUXE.

Located in a quiet canal-side neighborhood two blocks from Kailua Beach, **Sharon's Serenity** is a popular bed and breakfast with two rooms and a suite. Guests have use of the swimming pool and access to a comfortable spacious living room. Host Sharon Price serves breakfast and offers up plenty of advice to those who want it. This B&B can be booked directly; there is a three-day minimum stay. ~ 127 Kakahiaka Street, Kailua; 263-3634, 800-914-2271. MODERATE.

HIDDEN ► You can't get much closer to the water than **Schrader's Windward Marine Resort**. With about 50 units for rent, this unusual resting place consists of several woodframe buildings right on the edge of Kaneohe Bay. There are picnic tables, barbecue grills, a pool and

----

✔ **CHECK THESE OUT**

- Imagine you've been transported to the Orient while exploring the **Byodo-In Temple,** an exact replica of the famous Buddhist shrine near Uji, Japan. *page 134*
- Become a part of the neighborhood and get the local scoop when you stay in a **bed-and-breakfast** in Kailua, the bedroom community-turned-windsurfing capital. *page 138*
- Drop by **Ahi's Restaurant,** where you might think you're in the home of a new friend who wants to make sure you enjoy the shrimp. *page 140*
- Admire the exceptional collection of beautiful creations by Hawaiian artists at **Island Treasures,** a don't-miss shop located in Kailua. *page 141*
- Go birding, try your hand at catching a *papio* or snorkel in a well-protected crescent-shaped beach at tiny **Goat Island,** just off Oahu's shoreline. *page 146*

a spa on the two-acre property, as well as a tour boat that can take you snorkeling, kayaking or sightseeing on the bay. The guest rooms are cottage style with kitchenettes; many have lanais and bay views. Prices include continental breakfast. ~ 47-039 Lihikai Drive, Kaneohe; 239-5711, 800-735-5711, fax 239-6658. MODERATE.

The **Windward Bed & Breakfast** offers two rooms with private baths. The Victorian room features antiques and vintage paintings, while the Circus room has large circus posters, many of them originals, from around the world. This contemporary Hawaiian home has a shake roof and is furnished in antiques and Persian rugs. A full breakfast is served poolside every morning. ~ 46-251 Ikiiki Street, Kaneohe; phone/fax 235-1124, 800-235-1151. BUDGET TO MODERATE.

If you don't mind funky living, check out the **Countryside Cabins** in Punaluu. These old clapboard structures, complete with fading paint and linoleum floors, are set in beautiful garden surroundings across the street from the ocean. Depending on your taste, you'll find the one-room cottages either claustrophobic or quaint. But no one will find fault with the low prices on these units and the two-bedroom cottages, or with Margaret Naai, the charming Asian woman who runs this unique establishment. ~ 53-224 Kamehameha Highway, Punaluu; 237-8169. BUDGET

The **Roadway Inn Hukilau Resort** is a low-slung motel with two floors of rooms surrounding a swimming pool. This is a standard Coke-machine-in-the-courtyard facility located next to the Polynesian Cultural Center. Weekly rates available. ~ 55-109 Laniloa Street, Laie; 293-9282, 800-526-4562, fax 293-8115. MODERATE.

DINING

Kailua has a collection of eating establishments spread throughout the town. Among them is **Buzz's Original Steak House**, right across the street from the beach. The place is popular not only with windsurfers, but with Honolulu residents who drive out on the weekends to enjoy the surf and a meal at this upscale beach shack, which has been in business since 1932. Burgers, steaks and seafood are the specialties here, and all entrées include a trip to the salad bar. ~ 413 Kawailoa Road, Kailua; 261-4661. BUDGET TO MODERATE.

Assaggio Ristorante Italiano in the downtown Kailua Business Center is another restaurant that attracts the Honolulu crowds with its pasta, chicken, eggplant parmigiana and veal scallopine. ~ 354 Uluniu Street, Kailua; 261-2772. MODERATE TO DELUXE.

You can try **Times Coffee Shop** for fried rice, hamburger steaks or sandwiches. ~ 43 Oneawa Street, Kailua; 262-7122. BUDGET.

Saeng's Thai Cuisine is a freshly decorated ethnic restaurant with a hardwood bar and potted plants all around. Located in a strip mall, it nevertheless conveys a sense of elegance. The menu focuses on vegetarian, seafood and curry dishes. ~ 315 Hahani Street, Kailua; 263-9727. BUDGET.

Old World Bistro is a Continental restaurant that serves up fresh fish, steak and veal in an informal atmosphere. Closed Monday. ~ 20 Kainehe Street, Kailua; 261-1987. MODERATE TO DELUXE.

HIDDEN ►   Known for years as a prime breakfast and lunch place, **Cinnamon's Restaurant** eventually added dinner on Thursday and Friday nights. It draws a local crowd, which sits beneath the dining room gazebo or out on the patio. The menu is best described as Hawaiian-American as it's a traditional cuisine with a local spin—barbecued pork ribs, poached mahimahi, hamburger steak. My advice? Dinner is good but breakfast is best. ~ Kailua Square Shopping Center, 315 Uluniu Street, Kailua; 261-8724. MODERATE.

What sets **The Chart House at Haiku Gardens** apart is its idyllic setting. A terraced dining area overlooks sharp cliffs and peaceful flower beds, making this a choice stop for dinner (brunch is served on Sunday). Even though the atmosphere varies from the average Chart House, the menu remains the same: steak, seafood and prime rib. ~ 46-336 Haiku Road, Kaneohe; 247-6671. DELUXE.

In Kaneohe you might like **Koa Omelette House**. It's a tastefully appointed restaurant with a breakfast bill of fare that includes pancakes and crêpes suzette and a lunch menu with salads, sandwiches, teriyaki chicken and seafood. ~ 46-126 Kahuhipa Street, Kaneohe; 235-5772. BUDGET.

Or, if you want to take a snack to the beach, check out **Fuji Delicatessen and Restaurant** with its inexpensive sandwiches and Japanese plates. ~ 45-270 William Henry Road, Kaneohe; 235-3690. BUDGET.

HIDDEN ►   **The Ka'a'a Country Kitchen** is a roadside plate-lunch place. Located between the post office and the 7-11, it has four tables inside and an equal number in front. It offers the usual selection of plate lunches—teriyaki beef and fried fish—as well as burgers and other sandwiches. The food's not exceptional, but it's a place to meet the locals, who seem to like to eat here when they come to town to pick up their mail. ~ 52-4808 Kamehameha Highway, Kaaawa; 237-8484. BUDGET.

HIDDEN ►   The staff is so friendly at **Ahi's Restaurant** that dining in this family-run restaurant is kind of like eating in the home of a friend. The restaurant, in fact, was previously in the owner's house in Kahuku until it burned down and he relocated to Punaluu. The green woodframe building with stucco interior and screened-in porch catches the island breezes and provides a comfortable environment in which to dine. Although Ahi's serves a variety of meats, fish and chicken, the specialty is shrimp cooked in four different ways—scampi, cocktail, tempura and deep fried. There aren't too many places quite like this one. ~ 53-146 Kamehameha Highway, Punaluu; 293-5650. BUDGET TO MODERATE.

The **Crouching Lion Inn**, set in a vintage 1927 wood-shingle house, serves sandwiches and hamburgers, mahimahi and teriyaki steak for lunch. At dinner there's a surf-and-turf menu. Enjoying a beautiful ocean view, this attractive complex is popular with tour buses, so try to arrive at an off-hour. ~ 51-666 Kamehameha Highway, Kaaawa; 237-8511. MODERATE TO DELUXE.

Appropriately enough, you'll find the **Kahuku Sugar Mill Restaurant & Bar** in the old Kahuku Sugar Mill. The menu includes steak, shrimp and fresh fish. The dining room, with wood-paneled walls and ceiling fans, is located inside the sugar mill: Gaze past the glass lamps and it's all cogs and gears, conveyors and chains. ~ Kahuku; 293-5288. MODERATE.

Just down the way is **Giovanni's Shrimp Truck**, serving gourmet plate lunches that the locals claim are the best on Oahu. There's a choice of scampi, grilled shrimp or hot and spicy shrimp, and, like all plate lunches, they come with two scoops of rice. Seven picnic tables sit under an awning for this rain-or-shine outdoor eating spot. ~ Beside The Mill, Kamehameha Highway, Kahuku. MODERATE.

◀ *HIDDEN*

GROCERIES

In Kailua and Kaneohe, you'll encounter large supermarkets. In the Kailua Shopping Center there's **Times Supermarket**. ~ Kailua Road, Kailua; 262-2366. **Foodland** is in the Windward City Shopping Center. ~ At Kamehameha Highway and Kaneohe Bay Drive, Kaneohe; 247-3357.

For health food, you might try the **Vim and Vigor** store. ~ 345 Hahani Street, Kailua; 261-4036.

These are good places to stock up, since the next large supermarket is **Lindy's Food**. ~ Hauula Kai Center on Kamehameha Highway, Hauula; 293-9722.

Between these major shopping complexes there are smaller facilities such as the **7-11**. ~ 51-484 Kamehameha Highway, Kaaawa; 237-8810.

You can get fresh fish at **Masa and Joyce Fish Market** in the Temple Valley Shopping Center. ~ Kahekili Highway (Route 83), just north of Kaneohe; 239-6966.

There's a large **Foodland** grocery store in the Laie Village Shopping Center. ~ Kamehameha Highway, Laie; 293-4443.

All along the Kamehameha Highway in Waiahole and Waikane valleys, there are small stands selling fresh fruit grown right in this lush area.

SHOPPING

Kailua Shopping Center offers a wide range of services at 40 stores. ~ Kailua Road, Kailua; 262-0292. **Kaneohe Shopping Center** also serves the region with 26 stores. ~ 45-934 Kamehameha Highway, Kaneohe; 537-4519. These malls represent the prime shopping opportunities on this side of the island and provide a full assortment of shops.

Island Treasures offers an exceptional collection of pottery, wooden boxes, bark cloth notebooks, paintings, handcrafted wooden furniture, shell candles and etched crystal with island designs, all created by artists living in Hawaii. ~ 629 Kailua Road, Kailua; 261-8131.

Another similar store in Kaneohe chock full of treasures by local artists is **Jeff Chang Pottery & Fine Crafts Shop**. Among the items are ceramics, glass clocks, jewelry and figurines. ~ 45-781-B Kamehameha Highway, Kaneohe; 235-2808.

The **Livingston Galleries** at the Crouching Lion Inn sells paintings and prints by local and mainland artists, as well as art photography in color and black and white. ~ 51-666 Kamehameha Highway, Kaaawa; 237-7165.

HIDDEN ▶   Up in Punaluu, the **Punaluu Art Gallery** features batik work, calabash bowls, pottery, oil paintings, photography, blown glass, hand-carved candles and unusual pieces like landscapes made from banana leaves, all by local artists. ~ 53-352 Kamehameha Highway, Punaluu; 237-8221.

HIDDEN ▶   Hidden behind Punaluu Art Gallery in a small cottage, **Punaluu Trading Company** specializes in sarongs and shorts, with what the owner claims are the best prices on the island (except at the swap meet).

If you'd like to try a bit of fishing, be sure to stop at **Ching's Punaluu Store**, which has an entire section of fishing gear, poles, nets and lines. ~ 53-360 Kamehameha Highway, Punaluu.

Between Laie and Kahuku, **Planet Surf** sells beach attire, shorts and sandals, and sells and rents surfboards and boogie boards. ~ 55-730 Kamehameha Highway; 293-2392.

Calling itself **The Only Show In Town** is a slight (very slight) exaggeration, but claiming to be "Kahuku's largest antique and vintage collectible shop" is definitely warranted. Some store specialties include Japanese glass fishing floats, ivory and Coca-Cola memorabilia. Fittingly, this wonderful antique store is located in the old Tanaka Plantation Store, an early 20th-century woodframe building. ~ 56-931 Kamehameha Highway, Kahuku; 293-1295.

NIGHTLIFE   Nights on the Windward Coast are quiet and peaceful, and most people like it that way. For those who prefer a bit of action, however, there are a few choices.

In Kailua, you can catch live entertainment every Thursday, Friday and Saturday at **Jaron's Restaurant**. On Thursday, it's contemporary Hawaiian music and on the weekends dance tunes from reggae to rock. Occasional cover on Friday and Saturday. ~ 201 Hamakua Drive #A, Kailua; 261-4600.

The **Kahuku Sugar Mill Restaurant & Bar** has karaoke, a pool table, darts and sports via satellite television. ~ Kamehameha Highway, Kahuku; 293-5288.

BEACHES & PARKS   **KAILUA BEACH** 🛶 🏊 🏄 Stretching for two miles with white sand all the way and tiny islands offshore, this is one of the prettiest beaches around. It's in the suburban town of Kailua, so you'll trade seclusion for excellent beach facilities. The center of activity is Kailua Beach Park at the end of Kailua Road near the south end of the beach. This 30-acre facility has a grassy expanse shaded by ironwood and coconut trees and perfect for picnicking. There are restrooms, lifeguards and a pavilion with a snack bar. Kalama Beach County Park, a small park with restrooms in the middle of Kailua Beach, is less crowded. Swimming, surfing and bodysurfing are good all along the strand and windsurfing is excellent; but exercise caution. ~ You can also access Kailua Beach farther north via side streets off Kalaheo Avenue; Kalama Beach County Park is located at 250 North Kalaheo Avenue.

LANIKAI BEACH Everyone's dream house is on the beach at Lanikai. This sandy stretch, varying from 20 to 100 feet in width, extends for over a mile. The "Twin Islands," tiny bird sanctuaries, rest offshore. The entire beach in this residential community is lined with those houses everybody wants. The water is the color of cobalt and the protecting reef offshore makes the entire beach safe for swimming. The nearest facilities are at Kailua Beach. ~ The strand parallels Mokulua Drive in Lanikai, which in turn is reached by driving south along the beachfront roads in Kailua.

> Follow Kahana Valley State Park's five-mile trail up into the lush valley and you'll pass a succession of old Hawaiian farms.

KUALOA REGIONAL PARK You could search the entire Pacific for a setting as lovely as this one. Just 500 yards offshore lies the islet of Mokolii, better known as Chinaman's Hat. Behind the beach the *pali* creates a startling background of fluted cliffs and tropical forest. The beach is a long and narrow strip of sand paralleled by a wide swath of grass parkland. Little wonder this is one of the Windward Coast's most popular picnic areas. It's also a favorite for swimming, snorkeling, windsurfing and fishing (common catches are *papio*, bonefish, milkfish and goatfish). Facilities include lifeguards, picnic areas, restrooms and showers. ~ Located along Kamehameha Highway (Route 83) about ten miles north of Kaneohe.

▲ Tent camping permitted. County permit required.

SWANZY BEACH PARK, PUNALUU BEACH PARK AND HAUULA BEACH PARK These three county facilities lie along Kamehameha Highway (Route 83) within seven miles of each other. Swimming is generally good at each. Along this coast the most abundant fish is *papio*, followed by bonefish, milkfish and goatfish. Camping is allowed at all except Punaluu, but none compare aesthetically with other beaches to the north and south. Swanzy is located on the highway but lacks a sandy beach. However, it has the best diving. Its surf break, "Crouching Lion," is for experts only; Punaluu, though possessing a pretty palm-fringed beach, is cramped; and Hauula, a spacious park with a beach and a winter surf break for beginners, is visited periodically by tour buses. So put these beach parks near the bottom of your list, and bring them up only if the other beaches are too crowded. All three beaches have picnic areas and restrooms; all are within a few miles of markets and restaurants. ~ These parks are all located along Kamehameha Highway (Route 83). Swanzy lies about 12 miles north of Kaneohe, Punaluu is about four miles north of Swanzy, and Hauula is about three miles beyond that.

▲ Tent and trailer camping allowed at Hauula Beach Park as well as at Swanzy Beach Park on weekends. County permit required.

KAHANA VALLEY STATE PARK 🏃 🏄 🚙 This 5228-acre paradise, set on a white-sand beach, offers something for every adventurer. You can pick fruit in a lush forest, picnic in a coconut grove and sightsee the ancient Huilua Fishpond. You can also fish for *papio*, bonefish, milkfish and goatfish. Swimming is generally good. Surfing is a possibility but is mediocre at best. There are picnic areas and restrooms; markets and restaurants are nearby. ~ Located along Kamehameha Highway (Route 83) about 14 miles north of Kaneohe.

▲ There's camping across the street at Kahana Beach Park. State permit required.

KOKOLOLIO BEACH PARK 🏄 🎣 🚙 Here's one of the prettiest beaches on the Windward Coast. With trees and a lawn that extends toward the white-sand beach, it's a highly recommended spot for day-tripping. It's also a good beach for swimming and snorkeling and in winter there are breaks up to six feet, with right and left slide. Common catches include *papio*, bonefish, goatfish and milkfish. There are picnic areas and restrooms. ~ Located at 55-051 Kamehameha Highway (Route 83) in Laie about 20 miles north of Kaneohe.

POUNDERS BEACH 🏄 🚙 Named for the crushing shorebreak that makes it a popular bodysurfing beach, this quarter-mile-long strand features a corridor of white sand and a sandy bottom. Swimming is good near old landing at the western end of the beach. Anglers try for *ono*, *moi* and *papio*. There are no facilities here but restaurants and markets are nearby. ~ Located along Kamehameha Highway north of Kakela Beach.

HUKILAU BEACH 🏄 🎣 🏃 🚙 This privately owned facility fronts a beautiful white-sand beach that winds for more than a mile. Part of the beach is lined with homes, but much of it is undeveloped. Several small islands lie anchored offshore, and the park contains a lovely stand of ironwood trees. All in all this enchanting beach is one of the finest on this side of the island. Swimming is good; bodysurfing is also recommended. Snorkeling is usually fair and there are small surfable waves with left and right slides. The principal catch is *papio*; milkfish, bonefish and goatfish are also caught. There are no facilities here, but you'll find both

Windsurfing

There's no better place to learn windsurfing than on Oahu. The water is warm and the conditions are near perfect. Although not a particularly easy sport to learn, in a week or two you could be holding your own as you glide over the waves.

Windsurfing, also known as boardsailing, is a technique sport rather than a muscle sport, no doubt one of the reasons women can learn to do it faster than men. At the beginning you will use a 12-foot board, known as a learner board, or in sailboard slang, an aircaft carrier. These have a dagger board for stabilization and a small soft sail that flutters in the wind as you move slowly across the water. Most people spend just a few days learning on one of these boards, before progressing to a shorter or "fun board."

The shorter the board, the more wind you need. For an eight-and-a-half-foot board, 15 to 20 knots of wind are required. Because these boards don't usually have a dagger board, sailors use the wind to steer by tipping their board in the direction they want to go.

In order to sail, you have to be balanced. And in order to be balanced, you have to position yourself properly on the board. The faster you go, the more the board is out of the water. Your feet should be in the center of the "wetted" surface, the part of the board that's in the water. Advanced sailors wear a harness around their waists. The harness has a hook that fits into loops hanging from the boom. It helps sailors hold the sail without effort.

If you would like to learn how to windsurf, there's no place better than Kailua, a bedroom community on Oahu, to do so. It is the state's best spot for those who are at beginning and intermediate levels in the sport. A protective reef and no breakers mean the waters aren't too rough, and the local community has established scores of low-key B&Bs to cater to the windsurfing crowd.

markets and restaurants are nearby. ~ Located on Kamehameha Highway (Route 83) in Laie about 22 miles north of Kaneohe.

HIDDEN ►

MALAEKAHANA STATE RECREATION AREA AND GOAT ISLAND This is a rare combination. The Malaekahana facility is one of the island's prettiest parks. It's a tropical wonderland filled with palm, *hala* and ironwood trees, and graced with a curving, white-sand beach. And then there's Goat Island, just offshore. Simply put, if you visit Oahu and don't explore Goat Island, you'll be missing an extraordinary experience. I hope you'll make an extra effort to get here. It's a small, low-lying island covered with scrub growth and scattered ironwood trees. On the windward side is a coral beach; to leeward lies a crescent-shaped white-sand beach that seems drawn from a South Seas dream and is the best place on the island to swim because it is shallow and well-protected. There are also good places for snorkeling and in winter you can paddle out to a break with a left slide. Feel like fishing? You may well reel in *papio*, the most abundant fish along here; goatfish, milkfish and bonefish are also caught. Goat Island (which no longer contains goats) is now a state bird refuge, so you might see wedge-tailed shearwaters nesting. Whatever activity you choose, make sure you don't disturb the birds. Goat Island will return the favor—there'll be nothing here to disturb you either. Facilities include showers, bathrooms, barbecue pits and electricity in the cabins. ~ Located on Kamehameha Highway (Route 83) in Laie about 23 miles north of Kaneohe.

▲ Tent camping allowed. State permit required. There are also very rustic cabins available a mile down the road at Malaekahana Beach Park. These beachfront units rent from $35 per night (one-bedroom tent cabin) to $250 per night (six-room cabin). Tent sites are $5 for a single person, or $4.50 per person for a group per night. Bring your own bedding and cooking gear and be prepared for funky accommodations. For information, call 293-1736.

KAHUKU GOLF COURSE PARK Other than Goat Island, this is about the closest you'll come to a hidden beach on the Windward Coast. Granted, there's a golf course paralleling the strand, but sand dunes hide you from the duffers. The beach is long, wide and sandy white. Swimming is fair, but exercise caution. In winter, surfers work the "Seventh Hole" breaks, which reach up to eight feet and have a right and left slide. *Papio*, bonefish, goatfish and milkfish are common catches. There are restrooms at the golf course; a restaurant and market are nearby. ~ In Kahuku, about 25 miles north of Kaneohe, turn off Kamehameha Highway (Route 83) toward the ocean. Park at the golf course, then walk the gated road to the beach.

▲ Unofficial camping perhaps.

NINE

North Shore

Wide, wide beaches heaped with white, white sand roll for miles along the North Shore, which curves from Kahuku Point in the east to Kaena Point in the west. Although they can compete with the most beautiful beaches anywhere, it's not the sand or their size that is the main attraction here. Rather it is the waves, and these waves have made Oahu's North Shore legendary. Surfers come from around the world to try their skill at one of the world's best spots for the sport.

If you have ever owned a surfboard, or even a Beach Boys album, you will know Waimea Bay and Sunset Beach. The names are synonymous with surfing. They number among the most challenging and dangerous surfing locales anywhere. During the winter, 15- to 25-foot waves are as common as blond hair and beach buggies. The infamous "Banzai Pipeline," where surfers risk limb and longevity as thunderous waves pass over a shallow reef, is here as well.

The surf is not only superb. The setting is stunning. Oahu's two mountain ranges form the backdrop, while 4025-foot Mt. Kaala, the island's highest peak, towers above all. Small ranches and farms checkerboard the tableland between the mountains and the sea. The old-time farmers, the surfers and the counterculture types who live in the area all come to Haleiwa for shopping, dining and socializing. Haleiwa, a restored plantation town with old clapboard buildings and wooden sidewalks, preserves the spirit of a rural way of life that is rapidly disappearing.

The plantations that established Oahu's economic base may one day be no more. In fact, the last sugar mill on the island, located in the North Shore town of Waialua, shut down in late 1996, marking the end of a major chapter in Oahu's history. Although the Waialua Sugar Company now no longer processes cane, this low-key village west of Haleiwa, still has the feel of a sugar town. The mill, which stands at its center, and the Sugar Bar, a bar and pizza place in the old Bank of Hawaii building, serve as reminders of a past that just yesterday was the present.

Stretching for two miles and averaging 200 feet in width, **Sunset Beach** (Kamehameha Highway) is one of Hawaii's largest strands. When the surf is up you can watch world-class athletes shoot the curl. When it's not, Sunset becomes a great place to swim. The best place to go is **Ehukai Beach Park,** just off Kamehameha Highway about seven miles northeast of Haleiwa. Just 100 yards to the west sits the **Banzai Pipeline** (Ke Nui Road), where a shallow coral shelf creates tubular waves so powerful and perfect they resemble pipes. First surfed in 1957, it lays claim to cracked skulls, lacerated legs and some of the sport's greatest feats.

HIDDEN ►

On a plateau between Sunset Beach and Waimea Bay is **Puu o Makuha Heiau,** Oahu's oldest temple. A split-level structure built of stone, it once was used for human sacrifices. Today you will encounter nothing more menacing than a spectacular view and perhaps a gentle breeze from the ocean. To get there from Kamehameha Highway, turn left near the Sunset Beach Fire Station onto Pupukea Road, then follow the Hawaii Visitors and Convention Bureau signs.

At **Waimea Valley** you can wander through a tropical preserve stretching across 1800 acres. Once a Hawaiian village, it is an amazingly luxurious area crisscrossed with hiking trails and filled with archaeological ruins. A tram carries visitors to the famous **Waimea Falls,** where you can swim or picnic. The arboretum in the park features tropical and subtropical trees from around the world. There are also beautiful botanical gardens, including a particularly fascinating one featuring local Hawaiian species. Then there are the birds, caged and wild, that populate the complex; since this nature park serves as a bird sanctuary, it attracts a magnificent assortment. Admission. ~ Kamehameha Highway, five miles northeast of Haleiwa; 638-8511.

Across the street looms **Waimea Bay,** another fabled place that sports the largest surfable waves in the world. When surf's up in winter, the monster waves that roll in are so big they make the ground tremble when they break. Salt spray reaches as far as the highway. Thirty-foot waves are not uncommon. Fifty-foot giants have been recorded; though unsurfable, these are not tidal waves, just swells rising along the incredible North Shore. In summer Waimea is a pretty blue bay with a white-sand beach. The water is placid and the area perfect for picnicking and sunbathing. So when you visit Waimea, remember: swim in summer, sunbathe in winter.

Next, the Kamehameha Highway crosses a double rainbow–shaped bridge en route to **Haleiwa,** an old plantation town with a new facelift. Fortunately, the designers who performed the surgery on this village had an eye for antiquity. They planned it so the modern shopping centers and other facilities blend comfortably into the rural landscape. The community that has grown up around the new town reflects a rare combination of past and future. The old Japanese, Filipinos and Hawaiians have been joined by blond-

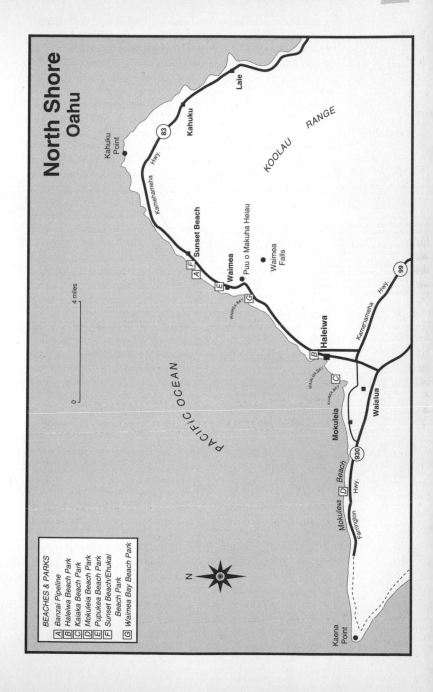

North Shore
Oahu

KOOLAU RANGE

Kahuku Point

Laie

Kahuku

83

Kamehameha Hwy.

Sunset Beach

[F]
[A]

Puu o Makuha Heiau

Waimea

Waimea Falls

[E]
[G]

WAIMEA BAY

99

Kamehameha Hwy.

Haleiwa

[B]

WAIALUA BAY

[C]

KIAKA BAY

Waialua

Mokuleia

PACIFIC OCEAN

930

Mokuleia Beach

[D]

Farrington Hwy.

4 miles

0

N

Kaena Point

BEACHES & PARKS
[A] *Banzai Pipeline*
[B] *Haleiwa Beach Park*
[C] *Kaiaka Beach Park*
[D] *Mokuleia Beach Park*
[E] *Pupukea Beach Park*
[F] *Sunset Beach/Ehukai
    Beach Park*
[G] *Waimea Bay Beach Park*

mopped surfers and laidback counterculturalists. As a result, this clapboard town with wooden sidewalks has established itself as the "in" spot on the North Shore. Its stylish nonchalance has also proved popular among canny travelers.

From here, head west and pick up Farrington Highway (Route 930). This country road parallels miles of unpopulated beachfront, and arrives at Dillingham Airfield, where you can take **The Original Glider Ride** along the Waianae Mountains. ~ 677-3404.

Beyond this landing strip, the road continues for several miles between ocean and mountains before turning into a very rugged dirt track. Along this unpaved portion of roadway you can hike out about ten miles to **Kaena Point** on Oahu's northwest corner (see the "Hiking" section in Chapter Two).

LODGING   For a resort experience in a rustic setting, consider the **Turtle Bay Hilton**. This rural retreat sprawls across 808 acres on a dramatic peninsula. With a broad beach at the doorstep and mountains out back, it's an overwhelming spot. Add to that riding paths, two golf courses, tennis courts and a pair of swimming pools. Every guest room features a sea view. ~ 57-091 Kamehameha Highway, Kahuku; 293-8811, 800-445-8667, fax 293-9147. ULTRA-DELUXE.

Located on the grounds of the Turtle Bay Hilton but independently operated, **The Estates at Turtle Bay** offers studio, as well as one-, two- and three-bedroom loft resort condominiums, each with stove, refrigerator, dishwasher, microwave, washer/dryer and cable television. There are five swimming pools and four tennis courts on the property, and guests can arrange golf and horseback riding through the Hilton. ~ 56-565 Kamehameha Highway, Kahuku; 293-0600, fax 293-0471. MODERATE TO DELUXE.

Turtle Bay Condos has one-, two- and three-bedroom units with kitchen facilities and private lanais that overlook a nine-hole golf course. Studios run $85 to $105; one-bedrooms units with a loft sleeping up to four guests are $130 to $145. ~ 56-565 Kamehameha Highway, Kahuku; 293-2800, fax 293-2169.

Surfers, scuba divers and budget-minded travelers will find two ideal addresses along Oahu's vaunted North Shore. Managed by the same folks, and within walking distance of each other are **Vacation Inn** and **Plantation Village**. The first consists of a central building that provides hostel-style rooms and features a TV lounge and kitchen. There's also a back house with private rooms that share a kitchen and bath. Like the hostel it's budget-priced. Across the street, and directly on the beach, there's a house with private apartments that include their own kitchen and bathroom and are moderately priced. Plantation Village consists of nine restored plantation houses with shared kitchens and baths. Set on a landscaped acre, the accommodations are moderate-to-deluxe in price, but budget-priced hostel facilities are also available. Both the Vacation

Inn and Plantation Village have laundry facilities and barbecue areas for guests. They also sponsor daily activities and provide excellent opportunities for meeting other travelers. ~ 59-788 Kamehameha Highway, Haleiwa; 638-7838, fax 638-7515. BUDGET TO DELUXE.

Offering houses right on the beach, **Ke Iki Hale** is located between the Banzai Pipeline and Waimea Bay. You'll find moderate- and deluxe-priced duplexes and an ultra-deluxe-priced cottage on an acre-and-a-half of palm-shaded property. They are basic wood-frame buildings with plain furnishings. The complex includes barbecue facilities and a volleyball court. ~ 59-579 Ke Iki Road, Haleiwa; phone/fax 638-8229, 800-377-4030. MODERATE TO ULTRA-DELUXE.

DINING

The Turtle Bay Hilton features two good restaurants. At the **Palm Terrace**, overlooking the hotel's lovely grounds, you'll encounter moderate-priced dining in an attractive environment. The restaurant, serving three meals, offers everything from burgers to *saimin* and teriyaki to linguine. Or, for a splurge meal, try **The Cove**. This gourmet establishment serves lobster, lamb chops, filet mignon, a seafood gumbo dish and a host of other delights. Reservations are required at The Cove. ~ 57-091 Kamehameha Highway, Kahuku; 293-8811. MODERATE TO DELUXE.

Otherwise, the best place to chow down is in Haleiwa, the main town on the North Shore. When you're around Sunset Beach, **D'Amico's** is quite convenient. It's a roadside restaurant serving pizzas, pasta, sandwiches and other surfer fare. ~ 59-026 Kamehameha Highway, Haleiwa; 638-9611. BUDGET.

◄ HIDDEN

Also in the area, the **Sunset Diner** packs local crowds into its awning-covered picnic tables, with plate lunches of barbecue chicken, *kalbi*, teri-beef, kalua pig and roast pork plates, as well as chili, burgers and a selection of fruit smoothies. ~ 59-176 Kamehameha Highway, Haleiwa; 638-7660. BUDGET.

For a fashionable spot overlooking the ocean, try **Jameson's By The Sea**. This split-level establishment features a patio downstairs and a formal dining room upstairs. For lunch there are sandwiches, chowders and fresh fish dishes; at dinner they specialize in seafood.

◆◆◆

KUA AINA IS DA KINE

Surfers pour into **Kua Aina Sandwich**, where they order hamburgers, fries and mahimahi sandwiches at the counter, then kick back at one of the roadside tables. Great for light meals, the place is a scene and a half. ~ 66-214 Kamehameha Highway, Haleiwa; 637-6067. BUDGET.

~ 62-540 Kamehameha Highway, Haleiwa; 637-4336. MODERATE TO DELUXE.

Haleiwa Beach Grill, a small café in the center of Haleiwa, is as colorful as coral. Matter of fact, the tropic-hued walls are adorned with a wide range of vintage albums from the '60s and '70s. Read the menu and you'll discover fried chicken, grilled sandwiches, burritos and "islander plates." There are *kalbi* ribs, teriyaki chicken and a mixed grill dish that includes mahimahi. ~ 66-079 Kamehameha Highway, Haleiwa; 637-3394. BUDGET.

At **Café Haleiwa** surfers swear by the huevos rancheros, pancakes and "the Barrel"—a blend of eggs, potatoes, green salsa and cheese wrapped in a tortilla. Located in a century-old building featuring local artwork, surfboards and surfing memorabilia, this local favorite also serves an excellent quesadilla. ~ 66-460 Kamehameha Highway, Haleiwa; 637-5516. BUDGET.

Paradise Found has a juice bar and vegetarian restaurant serving sandwiches, soups and salads. ~ Inside Celestial Natural Foods, 66-443 Kamehameha Highway, Haleiwa; 637-4540. BUDGET.

Meg's Country Drive-In is a small eatery serving local-style plate lunches and daily specials such as fried noodles with teriyaki beef. You can take your meal to go or dine on the adjoining lanai. Lunch only. ~ 743 Waiakamilo Road, Haleiwa; 845-3943. BUDGET.

Pizza Bob's has, you guessed it, pizza. It also has burgers and pastas and a wonderful outdoor covered patio for dining. ~ Haleiwa Shopping Center, Haleiwa; 637-5095. BUDGET.

For dessert or an afternoon snack, head for **Flavor Mania**, which serves homemade ice cream, served plain or with mix-ins. Take a group and try the Big Wave Special banana boat, with four scoops of ice cream and four different toppings. ~ 66-145 Kamehameha Highway, Haleiwa; 237-9362. BUDGET.

✔ **CHECK THESE OUT**

- Cross the double-rainbow bridge en route to **Haleiwa**, a clapboard plantation town that is a haven for surfers and counterculturalists. *page 148*
- Check into a restored plantation house across the street from the beach at **Plantation Village**, a place frequented by budget-conscious travelers and set on an acre of land. *page 150*
- Enjoy the sunset from **Jameson's By The Sea**'s second-story dining room while the chef prepares a fresh-catch dinner for you. *page 151*
- Watch as artists fashion whales, sharks and turtles in exquisite designs at **Oceans in Glass**. *page 154*
- Surf the largest waves in the world during the winter months, or ride the gentle surf in summer at **Waimea Bay**, made famous by the sounds of the Beach Boys. *page 155*

Years ago Haleiwa was home to Da Cuppa Kope, a great café and gathering place. Today it has been supplanted by an even better coffeehouse, the **Coffee Gallery**. In addition to the best cappuccino on the island, this homespun restaurant, decorated with coffee sacks, serves pastries, waffles, bagels, pasta, pizza and a variety of sandwiches. ~ North Shore Marketplace, 66-250 Kamehameha Highway, Haleiwa; 637-5571. BUDGET.

◀ *HIDDEN*

Mexican restaurants in Hawaii are different from their counterparts elsewhere in one respect—fish tacos. True to the islands, **Rosie's Cantina** offers them. They also have a menu filled with the culinary features found in every south-of-the-border eatery. In the case of Rosie's, you also get a steam-pipe-and-raw-wood interior complete with colored lights. ~ Haleiwa Shopping Plaza, 66-165 Kamehameha Highway, Haleiwa; 637-3538. MODERATE.

Appropriately enough, **Portofino** captures an air of the Mediterranean with its cream-colored pastel walls, blond-wood furniture, overhead fans and breezy ambience. This Italian restaurant prepares rosemary chicken, penne capricciosa (with eggplant and shrimp) and a catch-of-the-day dish. So sink onto one of the upholstered banquettes or sidle over to the granite bar. ~ 66-250 Kamehameha Highway, Haleiwa; 637-2782. MODERATE.

GROCERIES

Haleiwa Supermarket, one of the few large markets on the entire North Shore, is the best place to shop. ~ 66-197 Kamehameha Highway, Haleiwa; 637-5004. Out by Sunset Beach you'll find a **Foodland Super Market**. ~ 59-720 Kamehameha Highway, Haleiwa; 638-8081. There's also **Sunset Beach Store**, which has a small stock but is also conveniently located near Sunset Beach. ~ 59-026 Kamehameha Highway, Haleiwa; 638-8207.

Celestial Natural Foods has an ample supply of health foods and fresh produce. ~ 66-443 Kamehameha Highway, Haleiwa; 637-6729.

SHOPPING

Trendy shoppers head for the burgeoning town of Haleiwa. During the past several years boutiques and galleries have mushroomed throughout this once somnolent town. Now there is a modern shopping center and an array of shops. Since Haleiwa is a center for surfers, it's a good place to buy sportswear and aquatic equipment.

Iwa Gallery features a unique collection of artwork by a number of local island artists. ~ 66-119 Kamehameha Highway, Haleiwa; 637-4865.

Sunset Hawaii Clothing carries Hawaiian wear for the whole family. Bathing suits, accessories, handmade books, dolls, toys and stuffed animals round out their inventory. ~ 66-226 Kamehameha Highway, Haleiwa; 637-4782.

Oceania offers women's wear and jewelry. ~ 66-218 Kamehameha Highway, Haleiwa; 637-1516.

The North Shore Marketplace is an eclectic collection of exceptional shops selling everything from surfing gear to handblown glass. **Polynesian and Global Handicrafts** (637-1288) sells handicrafts from Fiji, Tonga, Samoa and Hawaii. **Silver Moon Emporium** (637-7710) offers women's wear and jewelry. At **Pacific Marine Arts** (637-3203) you'll find creations that celebrate the sea, such as bronze sculptures of turtles and paintings of beaches and underwater scenes. **Jungle Gems** (637-6609) is a gallery of gorgeous jewelry made from semiprecious gems, crystals, kukui nuts and inlaid woods. Just in case you forgot your bathing suit, you can pick one from the scores of bikinis and swim suits on display at **Beachwear Unlimited** (637-6859) or order a custom-made creation. Two glass artists fashion whales, sharks, reef fish and turtles in elegant designs while you watch at **Oceans in Glass** (637-3366). **Hawaii Surf & Sail** (637-5373) has a huge selection of surfboards and gear. ~ North Shore Marketplace, 66-250 Kamehameha Highway, Haleiwa.

Silver Moon Emporium offers women's wear and jewelry. ~ 66-250 Kamehameha Highway, in the North Shore Marketplace, Haleiwa; 637-7710.

Strong Current stocks everything imaginable that's related to surfing. They even have a small "surfing museum," consisting of memorabilia from the sport's early days. Then there are the books, videos, posters, boards and other appurtenances, all relating to a single theme. ~ North Shore Marketplace, 66-250 Kamehameha Highway, Haleiwa; 637-3406.

NIGHTLIFE   Entertainment is a rare commodity on the North Shore, but you will find contemporary Hawaiian music at the **Bay View** at the Turtle Bay Hilton; on Friday and Saturday they feature disco music. ~ 57-091 Kamehameha Highway, Kahuku; 293-8811.

In Haleiwa, **Pizza Bob's** has occasional live entertainment on the weekends. ~ Haleiwa Shopping Center; 637-5095.

To mix with the locals, head to the **Sugarbar**, where you'll find live rock, rhythm-and-blues or Hawaiian music Wednesday, Friday and Sunday. ~ 67-069 Kealohani Street, Waialua; 637-6989.

BEACHES & PARKS   **SUNSET BEACH**   While Sunset Beach is actually only a single surfing spot, the name has become synonymous with a two-mile-long corridor that includes Banzai Beach and the adjacent Pipeline. As far as surfing goes, this is the place! I think the best way to do Sunset is by starting from **Ehukai Beach Park**. From here you can go left to the "Banzai Pipeline," where crushing waves build along a shallow coral reef to create tube-like formations. To the right lies "Sunset," with equally spectacular surfing waves. Swimming is fair in summer and lifeguards are on duty; however, in winter it is extremely dangerous. From September to

April, high waves and strong currents prevail. Be careful! Snorkeling here is poor. Game fish caught around Sunset include *papio*, *menpachi* and *ulua*. Ehukai Beach Park has picnic areas, restrooms and showers. ~ Ehukai Beach Park is off Kamehameha Highway (Route 83) about seven miles northeast of Haleiwa.

WAIMEA BAY BEACH PARK ⚓ 🏄 🏊 ⛵ If Sunset is *one* of the most famous surfing spots in the world, Waimea is *the* most famous. The biggest surfable waves in the world roll into this pretty blue bay. There's a wide white-sand beach and a pleasant park with a tree-studded lawn. It's a marvelous place for picnicking and sunbathing. During the winter crowds often line the beach watching top-notch surfers challenge the curl; in summer the sea is flat and safe for swimming; you can also bodysurf in the shorebreak and snorkel when the bay is calm. *Papio*, *menpachi* and *ulua* are common catches. Facilities include a picnic area, restrooms, showers and a lifeguard. ~ On Kamehameha Highway (Route 83) about five miles northeast of Haleiwa.

HALEIWA BEACH PARK ⚓ 🏄 ⛵ This is an excellent refuge from the North Shore's pounding surf. Set in Waialua Bay, the beach is safe for swimming almost all year; windsurfing is good. You can snorkel, although it's only fair. Surfing in not possible here but "Haleiwa" breaks are located across Waialua Bay at Alii Beach Park. Facilities include a picnic area, restrooms, showers, a snack bar, a ball field, a basketball court, volleyball courts and a playground. The primary catches at Haleiwa are *papio*, *menpachi* and *ulua*. ~ On Kamehameha Highway (Route 83) in Haleiwa.

KAIAKA BEACH PARK ⚓ 🏄 ⛵ The setting at this park is beautiful. There is a secluded area with a tree-shaded lawn and a short strip of sandy beach. A rocky shoreline borders most of this peninsular park, so I'd recommend it more for picnics than water sports. You *can* swim and snorkel but there's a rocky bottom. Fishing is good for *papio*, *menpachi* and *ulua*. The only facilities are a picnic area and restrooms. ~ Located on Haleiwa Road just outside Haleiwa.

⚓ Permitted; a county permit is required.

SNORKELER'S PARADISE

Some of the island's best snorkeling is at **Pupukea Beach Park**, a marine reserve on Kamehameha Highway six miles northeast of Haleiwa. This 80-acre park, fringed by rocky shoreline, divides into several sections. Foremost is "Shark's Cove," located on the north side of the fire station, which contains spectacular tidepools and dive sites.

HIDDEN ▶   **MOKULEIA BEACH PARK AND MOKULEIA BEACH** 🏊 🚣

🎣 ⚓ ♩ The 12-acre park contains a sandy beach and large un-shaded lawn. An exposed coral reef detracts from the swimming, but on either side of the park lie beaches with sandy ocean bot-toms. If you do swim, exercise caution, especially in winter months; there's no lifeguard. There's good snorkeling and in winter the surf breaks up to ten feet near Dillingham Airfield. Anglers try for *papio*, *menpachi* and *ulua*. Whatever your activity of choice, you'll have to contend with the noise of small planes from nearby Dillingham Airfield. The park is also an ex-cellent starting point for exploring the unpopulated sec-tions of Mokuleia Beach. Facilities include picnic areas, rest-rooms and showers. ~ On Farrington Highway (Route 930) about seven miles west of Haleiwa. To the west of the park, this beach stretches for miles along a secluded coast. You can hike down the beach or reach its hidden realms by driving farther west along Far-rington Highway (Route 930), then turning off onto any of the nu-merous dirt side roads.

At Mokuleia, watch for skydivers and hang gliders, who often use the beach for their landings.

▲ Tent and trailer camping are allowed with a county permit. Unofficial camping along the undeveloped beachfront is common.

TEN

Central Oahu and Leeward Coast

Visitors often ignore Central Oahu and the Leeward Coast, which together make up the western half of Oahu. They'll buzz down Route 99, which intersects the island, on their way to or from the North Shore, and they'll avoid the Leeward Coast entirely, having been warned of potential problems with the locals. But they shouldn't. The very fact that people don't often visit these two places makes them worth going to for a glimpse of Oahu that hasn't been transformed by tourism.

The 1000-foot-high Leilehua Plateau, a rich agricultural region planted with sugar cane and pineapple, extends from the North Shore to the southern reaches of Oahu. Spreading across the middle of the island between the Waianae and Koolau ranges, this tableland nurtures the last of the large plantations that once formed the backbone of Oahu's agricultural infrastructure. It also has become a vital nerve center for the military. Wheeler Air Force Base, Schofield Barracks and several other installations occupy large plots of land here.

Out along the west coast of Oahu, less than 30 miles from the sands of Waikiki, Hawaiian culture is making a last stand. Here on the coastal shelf that separates the Waianae Range from the ocean, the old ways still prevail. This is a region of stark beauty. Some parts resemble the American Southwest, with rocky crags and cactus-studded hills. Farther north, the spartan scenery gives way to wide vistas of massive mountains sloping gracefully to the sea.

Hawaiian and Samoan farmers tend small fields and raise chickens. Side roads off the main highway pass dusty houses and sunblasted churches before turning into dirt tracks that keep climbing past truck farms and old homesteads. For entertainment, there are birthday luaus, cockfights and slack-key guitar playing.

The Leeward coast has become the keeper of the old ways, and residents jealously guard the customs and traditions that they see slipping away in the rest of the state. Although there have been reports of outsiders being hassled by local residents, the reality, in fact, is usually the reverse. Here, far from the madding crowds of tourists and tourist businesses, the true spirit of aloha is alive and well. But who knows for how long?

"Second City," a major new development already being built near the town of Ewa, will eventually add thousands of houses to Central Oahu. And in the southwest corner of the island, the ultramodern Ihilani Resort & Spa is only the beginning of a major tourist complex. So you should consider this side of the island one of those places that needs to be seen and seen soon, before the forces of change sweep through.

CENTRAL OAHU   From Haleiwa south to Wahiawa you can take Route 803, Kaukoahuna Road, a pretty thoroughfare with excellent views of the Waianaes, or follow Route 99, the Kamehameha Highway, which passes through verdant pineapple fields. The **Dole Pineapple Plantation**, often crowded with tourists, sells (who would have guessed) pineapple products. ~ 64-1550 Kamehameha Highway, Wahiawa; 621-8408. And the **Pineapple Variety Garden** displays many different types of the fruit in a garden museum. ~ Kamehameha Highway and Kamananui Road, Wahiawa.

HIDDEN ▶

The highway also passes near **Kukaniloho**, a cluster of sacred stones marking the place where Hawaiian royalty gave birth to the accompaniment of chants, drums and offerings. Studded with eucalyptus trees, this spot has held an important place in Hawaiian mythology and religion for centuries. ~ Follow the dirt road across from Whitmore Avenue just north of Wahiawa.

For a scenic and historic detour from Route 99, pull up to the sentry station at Schofield Barracks and ask directions to **Kolekole Pass**. On that "day of infamy," December 7, 1941, Japanese bombers buzzed through this notch in the Waianae Range.

You'll be directed through Schofield up into the Waianaes. When you reach Kolekole Pass, there's another sentry gate. Ask the guard to let you continue a short distance farther to the observation point. From here the Waianaes fall away precipitously to a plain that rolls gently to the sea. There's an astonishing view of Oahu's west coast. If you are denied permission to pass the sentry point, then take the footpath that begins just before the gate, leading up the hill. From near the cross at the top, you will have a partial view of both the Waianaes' western face and the central plateau region.

Wahiawa Botanical Gardens, spreading across 27 acres, offers a handsome retreat studded with tropical vegetation. There are plants from Africa and Australia, Asian camphor trees and gum trees from New Guinea. ~ 1396 California Avenue, Wahiawa; 621-7321.

From Wahiawa, Route H-2 provides the fastest means back to Honolulu; the most interesting course is along Route 750, Kunia Road, which skirts the Waianaes, passing sugar cane fields and stands of pine.

Along the way you can take in the **Hawaiian Plantation Village**, a partially re-created and partially restored village that spreads

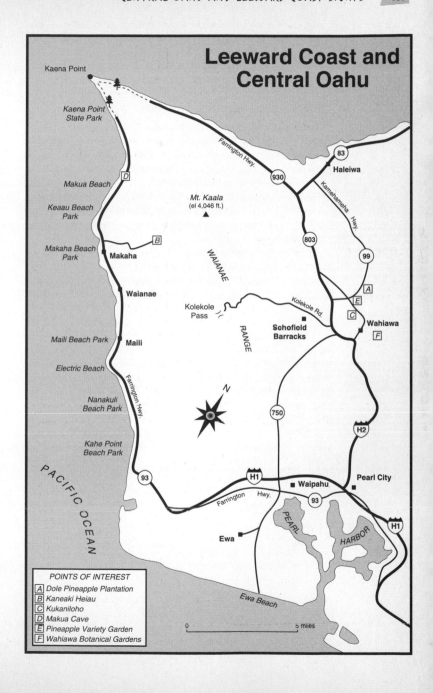

Leeward Coast and Central Oahu

Kaena Point

Kaena Point
State Park

Makua Beach

Keaau Beach
Park

Makaha Beach
Park

Makaha

Waianae

Maili Beach Park

Electric Beach

Nanakuli
Beach Park

Kahe Point
Beach Park

Farrington Hwy.

930

Mt. Kaala
(el 4,046 ft.)

WAIANAE

RANGE

Kolekole
Pass

83

Haleiwa

Kamehameha Hwy.

803

99

Kolekole Rd.

Schofield
Barracks

A

E

C   Wahiawa

F

Maili

N

750

H2

PACIFIC OCEAN

93

H1   Waipahu   Pearl City

93

PEARL

HARBOR

H1

Ewa

Ewa Beach

POINTS OF INTEREST

A Dole Pineapple Plantation
B Kaneaki Heiau
C Kukaniloho
D Makua Cave
E Pineapple Variety Garden
F Wahiawa Botanical Gardens

0   5 miles

across three acres of Waipahu Cultural Park in Waipahu. Comprised of over two dozen buildings, it includes a Japanese Shinto shrine, company store and a Chinese Society building. Hawaii's many ethnic groups are represented in the houses, which span several architectural periods of the 19th and 20th centuries. Together they provide visitors with a window into traditional life on a plantation. Closed Sunday. ~ 94-695 Waipahu Street, Waipahu; 676-6727.

LEEWARD COAST   From Honolulu you can visit the region by traveling west on Route H-1 or Route 90. If you want to tour a prime sugar-growing area, take Route 90 past Pearl Harbor, then turn left on Fort Weaver Road (Route 760). This country lane leads to the plantation town of Ewa. With its busy sugar mill and trim houses, Ewa is an enchanting throwback to the days when sugar was king. This town is a slow, simple place, perfect for wandering and exploring.

Near Oahu's southwest corner, Routes H-1 and 90 converge to become the Farrington Highway (Route 93). If you turn up Maili-ilii Street in **Waianae**, you'll pass placid Hawaiian homesteads and farmlands. This side road also provides sweeping views of the Waianae Range. Kaena Point Satellite Tracking Station sits atop the Waianae Range.

Makaha Beach, one of Hawaii's most famous surfing spots, is the site of an international surfing championship every year. The Makaha Valley, extending from the ocean up into the Waianaes, is home to the **Kaneaki Heiau**, a 17th-century temple dedicated to the god Lono and used as a site for human sacrifices. You can wander past prayer towers, grass huts and the altar used for the gruesome ritual. Closed Monday. ~ 695-8174.

The highway continues along the coastline past several beaches and parks. Across from Kaena Point State Park you'll come upon

✔ CHECK THESE OUT

- Learn about the daily life of plantation workers of the past while visiting **Hawaiian Plantation Village**, a partially restored village where Polynesian traditions are still carried on. *page 158*
- Hide away in the sumptuous **Ihilani Resort & Spa** and visit the spa, play a round of golf or luxuriate on one of the crescent beaches on a beautiful lagoon. *page 161*
- Check out the chicken *katsu* at **L & L Drive-Inn** and see if this chain deserves its reputation for the best plate lunch on Oahu. *page 162*
- Grab your snorkel and fins and skindive at **Makaha Beach Park**, a special place to find seashells when the surf's not up. *page 164*

Makua Cave, a lava cavern large enough for exploring. Beyond that, where the road turns to dirt, lies Yokohama Bay, with its curving sand beach and inviting turquoise waters.

The road past Yokohama is partially passable by auto, but it's very rough. If you want to explore Kaena Point from this side of the island, you'll have to hike. It's about two miles to the north-west corner of Oahu, past tidepools teeming with marine life.

LODGING

While the premise of "Hidden Oahu" is that you'll save money by uncovering secluded places, sometimes the remote comes with a hefty price tag. Take the Ihilani Resort & Spa. Backed by the Waianaes and facing a curved expanse of ocean, this 387-room hideaway is part of the 640-acre Koolina Resort. There's a golf course, six tennis courts, four restaurants and a sophisticated spa facility. More important, you'll find a string of four lagoons, each with a crescent beach and a cluster of islets that protects the mouth of the lagoon. All this material and natural splendor lies way out in the southwestern corner of Oahu. The entire complex is quite beautiful, from the trim green grounds to the atrium lobby to the spacious and elegant rooms. ~ 92-1001 Olani Street, Koolina Resort; 679-0079, 800-626-4446, fax 679-0080. ULTRA-DELUXE.

Makaha Shores, a six-story resort condo complex, overlooks pretty Makaha Beach County Park, one of Hawaii's top surfing beaches. There are studios and one- and two-bedroom units, each individually decorated by their owners. The minimum stay is one week, and the units are handled by different agents. Hawaii Hatfields (696-8415) handles most of them. ~ 84-265 Farrington Highway, Makaha. MODERATE.

Makaha Surfside offers one-bedroom units in a sprawling facility that fronts a rocky beach and has two swimming pools, a sauna and a jogging path. Units are $625 per month. ~ 85-175 Farrington Highway, Makaha; 696-6325, fax 696-7871.

Makaha Valley Towers is a highrise set along the slopes of Makaha Valley. Units range from studios to two-bedrooms, with nightly, weekly and monthly stays available. Studios for one week cost $550. ~ End of Kili Drive, Makaha; 696-4499, fax 696-1805.

Hawaii Hatfields Realty Corporation manages privately owned condominiums. One-week minimum; $400 to $1200 per week. ~ 85-833 Farrington Highway, Suite 201, Waianae, HI 96792; 696-4499, fax 696-1805.

DINING

By way of resort restaurants, Ihilani Resort & Spa has several deluxe- and ultra-deluxe-priced dining rooms. Foremost is Azul, where the lamb chops come with couscous, the lobster is served in *pistou* and the ideas are Mediterranean. Ushiotei is the ultimate in Japanese cuisine. And Naupaka, a poolside terrace serving cross-cultural dishes, is the Ihilani's answer to informality and easy elegance. ~ 92-1001 Olani Street, Koolina Resort; 679-0079. DELUXE TO ULTRA-DELUXE.

This sparsely populated strip of shoreline has several other dining spots. All are located on Farrington Highway, the main road, and most are in the town of Waianae. **Cathay's Inn Chop Suey** is a good choice for Chinese food. ~ 86-088 Farrington Highway, Waianae; 696-9477. BUDGET TO MODERATE.

Close by is **Hannara Restaurant** offering Korean and Hawaiian cuisines. ~ 85-888 Farrington Highway, Waianae; 696-6137. BUDGET TO MODERATE.

Nearby **E. J.'s** offers homestyle cooking in a casual, country-style atmosphere. Breakfast favorites include burritos, banana pancakes and home fries. Burgers, salads and sandwiches are prepared for lunch. Dinner entrées may include filet mignon, vegetarian lasagna or baked mahimahi. ~ 84-275 Farrington Highway, Waianae; 696-9676. BUDGET TO MODERATE.

Waianae has a number of drive-ins, but no doubt the most popular is **L & L Drive-Inn,** which serves breakfast, lunch and dinner. The breakfast combo includes eggs, Portuguese sausage, Spam and rice. Among the hearty plate lunches offered the rest of the day are breaded pork chop with hamburger steak and shrimp curry with chicken *katsu.* ~ 85-080 Waianae Valley Road; 696-3294. BUDGET.

Out at the Sheraton Makaha Resort Golf Course there is the **19th Hole,** an open-air café overlooking the golf course, serves scrambled eggs in the morning and *saimin,* hot dogs, sandwiches and plate lunches at lunchtime. ~ 84-626 Makaha Valley Road, Makaha; 695-7525. BUDGET.

GROCERIES   **Sack 'n Save Foods** is one of the prime markets in this area. ~ 87-2070 Farrington Highway, Waianae; 668-1277.

Another popular place to shop is **The Waianae Store,** a full-service supermarket that includes a bakery and delicatessen. ~ 85-863 Farrington Highway, Waianae; 696-3131.

NIGHTLIFE   **Naupaka Terrace** features nightly live entertainment. The Ililani is also home to the **Hokulea,** a nightspot that often has live music. ~ Ililani Resort & Spa, 92-1001 Olani Street, Koolina Resort; 679-0079.

BEACHES & PARKS   **HAWAIIAN ELECTRIC BEACH PARK** This once privately owned park, across the highway from a monstrous power plant, is now run by the county. There's a rolling lawn with palm and *kiawe* trees, plus a white-sand beach and coral reef. You can swim, snorkel, surf year-round and fish for *papio, ulua, moano* and *menpachi.* The drawbacks are the lack of facilities (there are restrooms and a picnic area) and the park's proximity to the electric

The
Endangered
Wildlife
of Oahu

Away from the crowds of Waikiki and the hubbub of downtown Honolulu and high in the mountains of Windward Oahu, a preserve operated by The Nature Conservancy is helping to save some of the island's and the world's endangered flora and fauna. The organization is trying to ensure that the land on which these threatened species exist will remain undeveloped and untouched so that the natural history of Oahu can be perpetuate, not only for the present generation but for those to come.

The 3692-acre forest preserve stretches along the southern Waianae Mountains and down their eastern slopes. Incorporated within its boundaries are what is left of a diverse native ecosystem once common on Oahu.

The preserve harbors plant and animals species that are, or have the potential to be, endangered. Several birds, including the *pueo* (Hawaiian owl), the flycatching *elepaio*, the crimson-feathered *apapane* and the yellow-green *amakihi*, live in the Honouliuli forests. Two endangered tree snails endemic to Oahu and found nowhere else also call the preserve their home.

Animals aren't the only living things that Honouliuli Preserve helps to spare. Four plants found here grow nowhere else on the planet. Two of these are mint species and two are flowering lobelia species.

Because the preserve is in a remote part of the Waianae Mountains, The Nature Conservancy recommends visiting it only as part of a regularly scheduled—usually twice-monthly—guided hike or work project. For more information and to join in the organization's efforts to preserve Honouliuli, contact them at 1116 Smith Street, Suite 201, Honolulu, HI 96817; 537-4508, fax 545-2019.

company. ~ Located on Farrington Highway (Route 93) about seven miles south of Waianae.

▲ Not allowed here; but tent and trailer camping are okay at nearby Kahe Point Beach Park, with a county permit.

NANAKULI BEACH PARK 🏊 🎣 🚿 This park is so large that a housing tract divides it into two parts. The main section features a white-sand beach, *kiawe*-studded camping area and a recreation complex. It's simply a park with everything, unfortunately including weekend crowds. Needless to say, the swimming and snorkeling are good; lifeguards are on duty. There are winter breaks with right and left slides. Fishing often rewards with *papio*, *ulua*, *moano* and *menpachi*. Facilities include picnic areas, restrooms, showers, a ball field, a basketball court and a playground. ~ Located on Farrington Highway (Route 93) about five miles south of Waianae; 668-1137.

▲ Tent and trailer camping are allowed, but a county permit is required.

MAILI BEACH PARK 🏊 🎣 🚶 🚿 A long winding stretch of white sand is the high point of this otherwise unimpressive facility. The swimming is good; snorkeling is only fair. There are winter surf breaks with a right slide. The principal game fish caught here are *papio*, *ulua*, *menpachi* and *moano*. The park contains shade trees and a spotty lawn. There are lifeguards, restrooms and showers. ~ Located on Farrington Highway (Route 93) in Maili a few miles south of Waianae.

▲ Not permitted here, but tent camping, with a county permit, is allowed in the summer at nearby **Lualualei Beach Park**.

MAKAHA BEACH PARK 🏊 🚶 🚿 Some of the finest surfing in the world takes place right offshore here. This is the site of international competitions, drawing championship surfers from all across the Pacific. For more relaxed sports, there's a white-sand beach to sunbathe on and some good places to skindive. Swimming and snorkeling are both good when the sea is calm; otherwise, exercise extreme caution. Anglers try for *papio*, *ulua*, *moano* and *menpachi*. The precipitous Waianae Mountains loom behind the park. There are lifeguards, picnic tables, restrooms and showers. ~ Located on Farrington Highway (Route 93) in Makaha, two miles north of Waianae.

KEAUU BEACH PARK 🏊 🎣 🚶 🚿 Except for the absence of a sandy beach, this is the prettiest park on the west coast. It's a long, narrow grassy plot spotted with trees and backdropped by the Waianaes. Sunsets are spectacular here, and on a clear day you can see all the way to Kauai. There's a sandy beach just west of the park. Unfortunately, a coral reef rises right to the water's edge, making entry into the water difficult. But once you're in there's great snorkeling, swimming and bodysurfing. In summer there are good surf breaks with a left slide. People fish for *papio*, *ulua*, *moano* and *menpachi*. There are picnic areas, restrooms and showers. ~ Located on Farrington Highway (Route 93) about five miles north of Waianae.

▲ Tent and trailer allowed. County permit required.

KAENA POINT STATE PARK (YOKOHAMA BAY) ◄ *HIDDEN*
This curving stretch of white sand is the last beach along Oahu's northwest coast. With the Waianae Range in the background and coral reefs offshore, it's a particularly lovely spot. Though officially a state park, the area is largely undeveloped. You can walk from Yokohama Bay past miles of tidepools to Oahu's northwest corner at Kaena Point, the legendary home of Nanue the Shark Man. Keep an eye out for dolphins. Yokohama Bay is a prime region for beach lovers and explorers both. When the sea is calm the swimming is good and the snorkeling is excellent but exercise extreme caution if the surf is up. There are summer breaks up to 15 feet over a shallow reef (left slide). Fish caught in this area include *papio*, *ulua*, *moano* and *menpachi*. Restrooms and showers are the only facilities. ~ Located at the end of the paved section of Farrington Highway (Route 93), about nine miles north of the town of Waianae.

Index

Adventure travel, 35
Aerial tours, 22–23
Air travel, 17–19
Ala Moana Regional Park, 110–11
Aliiolani Hale, 96
Aloha Patrol, 89
Aloha Tower, 98
American Hawaii Cruises, 98
Animals, 29–32
Arizona (battleship) Memorial, 116
Atlantis Submarine, 72

Banzai Pipeline, 148
Bed and breakfasts, 11–12; referral
    services, 11–12, 82–83, 138. *See also*
    Lodging *in area and town entries; see
    also Lodging Index*
Bellows Beach Park, 132
Biking, 44–45
Birds, 31–32
Bishop Museum, 114
Bowfin (submarine), 116
Brigham Young University (Hawaii cam-
    pus), 137
Byodo-In Temple, 134

Calendar of events, 6–9
Camping, 32–33. *See also* Camping *in area
    and town entries*
Car rentals, 19–20
Central Oahu and Leeward Coast, 5,
    157–65; addresses and phone numbers,
    24; beaches and parks, 162, 164–65;
    camping, 164, 165; dining, 161–62;
    groceries, 162; lodging, 161; map, 159;
    nightlife, 162; sights, 157–61
Children, traveling with, 13–14
Chinaman's Hat, 136
Chinatown (Honolulu), 99–100
Condos, 12, 83–84, 150, 161
Contemporary Museum, 114
Coral Queen (boat), 136
Coral reefs, 21
Coronation Pavilion, 96
Crabbing, 36
Crouching Lion, 136
Cruises, 98
Cuisine, 65–66, 104
Cultural Plaza, 100
Culture, 63–70

Damien Museum, 74–75
Diamond Head, 76–77
Diamond Head Beach Park, 118, 123
Diamond Head Lighthouse, 118
Dining, 12–13. *See also* Dining *in area and
    town entries; see also Dining Index*
Disabled travelers, 15
Diving, 37–39
Dole Cannery Square, 100–101
Dole Pineapple Plantation, 158
Downtown Honolulu, 4, 94–111; beaches
    and parks, 110–11; camping, 111; din-
    ing, 101–107; groceries, 107; lodging,
    101; map, 97; nightlife, 109–10; shop-
    ping, 107–109; sights, 95–101

East-West Center, 118
Ehukai Beach Park, 148, 154–55

Falls of Clyde (ship), 96
Fauna, 29–32
Fish and fishing, 29–31, 34, 36
Flora, 26–29
Foreign travelers, 16–17
Fort De Russy Beach, 72, 74, 93
Fort Street Mall, 98
Foster Botanical Garden, 100
Fruits, 27–28

Gay and lesbian travelers, 14–15; lodging,
    80–81; nightlife, 92–93; shopping, 88
Geology, 26
Goat Island, 146
Golf, 42–44
Greater Honolulu, 4, 112–23; addresses
    and phone numbers, 23–24; beaches and
    parks, 122–23; camping, 123; dining,
    120–22; groceries, 122; lodging, 118–20;
    map, 115; neighborhoods, 117; nightlife,
    122; shopping, 122; sights, 112–18

Haiku Gardens, 134
Haleiwa: dining, 151–53; groceries, 153;
    lodging, 150–51; nightlife, 154; shop-
    ping, 153–54; sights, 148, 150
Haleiwa Beach Park, 155
Halona Blowhole, 125
Halona Cove Beach, 129–30
Hanauma Bay and Beach, 125
Hanauma Bay Nature Preserve, 129

Hang gliding, 42
Hauula: groceries, 141; sights, 137
Hauula Beach Park, 143–44
Hauula Congregational Christian Church, 137
Hauula Door of Faith Church, 137
Hawaii Kai: dining, 128; groceries, 129
Hawaii Maritime Center, 96, 98
Hawaii Theatre, 98
Hawaiian Electric Beach Park, 162, 164
Hawaiian language, 66–68
Hawaiian Plantation Village, 158, 160
Heeia State Park, 136
Hiking, 45–48
History, 49–63
Hitchhiking, 22
Honolulu. See Downtown Honolulu; Greater Honolulu; Waikiki
Honolulu Academy of Arts, 100
Honolulu Hale, 95
Honolulu International Airport, 17
Honolulu Memorial Park, 113
Honolulu Zoo, 76
Honouliuli Preserve, 162
Hoomaluhia Botanical Garden, 134
Hostels, 78, 81–82, 119
Hotels, 11–12. See also Lodging in area and town entries; see also Lodging Index
Hukilau Beach, 144, 146
Hula, 70

Ilikai Hotel, 72
International travelers, 16–17
Iolani Barracks, 96
Iolani Palace, 95–96
Izumo Taishakyo Mission, 100

Jeep rentals, 20
Jelly fish, 21

Kaaawa: dining, 140–41; groceries, 141; shopping, 142
Kaalawai Beach, 123
Kaena Point, 150, 161
Kaena Point State Park, 165
Kahala Beach, 123
Kahala District (Honolulu), 117, 118
Kahana Bay, 137
Kahana Valley State Park, 144
Kahanamoku Beach, 72, 93
Kahuku: dining, 141, 151; lodging, 150; nightlife, 142, 154; shopping, 142; sights, 137
Kahuku Golf Course Park, 146
Kahuku Sugar Mill, 137
Kaiaka Beach Park, 155
Kailua: dining, 139–40; groceries, 141; lodging, 138; nightlife, 142; shopping, 141; sights, 133–34

Kailua Beach, 142–43
Kalama Village: dining, 128
Kalihi neighborhood (Honolulu), 117
Kamehameha Statue, 96
Kaneaki Heiau, 160
Kaneohe: dining, 140; groceries, 141; lodging, 138–39; shopping, 141, 142; sights, 134, 136
Kaneohe Bay, 136
Kapiolani Park, 75
Kawaihao Church, 95
Kayaking, 41
Keaiwa Heiau State Recreation Area, 122–23
Keauu Beach Park, 164–65
Kewalo Boat Basin, 98
Kodak Hula Show, 76
Koko Crater, 124
Koko Crater Botanical Gardens, 125
Koko Head, 124
Kokololio Beach Park, 144
Kolekole Pass, 158
Koolau Range, 126
Kualoa Regional Park, 143
Kuhio Beach Park, 74, 93
Kuilei Cliffs Beach Park, 123
Kukaniloho, 158

Laie: groceries, 141; lodging, 139; sights, 137
Laie Point, 137
Language, 66–68
Lanikai Beach, 143
Leeward Coast. See Central Oahu and Leeward Coast
Leis, 19
Lesbian travelers. See Gay and lesbian travelers
Lodging, 11–12. See also Lodging in area and town entries; see also Lodging Index
Lyon Arboretum, 118

Mail, 17
Maili Beach Park, 164
Makaha: dining, 160; lodging, 161
Makaha Beach, 160
Makaha Beach Park, 164
Makapuu Beach Park, 126, 130
Makapuu Point, 125–26
Makua Cave, 160–61
Malaekahana State Recreation Area, 146
Manoa Valley neighborhood (Honolulu), 116, 117, 118
Marijuana, 28–29
Maunakea Marketplace, 99
Merchant Street neighborhood (Honolulu), 98–99
Mission Houses Museum, 95
Mission Memorial Building, 95

Mokuleia Beach and Beach Park, 156
Moped rentals, 22
Mormon Temple, 137
Music, 68–70

Nanakuli Beach Park, 164
Natatorium, 76
National Memorial Cemetery, 113
North Shore, 5, 147–56; addresses and
   phone numbers, 24; beaches and parks,
   154–56; camping, 155, 156; dining,
   151–53; groceries, 153; lodging, 150–51;
   map, 149; nightlife, 154; shopping,
   153–54; sights, 147–50
Nuuanu Avenue neighborhood (Honolulu),
   112–13
Nuuanu Pali Drive and Lookout, 116

Oahu: addresses and phone numbers,
   23–24; animals, 29–32; areas, 4–5; cal-
   endar of events, 6–9; culture, 63–70; ge-
   ology, 26; history, 49–61; maps, 73, 97,
   115, 127, 135, 149, 159; outdoor adven-
   tures, 32–48; plants, 26–29; transporta-
   tion, 17–20, 22–23; weather, 5–6
Ocean safety, 21
Old Sugar Mill, 136
Older travelers, 15
Olomana Peak, 126
Original Glider Ride, 150
Outdoor adventures, 32–48
Outrigger canoes, 76

Pacific Aerospace Museum, 17–18
Package tours, 9–10
Packing, 10–11
Pakalolo (marijuana), 28–29
Parasailing, 41–42
Pearl Harbor, 116
People, 64–65
Pidgin language, 66–68
Pineapple Variety Garden, 158
Plants, 26–29
Polynesian Cultural Center, 137
Portuguese man-of-wars, 21
Pounders Beach, 144
Price ranges: dining, 13; lodging, 11
Public transit, 22
Punaluu: dining, 140; lodging, 139;
   shopping, 142
Punaluu Beach Park, 143–44
Punchbowl, 113
Pupukea Beach Park, 155
Puu o Makuha Heiau, 148
Puu Ualakaa Park, 114

Queen Emma's Summer Palace, 114, 116
Queen Kapiolani Garden, 76
Queen's Surf, 75, 93

Rabbit Island, 126
Restaurants, 12–13. See also Dining in
   area and town entries; see also Dining
   Index
Riding stables, 42
Royal Hawaiian Hotel, 74
Royal Mausoleum, 113
Royal-Moana Beach, 74, 93

Sailing, 40–41
Sand Island State Recreation Area, 111
Sandy Beach, 125, 130
Sans Souci Beach, 76
Sea Life Park, 126
Sea urchins, 21
Seasons, 5–6
Seaweed, 43
Senator Fong's Plantation and Gardens,
   136
Senior travelers, 15
Sharks, 21, 30
Shellfish gathering, 37
Sheraton Moana Surfrider Hotel, 74
Sheraton Waikiki, 74
Skydiving, 42
Snorkeling. See Diving
Snuba, 39
Southeast Oahu, 4–5, 124–32; beaches and
   parks, 124–30, 132; camping, 130, 132;
   dining, 126, 128; groceries, 129; map,
   127; sights, 124–26
Spearfishing, 36
Squidding, 36–37
State Capitol Building, 96
Sunset Beach, 147–48, 154–55
Surfing, 39–40
Swanzy Beach Park, 143–44

Tantalus, 113–14
Tennis, 44
Tenrikyo Mission, 113
TheBus, 131
Toilet Bowl (tidepool), 125
Torchfishing, 36
Tours: aerial, 22–23; package, 9–10; walk-
   ing, 23, 100
Transportation, 17–20, 22–23

Ulupo Heiau, 134
University of Hawaii, 118
U.S. Army Museum of Hawaii, 74
USS Arizona Memorial, 116
USS Bowfin/Pacific Submarine Museum,
   116

Vegetables, 27–28
Visitor information, 9

Wahiawa: sights, 158

Wahiawa Botanical Gardens, 158
Waiahole Valley, 136
Waialae Beach Park, 123
Waialua: nightlife, 154
Waianae: dining, 162; groceries, 162; lodging, 161; sights, 160
Waikane Valley, 136
Waikiki, 4, 71–93; beaches and parks, 93; condos, 83–84; dining, 84–87; groceries, 87; lodging, 77–84; map, 73; nightlife, 90–93; shopping, 87–88, 90; sights, 72–77
Waikiki Aquarium, 75–76
Waikiki Beach, 93
Waimanalo: dining, 128; groceries, 129; sights, 126
Waimanalo Bay State Recreation Area, 130, 132
Waimanalo Beach Park, 130, 132
Waimea Bay, 148
Waimea Bay Beach Park, 155

Waimea Falls, 148
Waimea Valley, 148
Waipahu: sights, 158, 160
Walking tours, 23, 100
Waterskiing, 41
Wawamalu Beach Park, 130
Weather, 5–6
Western Oahu. See Central Oahu and Leeward Coast
Whales, 29
Windsurfing, 40, 145
Windward Coast, 5, 133–46; addresses and phone numbers, 24; beaches and parks, 142–44, 146; camping, 143, 144, 146; dining, 139–41; groceries, 141; lodging, 138–39; map, 135; nightlife, 142; shopping, 141–42; sights, 133–37
Women travelers, 14

Yokohama Bay, 161, 165

Lodging Index

Aston Waikiki Beach Tower, 83
Aston Waikiki Beachside Hotel, 79
Aston Waikiki Shore, 83
Atherton YWCA, 119

Bed & Breakfast Manoa, 119
The Breakers, 78–79

Coconut Plaza, 80
Countryside Cabins, 139

Diamond Head Beach Hotel, 82

Edgewater Hotel, 79
The Estates at Turtle Bay, 150
Ewa Hotel, 80

Fernhurst YWCA, 119

Hale Pua Nui, 78
Hawaii Hatfields Realty Corporation,
   161
Hawaiiana Hotel, 79
Holiday Inn Waikiki, 81
Honolulu International Youth Hostel, 119
Honolulu Prince Hotel, 79–80
Hostelling International—Waikiki, 78
Hotel Honolulu, 80–81

Ihilani Resort & Spa, 161
Interclub Waikiki, 78
Island Hostel/Hotel, 81

Kai Aloha Apartment Hotel, 78
Kailua Beachside Cottages, 138
Kaulana Kai Resort at Waikiki, 83
Ke Iki Hale, 151

Makaha Shores, 161
Makaha Surfside, 161
Makaha Valley Towers, 161
Malihini Hotel, 77
Mango House, 120
Manoa Valley Inn, 118–19
Mark Waikiki Grand Hotel, 81

Naish Hawaii, 138
Nakamura Hotel, 100
New Otani Kaimana Beach Hotel, 82

Nuuanu YMCA, 118

Outrigger Coral Seas Hotel, 79
Outrigger East, 80
Outrigger Village, 80
Outrigger Waikiki Surf Hotel, 81

Pacific Monarch, 83
Pagoda Hotel, 100
Patrick Winston's Hawaiian King Rentals,
   83
Plantation Village, 150–51
Polynesian Hostel Beach Club, 81–82

Queen Kapiolani Hotel, 82

Roadway Inn Hukilau Resort, 139
Royal Grove Hotel, 77
Royal Hawaiian, 82
Royal Kuhio, 83

Schrader's Windward Marine Resort,
   138–39
Sharon's Serenity, 138
Sheraton Moana Surfrider Hotel, 82

Town Inn, 100
Turtle Bay Condos, 150
Turtle Bay Hilton, 150

Vacation Inn, 150–51

Waikiki Banyan, 83
Waikiki Circle Hotel, 77–78
Waikiki Hana Hotel, 80
Waikiki Lanais, 83
Waikiki Prince Hotel, 78
White Sands Waikiki Resort, 80
Windward Bed & Breakfast, 139

YMCA Central Branch, 78

LODGING SERVICES
Bed and Breakfast Hawaii, 83
Bed and Breakfast Honolulu, 82
Condo Rentals of Waikiki, 84
Marc Resorts, 84
Pacific Hawaii Bed and Breakfast, 82–83
Waikiki Vacation Rentals, 81

Dining Index

A Little Bit of Saigon, 106
Acqua, 86–87
Ahi's Restaurant, 140
Anna Banana's, 121
Assaggio Ristorante Italiano, 139
Auntie Pasto's, 105–106
Azteca Mexican Restaurant, 121
Azul, 161–62

Bali-By-The-Sea, 86
Bananas, 85
Bautista's Filipino Kitchen, 85
The Beachside Café, 86
Bueno Nalo, 128
Buzz's Original Steak House, 139

Café Haleiwa, 152
Cathay's Inn Chop Suey, 162
Chart House at Haiku Gardens, 140
Choi's Kitchen, 85
Cinnamon's Restaurant, 140
Coconut Willy's Bar & Grill, 84
Coffee Gallery, 153
Compadres, 102
Crouching Lion Inn, 140–41

Daiei, 101–102
Daiei Food Court, 102
D'Amico's, 151
Dave's Ice Cream, 128
Double Eight Restaurant, 106
Duc's Bistro, 107

E. J.'s, 162
Elena's, 121
Ezogiku, 84–85

Fisherman's Wharf, 104
Flavor Mania, 152
Fuji Delicatessen and Restaurant, 140

Giovanni's Shrimp Truck, 141
Grace's Inn, 103

Hale Vietnam, 121
Haleiwa Beach Grill, 152
Hannara Restaurant, 162
Harpos, 102
Hau Tree Lanai, 86
Helena's Hawaiian Foods, 121

Hernando's Hideaway, 85

Ihilani Resort & Spa, 161–62
Indigo, 107
Internet Café, 120
Irifune, 120
Itochan Sushi, 106

The J. R.'s, 84
Jameson's By The Sea, 151–52
Jimbo's Restaurant, 105
John Dominus, 104
Jungle Waikiki, 84

Ka'a'a Country Kitchen, 140
Kahuku Sugar Mill Restaurant & Bar, 141
Kau Kau Corner Food Lanai, 104
Kelly's Restaurant & Bakery, 121–22
Keneke's Bar-B-Q, 128
Keo's Thai Cuisine, 120
King Tsin Restaurant, 105
Koa Omelette House, 140
Kua Aina Sandwich, 151

L & L Drive-Inn (Honolulu), 103
L & L Drive-Inn (Waianae), 162
La Mer, 87
Like Like Drive Inn, 103
Liliha Seafood Restaurant, 120

Mabuhay Cafe, 106–107
Makai Market, 101
Mama Mia, 121
Manapua, 102
Maunakea Marketplace, 106
Meg's Country Drive-In, 152

Naupaka, 161–62
Nick's Fishmarket, 86
19th Hole, 162

Ocean Terrace, 86
Old Spaghetti Factory, 102
Old World Bistro, 140
Ono Hawaiian Foods, 121
Orchids, 87

Pagoda Floating Restaurant, 104
Palm Terrace, 151
Paradise Found, 152

Patti's Chinese Kitchen, 101
Peking Garden, 85
People's Café, 106
Perry's Smorgy, 85
Philip Paolo's, 105
Pizza Bob's, 152
Poi Bowl, 101
Portofino, 153
Prince Court, 102

Rainbow Drive-In, 120–21
Rodeo Cantina, 104
Rosie's Cantina, 153
Roy's Restaurant, 128
Ryan's Grill, 102

Saeng's Thai Cuisine, 139
Sam Choy, 120
Scoozee's, 102
Shirokiya, 101
Shore Bird Beach Broiler, 85–86

Spaghetti! Spaghetti!, 84
Sunset Diner, 151
Sunset Grill, 102, 104
Sushi Robot, 102
Swiss Inn, 128

Thai Taste, 106
Thai Valley Cuisine, 128
Times Coffee Shop, 139
Treats, 85

Ushiotei, 161–62

Waikiki Broiler, 85
Waikiki Shopping Plaza, 84
Waimanalo Fish Market & Restaurant,
   128
Wisteria Restaurant, 105

Yong Sing Restaurant, 106
Yummy Korean Barbecue, 102

Notes

Notes

HIDDEN GUIDES
Adventure travel or a relaxing vacation?—"Hidden" guidebooks are the only travel books in the business to provide detailed information on both. Aimed at environmentally aware travelers, our motto is "Adventure Travel Plus." These books combine details on unique hotels, restaurants and sightseeing with information on camping, sports and hiking for the outdoor enthusiast.

THE NEW KEY GUIDES
Based on the concept of ecotourism, The New Key Guides are dedicated to the preservation of Central America's rare and endangered species, architecture and archaeology. Filled with helpful tips, they give travelers everything they need to know about these exotic destinations.

ULTIMATE FAMILY GUIDES
These innovative guides present the best and most unique features of a family destination. Quality is the keynote. In addition to thoroughly covering each destination, they feature short articles and one-line "teasers" that are both fun and informative.

Ulysses Press books are available at bookstores everywhere. If any of the following titles are unavailable at your local bookstore, ask the bookseller to order them.

You can also order books directly from Ulysses Press
P.O. Box 3440, Berkeley, CA 94703
800-377-2542 or 510-601-8301
fax: 510-601-8307
e-mail: Ulypress@aol.com

Order Form

HIDDEN GUIDEBOOKS

____ Hidden Arizona, $13.95

____ Hidden Bahamas, $12.95

____ Hidden Baja, $14.95

____ Hidden Boston and Cape Cod, $11.95

____ Hidden Carolinas, $16.95

____ Hidden Coast of California, $16.95

____ Hidden Colorado, $13.95

____ Hidden Florida, $16.95

____ Hidden Florida Keys & Everglades, $10.95

____ Hidden Hawaii, $16.95

____ Hidden Idaho, $13.95

____ Hidden Maui, $12.95

____ Hidden Montana, $13.95

____ Hidden New England, $16.95

____ Hidden New Mexico, $13.95

____ Hidden Oahu, $12.95

____ Hidden Oregon, $13.95

____ Hidden Pacific Northwest, $16.95

____ Hidden Rockies, $16.95

____ Hidden San Francisco and
  Northern California, $15.95

____ Hidden Southern California, $16.95

____ Hidden Southwest, $16.95

____ Hidden Tahiti, $16.95

____ Hidden Tennessee, $15.95

____ Hidden Wyoming, $13.95

THE NEW KEY GUIDEBOOKS

____ The New Key to Belize, $14.95

____ The New Key to Cancún and
  the Yucatán, $14.95

____ The New Key to Costa Rica, $16.95

____ The New Key to Ecuador and
  the Galápagos, $16.95

____ The New Key to Guatemala, $14.95

ULTIMATE FAMILY GUIDEBOOKS

____ Disneyland and Beyond, $12.95

____ Disney World and Beyond, $13.95

Mark the book(s) you're ordering and enter the total cost here ⇨

California residents add 8% sales tax here ⇨

Shipping, check box for your preferred method and enter cost here ⇨

❏ BOOK RATE   **FREE! FREE! FREE!**

❏ PRIORITY MAIL $3.00 First book, $1.00/each additional book

❏ UPS 2-DAY AIR $7.00 First book, $1.00/each additional book

Billing, enter total amount due here and check method of payment ⇨

❏ CHECK   ❏ MONEY ORDER

❏ VISA/MASTERCARD _____ EXP. DATE _____

NAME _____ PHONE _____

ADDRESS _____

_____

CITY _____ STATE _____ ZIP _____

MONEY-BACK GUARANTEE ON DIRECT ORDERS PLACED THROUGH ULYSSES PRESS.

ABOUT THE AUTHOR

RAY RIEGERT is the author of eight travel books, including *Hidden San Francisco & Northern California*. His most popular work, *Hidden Hawaii*, won the coveted Lowell Thomas Travel Journalism Award for Best Guidebook as well as a similar award from the Hawaii Visitors Bureau. In addition to his role as publisher of Ulysses Press, he has written for the *Chicago Tribune*, *Saturday Evening Post*, *San Francisco Examiner & Chronicle* and *Travel & Leisure*. A member of the Society of American Travel Writers, he lives in the San Francisco Bay area with his wife, co-publisher Leslie Henriques, and their son Keith and daughter Alice.